FRUIT BEVERAGES AND PROCESSING WITH MANGO PRODUCTS

FRUIT BEVERAGES AND PROCESSING WITH MANGO PRODUCTS

Written By

EIRI BOARD OF CONSULTANTS & ENGINEERS

ENGINEERS INDIA RESEARCH INSTITUTE

4449, Nai Sarak, Main Road, Delhi - 110006 (India)

Ph: 91-11-23918117, 23916431, 23840361

Fax: 91-11- 2391 6431, 2391 8117

* E-Mail: eirisidi@bol.net.in

*Website: www.eiriindia.org

Also at

4/54 ROOP NAGAR, OPP. SHIV MANDIR, DELHI -110007

PRINTED & PUBLISHED BY

ENGINEERS INDIA RESEARCH INSTITUTE

4449, Nai Sarak, Main Road, Delhi - 110006 (India)
Ph: 91-11-23918117, 23916431, 23840361
Fax: 91-11- 2391 6431, 2391 8117
*** E-Mail: eirisidi@bol.net.in**
***Website: www.eiriindia.org**

Sole Distributors:

EIRI PROJECT CONSULTANTS AND PUBLISHERS
4/54 Roop Nagar, Delhi-110007

ISBN: 978-81-89765-24-8

Printed in New Delhi (INDIA)

Rs. 750/-

Printed & Published by Sudhir Gupta for "Engineers India Research Institute", 4449 Nai Sarak, Main Road, New Delhi -110006

Preface

The mango is one of the most important and widely cultivated fruits of the tropical world. Its juicy fruit is a rich source of Vitamins A, C and D. In India there are over100 varieties of mangoes, in different sizes, shapes and colours. Mangoes, have been cultivated in India from time immemorial. The poet Kalidasa sang its praises. Alexander savoured its taste, as did the Chinese pilgrim Hieun Tsang. Akbar planted 100,000 mango trees in Darbhanga, known as Lakhi Bagh. A fleshy fruit, eaten ripe or used green for pickles etc., of the tree *Mangifera indica*.

Mangoes belong to the genus ***Mangifera***, consisting of numerous species of tropical fruiting trees in the flowering plant family *Anacardiaceae*. The mango is indigenous to eastern Asia, Burma, and Assam. Cultivated in many tropical regions and distributed widely in the world, mango is one of the most popularly exploited fruits for food, juice, flavor, fragrance and colour. Its leaves are ritually used as floral decorations at weddings and religious ceremonies.

The name *mango* is ultimately from the Kodagu *mange*, the Malayalam *manga*, or the Tamil *mangai*, and was loaned into Portuguese in the early 16th century, and from Portuguese passed into English.

The fruit flesh of a ripe mango is very sweet, with a unique taste. The texture of the flesh varies markedly between different cultivars, some having a soft, pulpy texture similar to an over-ripe plum, while others having firmer flesh like a cantaloupe or avocado. In some cultivars, the flesh has a fibrous texture. Mangoes are juicy with a sweet taste and high water content making them refreshing to eat.

Mangoes are widely used in chutney, Juices, Fruits in Syrup, Sauces, Jams, Pulps and Nectars, Canned Products. In the Indian subcontinent is usually made with sour, unripe mangoes and hot chilis or limes, mango shake padturised juice etc. In India, ripe mango is often cut into thin layers, desiccated, folded, and then cut and sold as bars that are very chewy. These bars, known as amavat or halva in Hindi, are similar to dried guava fruit bars available in Colombia. In many parts of India, people eat squeezed mango juice (called Ras), the thickness of which depends on the type of mango, with variety of bread items and is part of the meal rather than a dessert. Unripe mangoes (which are extremely sour) are eaten with salt, and in regions where food is hotter, with salt and chili.

In other parts of South-east Asia, mangoes are very popular pickled with fish sauce and rice vinegar.

The book contains 26 chapters on various aspects on presevation technologies, "Hot Fill" Procedure, Canned Products Processing etc.i.e. *Mango, Preservation Technologies, Mango Processing Unit -Mango Juice in Bags "Hot Fill" Procedure, Fruit and Vegetable Processing Flow Sheets (Simple Processing), Fruits/Vegetables Processing (Drying/Dehydration), Juices, Fruits in Syrup, Sauces, Jams, Pulps and Nectars, Canned Products Processing, Standards for Grades of Dried Apricots, Recipe Guidelines: Dried Fruit and Vegetables, Mango Products, Method of Preparation and Keeping Quality of Reconstituted Skim Milk-based Mango Beverage, Ready to Serve (RTS) Beverage based on Pomegranate and Mango, Mango (Mangifera indica L.) Varieties for Wine-making, Membrane Technology in Fruit and Vegetable Processing, Value Aaddition to Fruits and Vegetables by Mechanical Washing, Packaging of Fruit Juices, Flexible Packages for Fruit and Vegetable Pulps, Developments in Packaging of Liquid Foods, Drying of Fruits and Vegetables, Dehydration Fruits and Vegetables by Vacuum Drying Method, Fruit Drink Rasna Type Mango and Pineapple Pulp and Concentrates. Jam, Jelly, Chutney, Pickles and Squashes, Mango Pappad (Aam Pappad), Mango Pulp Processing and Canning, Mango Powder, Mango Kernel Seed Powder (Starch)*

Director

ENGINEERS INDIA RESEARCH INSTITUTE

Nai Sarak, New Delhi (INDIA)
E-Mail: eirisidi@bol.net.in

Contents-cum Index

Chapter 10

Chapter 11

Chapter 12

1

Mango

The mango (*Mangifera indica* L.) is considered to be the king of fruits. It is, undoubtedly, one of the choicest and most ancient fruits known to mankind. In India, it has always been a prized and favourite fruit throughout the recorded history of this country. The fruit not only finds a prominent mention in the old Sanskrit literature but almost all the foreigners, right from the Chinese pilgrims who traveled here in Seventh century, A.D. down to the modern writers, have spoken in glowing terms about this fruit, during the Mughal rule, mango was honoured with a real patronage. The well-known **Lakh Bagh**, known to be stocked with 1,00,000 mango trees, was planted neat Darbhanga in Bihar state by Akbar. Some mango orchards planted during that period notably the Shalimar Garden of Lahore and Mughal Gardens at Pinjore near Chandigarh are still preserved and bear testimony to the high esteem this fruit enjoyed in the past. The mango occupies the same position in the tropical and sub-tropical regions, which is enjoyed by the Apple in temperature regions.

Origin, History and Distribution

Several authorities have testified to the origin of mango in the Indo Burma region, where it has been in cultivation for atleast 4000 years. This fruit has become deeply interwoven with religious rites and folklore of the inhabitants of this country due to its antiquity, popularity, and usefulness. It is a fruit par excellence for millions of people in the Orient, especially those in India. The mango which combine utility with beauty has the status of the national tree of India and is very rightly considered 'King' among fruits grown in the country.

The mango spread quite early in eastern part. Some Chinese travellers who came in India in seventh century, they described that mango is very sweet and delicious fruit. Even earlier than that in the Buddhist and Hindu temples their is life like images of mango. Mango traveled to the west only after the sea-route was discovered. Alexander saw first mango tree in Indus Valley, which proves that it did not travel towards the Western countries before Alexander, Portuguese people took mango fruit to South Africa and Brazil in about 1700 A.D. Spanish people introduced in Philippines. Mango was introduced in Jamica around 1782. From Mexico, it was introduced in Florida during 1833. In 1869 grafted mango trees were taken to Florida from India. Mango was introduced in Israel in 1929 through seeds brought from Egypt. This fruit is grown on commercial scale in countries like India, Bangladesh, USA (florida), Indonesia, Philippines, Malaya, Myanmar, Cylon, Pakistan, Egypt, Sudan, South Africa, West Indies, Hawai, California, etc.

Area and production

In India, mango occupies 31.25 per cent of the total area under fruits comprising of 1.01 million hectares with a total production of 8.50 million tones. The main mango growing states in India and Uttar Pradesh, Andhra Pradesh, Bihar, West Bengal, Kerela, Karnataka, Punjab, Haryana; Himachal Pradesh and Jammu & Kashmir.

Of the various states, Uttar Pradesh has the largest area accounting for nearly 33.2 per cent of the total area in the country, followed by Bihar (13.5%) and Andhra Pradesh (13.4%). In Punjab, the total area under mango is approximately 14741 hectares with the annual production of 88446 tonnes. The production is far too low, with the result that this State has to import a bulk of fruit particularly of grafted varieties, from other States every year. About one-fourth of fruit acreage is found under mango alone.

The mango grows and prospers in almost all parts of the Punjab, barring very hot and dried zones of the south-west Punjab, where it fails to thrive. However, the best zones for the commercial cultivation of mango in Punjab are the sub-montane tracts of Gurdaspur, Hoshiarpur, Ropar and parts of Patiala district and U.T. Chandigarh. The sub-montane belt has numerous seedling mango trees, many of which are of enormous size and some of them over 100 years old.

India is the largest mango producing country, accounting for 66.0 per cent of world production. There are bright prospects of building up a flourishing trade fro the export of this fruit to other countries as well as of its products like 'Canned mango slices' and 'bottled mango juice'. Already mangoes are exported to nearly 20 countries, whereas its products are sent to over 40 countries. However, the present turn out is too meagre. Mango can thus earn for India a handsome foreign exchange, through the export of fresh mangoes and mango products. There are vast stretches of areas where the cultivation of this choice fruit could be developed and expanded usefully and profitably.

Importance and uses

Mango possess unique nutritional and medicinal qualities apart form being a rich source of vitamins A and C. besides its attractive form and appearance, delicious taste and appetizing flavour, the ripe mango fruit, according to nutritional experts, is also highly invigorating, fattening, laxative and diuretic.

Every part of mango, from root to top, is used in a variety of ways. The fruit itself, in the various stages of its development, is used in many ways. In its raw stage, the fruit is used for extraction of tannin and other astringent products as well as for the preparation of delightful chutneys, curries and pickles. Ripe fruits are a delicacy for the table, while the unmarketable and inferior ones can be converted into delicious squashes, juices, nectars, syrups, jams and jellies. Canned mango slices and pulp are indeed very popular. The stones, besides their use for propagation, can serve as a good stockfeed for cattle. The inside kernel of the stone, being rich in carbohydrates, calcium and fat, can be used as a source of food for certain industrial purposes. Thus the mango is a unique fruit, and possesses all the endearing qualities which justifiably lend to it a universal appeal.

Botany

Mango belongs to the family Anacardiaceae and genus Mangifera. The genus has 62 species, out of which only a few have edible fruits. In India only 3 species are found i.e. *Mangifera indica*, *Mangifera sylvatica* and *Mangifera coloncura*. The species Mangifera indica bears edible fruit.

Mangifera sylvatica is a wild species, grown in north east parts of India and fruit is not edible.

Mangifera Indica: It is a cultivated species of India. The tree is a medium in size, ranging from 10-13 meters in height. The tree top is oval or dome shaped. The trunk of the tree is mostly straight, cylindrical, 75-100 cm in diameter. Mango is a evergreen tree bearing numerous branches. In the upper portion the branches ascend gradually but in the center the branches are nearly erect type. The mango has simple, alternate, thick, leathery and short pointed leaves which may be either oblong, elliptical and lanceolate in shape. Leaves have short petiole, swollen at the base and irregularly placed around the twigs. The leaves are dark shinning, green from above and yellow green from below. Inflorescence of mango is large panicles which is known terminally. Sometimes inflorescence is axillary also. These panicles may be 6-40 cm long and 3-25 cm in diameter. Flowers are small in the inflorescence and both side of male and female flowers are borne in the same flower i.e. hermaphrodite. These flowers may be 6-8 mm in diameter. There are 4-5 stamens which are unequal in length, only one or two are fertile; the others are reduced to very purple or yellow white structure called staminodes which are infertile. The ovary is one called structure, oblique and slightly compressed. Sometimes the re may be a 3 carpels in a flower.

Mango fruit is drupe and mesocarp is the edible portion, fruit size, shape, colour, flavour and taste vary according to variety. In many varieties beak is very prominent especially in Langra. Skin of the fruit has many glands with dots. The colour of skin varies from green yellow, red or any shade of the colour. Pulp also varies from green yellow to orange in colour.

The number of panicles in mango varies from 200-300 per tree. The panicles may have 300-1000 flowers in each panicles.

Out of these flowers only few fruits are formed depends upon the season and variety. The panicles of male and hermaphrodite flowers varies 1:4, 1:1, 2:1. In Punjab, it was found that Dusehari and Langra varieties had on an average 77.9 and 66.8 per cent perfect flowers, respectively. This shows that the grafted plant has more hermaphrodite flowers than the seedling mango.

Flowering and Fruiting

During the first year of planting, the young mango grafts may being to flower. The first three years flowering should be removed as soon they appear. They seldom bear fruit and their presence would mean suppression of corresponding vegetative growth which is so essential in building up the young trees.

The grafted mango begins to bear fruit from the fourth or fifth year of planting. The time of flowering in different regions is greatly influenced by local weather conditions. In many parts of North India, the mango flowers late in January or in the beginning of February or even as late as March in some submontane districts. In Punjab the period of flushes take place between April and August but the heaviest flushes takes place in April-May. Flowering in mango continues in two or three distinct flushes for a period of 6 to 8 weeks on different branches or trees and it takes about 5 months for the fruit to mature and ripen after flowering.

Mango products blossoms and bears fruit mostly from the terminal buds of its shoots and very rarely from the axillary buds. Dry weather stimulated flowering and cloudy weather or winter rains tend to retard it. Inspite of a favourable dry weather after the month of October, the tree may not flower and it may produce vegetative or leafy shoots only. The chief internal factor that governs and control the entire phenomenon of flowering in mango is the maturity and age of its seasonal vegetative growth (leafy shoots) which are produced in distinct flushes at certain times of the year.

In Uttar Pradesh, the first flush is produced in March-April and the second in July-August. In Punjab, about five flushes are produced between April and August, but the April-May flushes are the heaviest. The flowers starts in February and continue well beyond the month of March.

In different flushes, the eight to ten month old mature shoots produce flowers. These shoots are produced in spring and early summer and cease growing at least four months prior to blossoming, other shoots produced in subsequent flushes during late monsoon and after October rarely blossom towards the end of winter or in the beginning of spring which is the flowering time throughout in India. The internal nutritional conditions of the tree favour differentiation of flower buds, if vegetative shoots produced in the spring and summer cease to grow early and accumulate sufficient time to grow, rest and mature for the purpose but the later formed growths do not get time to do so.

Flower-bud Differentiation

The first indication of the initiation of the flower bud is in the internal structure of the bud. Before this initiation takes place the apical end of the vegetative shoots become dome shaped. As far as the differentiation start. The main axil of the panicles enlongates slightly. The axil of he scale also elongate and slightly broaden at the base. The apex broaden slightly gets rounded off and becomes more regular and consists of meristematic cells. The scales grow longer. From the axil of the some of the scale, some conical growth arise which are sign of differential of fruit bud in mango.

The time of flower bud differentiation varies from place to place. In Punjab, fruit bud differentiation takes place in August and September. At Saharanpur, the fruit bud differentiation takes place in December. The application of nitrogen should be given before rainy season to the mango trees before the fruit bud differentiation, so that more flowering, more fruit set and more fruit is retained on the tree and thus increasing the yield of the fruit.

Pollination

Cross pollination is very important in mango and give good commercial crop. The cross pollination is done by insects. It has been sent hat honey be is not attracted by mango flowers. It is pollinated by mango fly, especially house fly. Even by cross pollination only 15 per cent or even less hermaphrodite flowers are pollinated, staminate flowers are not pollinated at all.

Monoembryony and Polyembryony: In mango monoembryoinic and polyembronic are the two distinct races, when the mango seed contains only one embryo and give rise to only one plant is termed as monoembryonic mango. When the seed contains several embryos which give to several plants which can be separated from one another on germination and planted as independent plants is termed as polyemberyonic mango.

In monoembroyonic mango, the embryo is generally a hybrid, being the product of natural crossing of the flowers of two trees of different varieties growing under the same environment, therefore, such seed gives rise to a plant which shows mixed characteristics of two different kinds and does not look like the parent tree from which the seed is obtained. This type of mango when grown from seed does not usually breed true-to-type.

In polyembryonic mango, out of several embryos in the seed only one embryo may be produced by the crossing of flowers of two different varieties. Even the one plant which is expected to be a product of sexual process is often suppressed and absent. As such, the seed of a polyembryonic mango gives rise to several plants which breed true to the parent.

Almost all the varieties of mango in India are monoembryonic and do not breed true to their parents when grown from seed. So, they have to be propagated by the asexual method. On the other hand, the polyembryonic types of mango are not to be found in any part of India, except in Malbar where few varieties of polyembroynic nature are found, the famous mango of this type i.e. 'Olour grown in Malabar is propagated from seed. The polyembroyonic mangoes are found growing in the moist tropics of South East Asia, such as Malaysia, Philippines and Indonesia.

Climate

Although known to be ramarkably tolerant of a wide range of climatic conditions, the mango should always be grown within specific and well-defined ranges of temperature and rainfall for its more profitable cultivation. In general, it does best in comparatively dry regions which receive good rainfall in hot weather from June to September, followed by a more or less dry spell in the subsequent period. A rainfall of about 125 cms falling mostly during the monsoon, is considered very suitable, but much less of it will suffice if irrigation facilities are available. Actually the quantum of rainfall is not so important as its distribution. Rain during the flowering and fruit-setting season (February to April) is particularly harmful as it interferes with pollination which is done by flies, bees, etc. During this periods, even thick fog or cloudy weather may ruin the prospects of a bumper crop. Dry and cloudless weather, before blossoming, has been found conductive to profuse flowering. Strong winds and cyclones during the fruiting season can incur immense damage by shedding the fruits.

Temperature is of a basic importance in determining success in mango-growing. Whereas the temperature ranges are not ideal, both the fruit and the fruit trees may be adversely affected, broadly speaking, temperature rising beyond 115°F and that falling below freezing point is not suitable for this fruit. In the regions where optimum temperature ranges do not prevail, cultivation of mango on a commercial scale is hazardous. Instances are not uncommon when young and even grown up trees were killed or damaged seriously due to abrupt fluctuations in temperatures beyond the safe limits, especially due to the fall of temperature below the freezing point.

The frequency of winds, their intensity and speed has also to be taken into account while selecting sites for mango orchards. Besides causing shedding of flowers and fruits, strong winds also cause mechanical injuries to the trees. The localities reasonably free from the onslaughts of winds should, therefore, be preferred. The damage caused by the winds can, however, be minimized by planting windbreaks of tall and hardy trees around mango groves, especially around those of grafted.

Selection of site and soils

Site

Mango is a long-lived tree. If maintained and looked after properly, it continues to yield profitable crops for a longer number of years than many other fruit trees. Its planting, therefore, requires a great deal of pre-planning in the matters of selection of site, provision of suitable drainage, adequate preparatory tillage, systematic lay-out, proper selection of plant material and after care, to achieve good measure of success. The common belief held by growers that mango does not need any special care for its planting and subsequent after care during fruit bearing is highly erroneous and fallacious. The care bestowed on preliminary operations including selection of site may make all the difference between success or failure of a mango orchard.

The site for a commercial mango orchard should be selected as far as possible in a region or locality where this fruit has been growing successfully in the past. Such a selection would ensure the suitability of climate and soils and the adaptability to the agro-climatic complex. Within the afore-mentioned regional concept, due consideration should also be given to factors like nearness to the market, road and railway station, availability of adequate irrigation facilities, topography of the soil and its physical and chemical composition, it may be borne in mind that while it is possible to improve, in some measure, the physical and chemical properties of the soil and its drainage, it is not possible to alter materially the advantages or disadvantages of its location. Hence one should be over cautious while selecting a site or locality.

Mango orchards should not be planted in the close vicinity of brick-kilns, as fumes emitted by the kilns result in the spoilage of fruit by causing blacktip disease. The safe distance of a brick-kiln from a mango plantation is about two kilometers. There should be no brick-kilns within this range, their chimneys should be raised to atleast 50 feet above ground and they should not be operated, if possible during the entire flowering and fruiting season of the mango.

Soils

Mango is not very fastidious for its soil requirements and can grow and crop well on a wide variety of soils. For its best performance, however, it requires deep and well-drained soils of loamy texture. Soils which lack proper drainage are not suitable for its successful cultivation. Likewise soils with a hard pan of a compact canker layer underneath or with a high water-lable or those liable to be flooded, are also unsuitable. On defective or unsuitable soils, the trees may just linger on with no prospects of profitable production.

Like most other fruit trees, it is not the upper eight to ten inches of soil that is of importance for mango but the sub-soil down below up to a depth of six to eight feet matters the most. Before planting an orchard, both soil and sub-soil should be got examined thoroughly by the experts.

Most of the mango-growing soils in India have a low soluble salt content ranging 0.04 to 0.05 per cent and high fertility status. The pH of the most well known mango regions varies from 5.5 to 7.5 (value of 7.0 being neutral while lower values indicate acidic reaction and higher values alkaline reaction). Soils with higher or lower values than the above optimum range should be avoided.

Varieties

The pre-historical existence of mango in India, its widespread cultivation all over the country and, above all, its propagation for centuries from seed, has all contributed to the multiplicity of its varieties. The vegetative propagation of mango, which seems to have come into vogue only about four centuries back, has helped in the preservation of outstanding varieties, all of which have originated as chance seedlings. According to reliable estimates, there are, at present, over a thousand recognised varieties of mango grown in India alone, if the countless sucking varieties found growing in various parts of the country are also taken into account, the number of mango varieties would become colossal indeed.

In a commercial orchard, selection of varieties has to be restricted to only a few, which are highly productive, possess superior quality and are well adaptable to the agro-climatic conditions of the tract. Experience has shown that different mango varieties are suited for cultivation in different climatic zones. For example, the Alphanso, a prize mango of the coastal areas of western India, has failed to do well in the interior and north India. Similar is the case with some northern and central Indian varieties, when planted in south India. But this rule does not apply with equal force to all the varieties. There are many instances when certain varieties have done well under diverse climatic conditions. Therefore, it is only through local experimentation and trials that the relative success or failure of a particular variety for a tract can be properly assessed and ascertained.

Bombay Green (Malda)

This is an early variety and has fruit of medium size with lettuce-green colour. The pulp is deep-yellow, firm and fibreless. The taste and flavour are excellent. The Sehroli of Delhi is similar to this variety and is believed to be a chance seedling selection of Bombay Green. Another popular selection from the same stock is Bombay Yellow. It starts ripening by the end of June.

Langra

This is another notable variety which is very popular in the Punjab. The tree is tall and spreading. The fruit ripens in mid-season, (first fortnight of July) and has got a lettuce-green colour. The pulp is lemon-yellow, moderately firm, juicy, creamy and fibreless. It has a very sweet-taste with a fine blend and flavour. Stone is oblong and comparatively small in size. Except for its irregular bearing habit, this variety ranks as one of the best in north India.

Dusehari

This variety is very successful and is becoming increasingly popular with the growers in the Punjab. The size of fruit is small to medium, with an elongated shape. The skin has got in primuline-yellow colour and is medium thick and tough. The pulp is very sweet, firm and fibreless. The fruit has got a good keeping quality and sells at a premium in the market. The tree, though medium in size, has a tendency towards regular bearing. Besides its superb quality, the fruit is highly suitable for canning. It is a mid-season cultivar, ripens in July.

Samarbahisht Chausa

Out of the late varieties grown in the North India, this is most popular. The tree is very tall and spreading but bears rather erratically. The fruit has a medium to large size and is a good keeper. On ripening, its skin assumes uniform yellowish tinge. The pulp is soft, fibreless, and yellowing creamy in colour, has a sweet taste with delightful flavour. It starts ripening from the end of July.

Fajri

This is another late variety, ripening by the middle of August. The fruit is large in size which remains green from outside even or ripening. It keeps well but its quality is not so good.

Sucking Mangoes

A good collection seedling mangoes with good sucking qualities; thin skin, abundant juice of excellent taste and flavour, less fibre, small stones and red blush on cheeks has been established at the Fruit Research Station, Gangian, PAU. The plants of outstanding seven selections under the code names GN1, GN2, GN3, GN4, GN5, GN6 and GN7 are being propagated for distribution to the growers.

Besides the above varieties, two mango hybrids have been released from IARI in recent years. Their important characters are given on next page:

Amarpalli

It is a cross between Dushehari X Neelam. It is very dwarf, regular, late and rich in Vitamin A content. It yields, on an average 16 tonnes/hectare and 1600 plants of this variety are reported to be planted in a hectare.

Mallika

It is across between Neelam X Dushehari varieties of mango. It is reported to be good quality variety with regular bearing habit. Fruit size is medium, shape oblong to elliptic and colour cadmium yellow. Fruit quality is good. Keeping quality is good. It is a midseason variety. It is, however, susceptible to bacterial canker in Northern India.

Planning and Planting

Before embarking upon a planting programme, all the preliminaries by way of leveling and demarcation of land, lay-out, digging of pits and their filling up, provision of irrigation channels and planting of windbreaks should be completed. It is also advisable to obtain the requisite number of plants and stock them in the nursery for some time for their proper acclimitisation, before their planting to the actual sites. Such a measure has been found to increase success percentage considerably.

Time of planting

There are two planting seasons for mango i.e. spring (February-March) and Monsoon (August-September). The latter season gives better results, particularly in the dry and arid tracts where intense summer heat of May-June results in heavy mortalities among the spring plantings.

Lay-out

Proper lay-out not only improves beauty and systematic look to the orchard, but it is as necessary as a sound foundation for a strong building, mango trees being long –lived, growers should be over-cautions to adopt a well-conceived plan of lay-out both in respect of immediate planting and future extensions. The area of immediate planting should be planned in such a way so as to take different blocks of early, mid-season and late varieties. It is a good idea to place late varieties in the centers and others outside. For mango planting, three systems of lay-out namely, square, hexagonal and quincunx are usually employed, of these, the square system is most commonly followed in the mango growing regions of the world. This system is easy to execute and permits intercultural operations cross-wise.

Planting distance

The distance of planting in mango depends upon a number of factors, such as locality, varieties to be grown and soil fertility, seedling mangoes which attain a much bigger size, need more spacing than the grafted trees. Within grafted varieties, certain varieties like Langra and Samarbahist Chausa, being more spreading, require greater space than varieties like Dushehari which ahs trees of rather small size. A distance of 10.5 metres for seedling mangoes and 9 metres for grafted mangoes is considered adequate.

Some growers have a tendency of giving less distance to their plants. Closely planted orchards become congested within a few years of their planting. Not only cultural operations in such plantations become difficult and costly, but the trees cannot get adequate amount of sunshine and air so vitally necessary for their proper growth and bearing. Given below, are the total numbers of plants that can be accommodated in and hectare with various systems:

Distance between Plants (metres)	Number of plants/ha		
	Square System	Hexagonal System	Quincunx System
9	123	137	220
10.5	90	100	162

Planting of Grafts

While planting, a hole slightly bigger than the earth ball of the plant, should be dug out in the filled up pit. The packing material around the ball of the graft should then be removed, care being taken that the ball is not injured in the process. Now the plant along with its ball is placed in the hole of the pit and with the help of the planting board, its position is set right. Moist surface soil removed from the hole earlier, should be used in refilling the vacant space and earth around the plant should be firmly pressed. As soon as planting is completed, the field should be watered.

While planting and setting the plant, it is advisable to keep its collar slightly higher in the pit than it was originally in the nursery, thus keeping a safe margin for setting down of the soil. It is unwise to allow the plants to set either too deep to too high. The graft union should be approximately 23 cm above the level of earth in the pit.

Care of the young Orchard

Young mango plants, in their early stages of orchard life, i.e. upto first four to six years, need utmost care and attention for their proper irrigation, training, hoeing, weeding and keeping them free of diseases and pests. In regions, where strong winds are rampant, it would be necessary to provide the plants with wooden stakes immediately after planting, it will be advantageous to coat the lower portions of the stakes with coaltar, to save them from white-ants.

Protection against frost

Mango trees are highly susceptible to frost injury. It has been observed that during years of severe frost, young unprotected plants five to six years old or even of more age have been found to have been killed to ground or damaged seriously. In the north India frost usually occurs during the months of December to February. Sometimes late frost may be experienced even in March. Adequate timely measures and precautions against frost are, therefore, necessary. Young plants, especially in the localities which are subject to frost, should always be well-covered up with thatches or kullies of Sarkanda, rice, sugarcane or some other farmwaste straw, keeping the south east side open for aeration and sunshine. When a frost is threatened or imminent, watering the filed has a healthy effect as it minimizes the chances of damage. Smudging, i.e., burning heaps of dry matter at several places in the orchard (which are kept ready for the purpose previously), also proves useful in warding off the ill-effects of frost. In short, the grower should keep himself fully equipped and ready to meet the menace of frost to save his valuable trees. Even a little slackness or negligence on this account, may prove disastrous for the young mango plants.

Protection against hot weather

In tracts, where the summer heat is intense and hot winds

'loo' blow, it is advisable to provide some sort of protection to the young mango trees against the vagaries of the hot weather, this can be accomplished by planting quick-growing plants like Jantar and Arhar around the basins or by constructing mud walls. The trunks of the young trees should be white-washed to afford them protection against sunburn injury. The practice of planting bananas around the newly-planted mango plants seems to be helpful in warding off intense heat by increasing humidity but care should be taken that the banana plants are kept reasonably away from the mango plants, because if the banana plants are put too closely, the practice may do more harm than good.

Windbreaks

Mango orchards should always be provided with effective windbreaks to afford protection against the onslaughts of windstorms chilly weather and other scourges. In fact, the planting of windbreak trees should proceed by 2-3 years the actual planting of mangoes so that by the time the plants grow up windbreak is there to provide proper protection, orchards sheltered by windbreaks are less prone to damage from frost than those which are exposed, without windbreaks. Moreover, in such orchards there is less evaporation of soil moisture as well as wastage of water through transpiration.

Under conditions obtaining in the Punjab, growing of tall and hardy trees, namely Tarminalia arjuna, simbal, Euclyptus and jaman is advocated for the purpose of establishing windbreak. Shisham and seedling mangoes are also equally good for this purpose. To make the windbreak more effective it is advisable if tall trees are planted alternating with short statured trees of mulberry and ber. Usually a distance of 21/2 to 41/2 metres is kept in between the windbreak trees.

Removal of early blossom

Young mango plants often being to flower in their tender age, which has a detrimental effect on their health and vigour, particularly, if such inflorescences are allowed to set fruit. Such fruiting is always at he expense of the growth of the tree which is so vitally necessary to build up a strong framework and proper size and shape of the tree. Such early inflorescences must always be nipped off immediately till the trees complete atleast four years of age and have attained sufficient size. With a large leaf canopy the tree becomes physiologically fit to bear a good fruit crop.

Propagation Techniques

Propagation by seed in mango is the oldest, cheapest and easiest method, but it has several serious defects. Seedlings raised from stones having an influence of mixed parentage seldom come true-to-type. Moreover, they also entail considerable longer period to attain bearing age, this method, therefore, has no place for use in commercial mango-growing where the grower is interested in the perpetuation of the quality of the selected varieties so as to produce fruits of known and superior quality.

As propagation of mango from seed has been practiced in different parts of the country from times immemorial, many groves and scattered plantations of mango still have a pre-ponderance of seedlings, the mango industry in the past has suffered tremendously on account of this drawback as the seedlings in most cases yield crops of unsatisfactory and inferior quality. Thanks to the propaganda and efforts made by the Agricultural Universities and State Department of Horticultural majority of the growers have now started going in for grafted varieties and new orchards are invariably stoked with grafted plants. This is a happy development and would go a long way to place our mango-growing industry on a better footing.

Vegetatively, the mango is mostly propagated thorough graftage. Inarching, veneer grafting and side grafting are the common methods of propagation, however, side grafting is considered the best method of multiplication of mango plants. Other methods like propagation from cuttings, chip budding, forkert method of budding and air layering, etc. are also employed, though on a limited scale.

Raising of Rootstock

Rootstock used for grafting is grown from stones of seedling trees. For this, the fruits from vigour, disease free and high yielding trees of seedling mangoes are collected during July-August. The stones are sown soon after they are removed from the ripe fruit as they loose their viability very soon. Mango stones gives only 10-15 per cent germination if they are sown after two months of their extraction from the fruit. Before sowing, the stones should be immersed in water and only those stones are sown which sink in water as these are considered to be viable.

The stones are sown in the beds which are prepared thoroughly after mixing well rotten farmyard manure. In the beds, the seeds are sown in lines which are 45 cm apart and distance of 60 cm is left after every two rows to facilitate the cultural practices and grafting of seedlings, the stones are sown at 15-20 cm distance within the line at the depth of 5 cm. the stones are placed in the soil with the pulmule up as it avoids distortion of seedlings. The stones after sowing are covered with the mixture of sand and farmyard manure. Mulching the beds with sarkanda, rice straw etc. increases seed germination. The beds are irrigated immediately after sowing the stones and subsequent irrigations are given to keep the soil moist but not in too much wet conditions.

The germination of stones starts after about three weeks. The seedlings will be ready for grafting when they have attained the height of about 45 cm and thickness of 0.75 to 1.5 cm. Most of the seedlings become graftable in the next April.

Preparation of scion

Mother trees from where the scion is to be taken should be healthy, vigorous and have sufficient record of good bearing. Before the actual grafting is done, the scion should be prepared carefully. For this, the healthy shoots of the last mature flush giving plump terminal buds are selected. These shoots are defoliated 7-10 days before they are detached from the mother tree for grafting, while defoliating the small petioles are left intact. The drop of these petioles and swelling of the terminal buds in week's period is good judgement of preparation of scion wood.

Inarching is done when the sap is flowing and plant is in active growth condition, during rains and dry periods, the process of inarching is avoided as this reduces the graft success. In Punjab, last week of July or the first week of August is the best period for inarching.

Side grafting can be carried out successfully from March to October, but success during the May and October is rather low.

Orchard Cultural practices

Training and Pruning

The training of the mango plants in the initial stages is very essential to give them proper shape. Specially when the graft has branched too low, the process of training becomes very important. Atleast 75 cm of the main stem should be kept free from branching and the first leader of main branch should be allowed after that. The main branches should be spaced in such a way that they grow in different directions and are atleast 20-25 cm apart otherwise there are every chances of breakage due to smaller crotch angles and heavy top.

Normally mango trees require very less or no pruning. During its first four years of orchard life, the mango plants need not be given any pruning except the removal of dead or diseased branches, if any. The side branches emerging too near the ground may also be removed but it is not a sound practice to cut away the small drooping lateral branches emerging from the head. Such a practice has been found to dwarf the tree and delay its bearing.

A dome-shaped top, neither too near the ground nor too high, avoids exposure to the trunk form the sunburn injury, should be the aim of ideal training and pruning in young mango trees. After the trees are well grown up, the crossed or too close braches which crowd the center of the trunk and weak branched underneath the main limbs which remain under perpetual shade, should be removed. Always restrict pruning to the barest minimum, as every healthy branch having foliage fully exposed to the sun, is an asset for its future fruiting and bearing. This rule of minimum pruning should apply to mango trees of all categories, young or old, grafted or seedling.

Top-working of inferior mango trees:

The old unproductive and inferior seedling trees which are

found in large numbers everywhere, can be rejuvenated and improved by the process of top-working. Conversion of inferior trees into superior varieties of proven performance, not only improves orchard performance, but increase the income from mango trees in the shortest time.

The selected scaffold limbs of inferior or unproductive trees; desired to be top-worked are headed back in February-March with a saw having 2-3 feet long stubs. The cut ends are applied with Bordeaux paint. Many shoots emerge within a short time below the stubs. Out of these, 2-3 vigorous shoots per branch or limb are selected and the remaining are removed. Since the new shoots are very weak at the points of emergence, they are suitably staked to make grow straight. These shoots make fast growth and become suitable for grafting by August-September of the same year.

Rejuvenation of old mango trees

The old mango trees have a tendency to develop hollows in their trunks and in main branches starting from crotch or the point of bifurcation. Rain water is deposited here and this causes the bark and wood inside it to rot. This process continues year after year, thus large cavities are formed. Similarly, when a branch is broken by wind or mechanically, the untrimmed stub left behind usually rots and dies. Old trees in neglected condition with unhealthy braches full of diseases and insect-pests need be rejuvenated. The stem-borers should be removed and suitable measures should bet taken to check the diseases. Add 100 kg of well-rotten farmyard manure to each plant, top-working of old mango trees be cleft-grafting, budding or bark grafting is practised. Such trees in weak health can also be invigorated by infusing fresh sap of younger seedlings into them. Many stocks are planted near the old trees and when these have attained the height of one metre or more from ground level they are headed back and the cut ends are then shaped to wedge and inserted into barks of the old tree and tied up.

Interculture

Interculture of the mango orchards is necessary not only to remove the weeds which compete for water and nutrients but also to ensure aeration which is so essential for the proper development of roots and shoots. Hoeing also serves the purpose of mulching and thereby reduces the frequency of irrigation. Interculture may help in reducing the insect-pest population by killing them physically. Frequency and the time of intercultural operations will vary with age of the orchard. If the intercrops are not being raised in the pre-bearing stage due to some reasons, then area in between the basin should also be ploughed atleast three times in a year i.e., pre-monsoon, post-monsoon and in the last week of November.

For the bearing mango orchards, interculture is also equally important. First cultivation should be done before the onset of rains. This help in checking run off losses and facilitate maximum intake of water into the soil. Orchard may be ploughed again after the rainy season is over so as to suppress the weed growth and also to break capillaries. Third cultivation may be dome in the last week of November or first week of December in order to check the population of mango mealy bug.

Irrigation

Amount and frequency of irrigation to be given depends upon the type of soil, climatic condition especially rainfall and its distribution and age of trees, the irrigation requirements of young and non bearing trees are different from those of the bearing trees.

The young non-bearing trees need to be irrigated more frequently in order to grow vigorously and rapidly. The newly planted young mango plants, upto their first four to six months should receive irrigations twice a week in the hot weather. Therefore, the interval of irrigation as well as quantum of water per irrigation may be progressively increased. For the first four to five years, the irrigation must be frequent and regular though of light intensity. During rainy season interval may be adjusted keeping in view the intensity of rainfall and its distribution.

In bearing trees, during the period of two or three months preceding flowering season, profuse irrigation is inadvisable. For the rest of the year, a mango tree should receive irrigation according to its needs which in turn would depend upon several factors such as soil structure, climatic conditions, variety and rootstock and age of the trees. In lighter soils, more frequent irrigation would be necessary than in case of heavy soils. Similarly, irrigation needs during hot, dry and windy weather will be heavier than in rainy and cold weather.

Generally intercrops are grown during the early years after plantation and hence method of application has to be adjusted accordingly. Upto 5 years after planting, it is better to make basins around the plants and connect them in series so that irrigation could be administered independent of the intercrop. For subsequent age, irrigation can be combined with that of intercrops. However, if intercrops are to be abandoned in fully-bearing orchards then basin system should be followed so as to economise on the water use. Then the basins may be connected in series or to a channel dug in between the rows.

Manuring and fertilization

Although mango grows well even in poor soils because of its deep root system but keeping in view the vegetative growth it has to attain and removal of nutrients through the harvest, it needs some amount of fertilizers. Nutrition requirements may vary wit the region depending upon the type of soil and age of the tree. The underfed and under-nourished trees fail to give satisfactory bearing of fruit.

The life cycle of the mango can be divided into five parts, viz. nursery stage, establishment in the field and non-bearing, bearing and a gain periods of trees. Broadly speaking, it falls under two main categories viz. non-bearing and bearing stages, while the chief requirements in pre-bearing age are a rapid growth and the development of a strong framework, during the bearing periods good cropping, regular bearing and high quality of fruit are the primary objectives. Nutritional requirements of the trees at different stages, therefore, vary a great deal and are discussed below separately.

Non-bearing trees

This stage extends form the planting of a tree in the orchard until it begins to yield fruits. As already stated above, the manurial programme during this period has to be designed in such a manner so as to achieve speedy development of the tree together with formation of strong limbs and sound framework. The young trees in this stage need to be given liberal doses of nitrogen, calcium and phosphorus. Potassium would also be needed in reasonable amounts. In soils where calcium content is inherently high and which have a pH ranging from 7.0 to 8.0, the surface application of calcium may not be necessary but in soils where pH is low, ranging between 5.5 to 6.5, it may be necessary to add calcium through delomitic lime. The quantities required to be applied would depend on soil reaction and in certain cases may run as high as 2 quintals per acre.

During the non-bearing period, nitrogen is particularly needed in rather heavy quantities to support healthy and fast growth. It would be advantageous to apply substantial portion of N in the form of organic matter, so that texture of the soil, its moisture holding capacity and ultimately the development of roots there in may be improved. Phosphorus would be needed to cope with high respiration rates and for translocation of carbohydrates. Potash would also be required to meet the need of photosynthesis.

The above different needs can be met roughly if N, p and K applied at the rate of 50-100, 40-80 and 100-200 g of actual nitrogen, phosphorous and potash for each year age of the tree with 40 to 80 per cent derived from organic source.

Bearing trees

During this stage the manurial programme should aim at two fold objectives, viz. (a) to maintain optimum vegetative growth from year to year, and (b) to ensure regular cropping with superior quality fruit.

In mango, which is a terminal bearer, the fruit-bud differentiation under most situations takes place about four to five months before flowering. There is an antagonism between growth and fruiting in the tree. In the year of heavy flowering and fruiting the vegetative growth remains suppresses which in turn affects adversely next year's crop. If the early flush of vegetative shoots does not come up due to heavy flowering and fruiting, very few mature shoots would be available at the time of fruit-bud differentiation or formation of floral buds and hence there would be little or no flowering next spring. Manuring of the mango is, therefore, quite complex problem and a grower has to keeping view all factors involved in order to get good results.

The following fertilizers schedule is recommended for mango trees:

Tree age (years)	Farm yard manure (kg)	Nutrient (g)		
		Nitrogen	Phosphorus	Potash
1-3	5-20	50-100	40-80	100-200
4-6	25-50	100-200	80-100	200-400
7-9	60-90	200-250	120-160	400-600
10 & above	100	250	160	600

The above does are for the 'off' year of crop. During the 'on' year apply one additional kg of CAN in June. Apply the whole quantity of farmyard manure and phsophatic fertilizer in December. Apply all nitrogen and potash in February. During 'on' year, split the nitrogen dose into two parts, first part is given at the time of flowering and the remaining half in the month of June.

DEFICIENCIES AND IMPORTANCE OF ESSENTIAL ELEMENTS

Mineral nutrition of mango plants is an important soil-management practice in an orchard. The life of plant is markedly influenced without these elements. Symptoms of deficiency and excess of essential nutrients have been discussed below.

Nitrogen

The total nitrogen content in mango orchard soils (0-15 cm depth) in different parts of the Punjab ranges between 0.018 to 0.045 per cent with a mean value of 0.032 per cent. The mango orchard soils around Malihabad (Lucknow) had total nitrogen content of 0.018 to 0.054 per cent.

The most striking symptom of nitrogen deficiency are the severe retardation of growth, yellow and under-sized leaves. Sand culture experiment of 'Langra' mango exhibits retardation of growth under all the degrees of deficiency of nitrogen. The fruit set is greatly reduced and leaves mature without attaining normal size. The leaf stalks form narrow angles with the stem. The mature leaves become yellow. The symptom first appear near the base of the current growth and progress toward the tip. Twigs become stiff and woody, limited in length and diameter. Under acute deficiency, the fruit size greatly, reduced, tended to ripe and drop prematurely.

The incidence of physiological disease like softnose is increased with an increase in nitrogen fertilization. This can be reduced by maintaining leaf-calcium at 2.5 per cent either by supplying nitrogen as calcium or by adding limestone or gypsum.

Phosphorus

The deficiency of phosphorus causes stunting of growth in mango. As the deficiency persists, causes premature defoliation following dying back from the tips. The younger leaves become excessively green ad slightly smaller than normal, the wood of the main trunk become thin and willowy and cause dying back in some branches.

While growing plants of 'Langra' mango in sand, it was observed that the phosphorus deficiency caused slow plant growth and delayed fruit maturity. An early symptom was the development of reddish purple colour on the underside of the leaf, first starting as spots, later spreading over the entire leaf with veins finally becoming reddish purple. The leaves were thick and stunted. The roots were also stunted. The plants were late in setting fruit.

The high level of phosphorus in shoots of Dusehari mango is found favourable of flower-bud formation. During August, there is not much difference in the level of different fractions of phosphorus in potential flowering and non-flowering shoots. As the time of flower-bud initiation approached nearer i.e. November-December, the level of phosphorus fractions except nucleic acid become quite high in the flowering stems. The leaves from the flowering shoots also has a high level of phosphorus but the differences are not so marked as in the case of stems.

Mango trees appear to be quite sensitive to heavy phosphorus fertilization accumulating as much as 0.84 per cent phosphorus in leaves on dry weight basis against 0.08–0.175 per cent in normal leaves. This excessive phosphorus resulted in a spotting of mature leaves in fall, first appearing on the lower surface, but later on also on the upper surface.

Necrotic areas also developed on the margins of some leaves. Leaves become chlorotic and sheds heavily. It also cause some drying of shoots.

Potassium

The mild potassium deficiency is confused with the symptoms of nitrogen deficiency. Pronounced symptoms of potassium deficiency appears as characteristic type of foliage necrosis. The leaves located near the middle or slightly below the middle of the current season's growth are the first to be affected. From this position, the injury spreads towards the distal and basal part of the affected twig. The scorch usually located along the leaf margin and proceeded by dark purplish discolouration, the intensity of the scorch varies with severity of the potassium deficiency.

In Florida, the leaf potassium of 0.3 to 0.8 per cent is suggested as a desirable range for mango. In Philippines, foliar spray of potassium nitrate at 12.5 g per litre induced early, uniform and profuse flowering in 'Carabao' mango, the fruiting was has not produced such a response in mango under Indian conditions.

Calcium

The calcium deficiency do not cause any definite leaf patterns but the trees deprived of calcium remain small and slightly lighter green than normal. Increasing the calcium level in the tree with heavy application of limestone or gypsum reduce the incidence of soft-nose.

Magnesium

Magnesium deficiency in mango growing in sand cause stunting of plants which become pale, smaller in height and girth, in the developing leaves, yellowing white areas between the main veins on both sides of the mid-rib run parallel toward the margin. Prominent yellowish specks first visible on both sides of the mid-rib and flows chlorosis.

It was reported that adding more than 98.5 kg of magnesium per tree per year in 'Kent' mangoes is not useful.

Sulphur

The general behaviour of the minus-sulphur trees is somewhat similar to that of phosphorus-deficient trees. In sulphur deficient plant growth is gradually reduced and severe defoliation occurred. The leaves turns very dark green but upon reaching maturity, they develop necrotic areas along the margins and absciss soon-after. The location of the dead leaf areas is the chief distinction between these two deficiencies, being a tip scorch in the case of phosphorus and a side scorch with sulphur.

High concentration of sulphur-dioxide in the atmosphere near the brick-kilns and other industrial units burning coal have resulted in Black tip in mango.

Manganese

Manganese deficiency of mango plants in sand culture cause paling and dropping of plants. Lightening of green between the principal veins develops which gradually turn yellow with a band of green along the mid-rib and the lateral veins in the young leaves. As the deficiency progress characteristic mottling of the leaf appears. Later, prominent yellow colour develop with dark-brown pinhead like spots scattered all over the leaf. This is followed by leaf fall, the size and shape of the leaves is quite normal but the number of the leaves and the twigs are less than the normal.

In an experiment, 800 ppm manganese in the nutrient solution proved highly toxic to mango seedlings, there was marginal necrosis of leaves with deep brown colour between the veins gradually proceeding toward the mid-ribs. This was followed by curling and drying of leaves from the margins inward. Apical buds died, growth remained stunted, ultimately resulting in the death of plants.

Copper

No characteristic uniform symptoms of copper deficiency on plants in sand-culture has been observed. However, severe tip burn in old leaves with grey-brown patches is noticed. The plants are pale green in appearance. The minus copper plants turns slightly lighter green than normal and ahs S-shape limb growth.

Boron

The deficiency of Boron on mango plants in sand culture cause stunted growth and short internodes in some plants, the new terminal leaves in the deficient plants are reduced in size, looking pale green, distorted and brittle, the older leaves are normal green but are smaller than those borne by the control plants. Some leaves curved on one side, the mid-rib turns brown from the ventral side.

Zinc

The zinc deficiency cause stunting of growth within the first six months in sand culture which become more prominent in the second year. The leaves turn pale yellow but less pale than those suffering from nitrogen deficiency, small, thin pointed, narrow and brittle with petioles making acute angle with the stem. Grey brown necrotic patches of irregular shape scattered all over the leaf surface. On some leaves, they spread across the whole leaf surface with distal portion dying, necrotic areas finally fell off giving a shot-hole appearance, root growth is also stunted.

Zinc deficiency first appears on terminal flushes with upper part of the tree. The symptoms consists of stunted growth of young leaves with interveinal chlorosis. The affected leaves curb backward giving a cup-shaped appearance. The tips and margins of the curled leaves become chlorotic. The leaves eventually broken down and detach from the lamina. It can be controlled by spraying 1 per cent zinc sulphate or 0.2 per cent zinc oxide, preferably at the beginning of the growing season, thoroughly wetting the foliage. At Ludhiana, a 0.2 per cent zinc sulphate spray gave complete recovery of zinc deficiency symptoms in mangoes growing under field conditions.

Iron

A pot-culture study on mango did not produce any symptoms of chemicals and environmental pollutants may have provided enough iron for normal growth of the plants in the minus-iron cultures. However, in Florida occasional chlorosis observed on young mango trees growing on lime stone area.

Chlorine

Chloride injury in mango manifests as a leaf scorch which starts from the leaf tip, generally 8-10 months after emergence. As the leaf gets older, the scorch becomes brick red and progresses along the leaf margins, slowly covering the major portion of the lamina. Nearly all the affected leaves which emerge in March start abscising in April of the next year. After a few years, the young twigs start drying, giving a sickly look to the tree. The chloride affected mango leaves had 0.02 to 0.09 per cent chlorine as compared with 0.01 per cent chloride in the healthy leaves on dry weight basis.

Intercropping

During the first few years of their non-bearing life and until the trees have grown to a big size, the vacant land in between the mango trees can be profitably utilized for the cultivation of harmless types of intercrops like fodders, farm crops, vegetables and pulses preferably of leguminous type. Intercropping should always be judicious and needs of the trees should receive primary consideration, otherwise the practice may prove extremely harmful. Intercropping helps to keep the weeds under check, which otherwise would rob the orchard soil of plant nutrients and moisture.

While intercropping, the trees should be provided with suitable wide basins and an independent irrigation system. They should also be given regular hoeings and weedings. When the trees grow up to a big size, as it usually happens after their 10-12 years of life, then discontinue the intercropping as at that stage it would impair with their normal growth and fruiting, in order to replenish the organic matter content of the soil, green manuring with leguminous corps like guara, hemp and senji may be carried out, depending upon the need of the soil. Instead of intercropping, temporary quick growing fruit trees can be grown as fillers which are removed when the mango trees assume big size. Papaya, peach, pulp, guava and phalsa are grown as fillers.

Harvesting and Handling of Fruits

Mango is highly perishable fruit, it should be harvested when they have attained full maturity but are not ripe. In successful orcharding, harvesting the fruit at its proper stage of maturity, its careful sorting, grading and marketing are the most vital processes. The factors like stage of fruit maturity at harvest, method of harvest, handling during transportation and temperature and method of ripening determine the development of typical aroma and taste. Marketing is dependent on quality of the fruit, faulty methods of harvesting cause a lot of damage and bruising of the fruits which is the main cause of fruit spoilage. The fruit should be properly handled to fetch better price in the market and to enhance the shelf life.

Harvesting and yield

Harvesting of fruit at its proper stage of maturity is of fundamental importance. The characteristic colour and typical flavour of a variety develop at appropriate stage of maturity, the stage of maturity at harvest effects the fruit quality and its storage life. In Northern Indian conditions, fruit of early varieties become usually ready for harvest by the end of June and the ripening season in case of late varieties may extend up to the end of August. If the fruits are picked when these are not fully mature, they develop white patches and the normal TSS/acid ratio is also not obtained. On the other hand, if the fruits are picked when over-mature or fully ripe, more microbial and physiological spoilage occurs due to the increased susceptibility of the fruits, thus reduced the shelf life considerable, therefore, the mango fruits should be harvested at the proper and correct stage of maturity, premature picking should be discouraged because such degreened fruits cannot develop proper taste and flavour.

The fruits are usually harvested when green in colour, fully mature but unripe. Generally, when a few ripe fruits have fallen on their own accord from the tree, the rest of the fruits are considered sufficiently mature, but this criterion is not always reliable and dependable. Development of characteristic colour of spots and appearance of bloom on the skin are also important criteria of fruit maturity, specific gravity and starch content of the hard fruit have observed to be associated with maturity, direct measurement of the percentage of starch in the flesh is found to be a comparatively accurate method for determining the degree of maturity in hard green fruits. Picking fruits at specific gravity give satisfactory results in respect of uniform ripening and keeping quality. Pressure test is also employed to determine the fruit maturity, a practical method of standardization of the stage of maturity for picking would be a combination of various methods for individual varieties in a particular region. Generally, the TSS 12-15 per cent, a pressure 1.75 – 2 kg per sq. cm and specific gravity will generally give a fair index of maturity. For judging maturity, the physical development of the fruit such as rounding of ventral edge, development of beak, out-growing of shoulders, filling up of the hollow at the stemend and development of the characteristic colour should also be considered together.

The fruit injured or even slightly bruised during the picking operation losses its keeping quality and becomes unfit for despatch of distant markets. The usual practices of knocking down the fruits or shaking the trees violently to get the fruit down need to be discouraged. If the fruit is hanging high, it should be picked up with the help of a step ladder. In no case the picker should climb up the tree as this practice is harmful both for the tree and the picker. The fruits should always be gently cut with special type of clipper and placed in canvas bags or padded baskets and carried to the packing house, a device known as mango-picker, fixed with a long pole, can also be usefully employed for picking of fruits hanging high on the trees, a small fruit stalk (button) should be kept with the fruit which helps in keeping the fruit in better condition in transportation and storage.

Grafted mango usually start bearing from the fourth to sixth year after their planting. Some trees of the varieties like Dusehari are precocious and start bearing even in the third or the fourth year. A grafted mango tree usually continue to bear till upto 50 years, but its most prolific years of bearing are generally from the tenth to the fourteenth years. During an 'on' years; a well looked after mango tree of 10 to 20 years bears a crop of about 500 to 1000 fruits, during 20 to 40 years its yield may will range between 1000-3000 fruits. Seedling trees usually take about eight years to come into bearing but their productive life is much longer, many old trees of 100 years of age in mango growing regions are known to be still bearing heavy crops.

Mango orcharding is indeed very paying, especially in the tracts highly suitable for mango culture. It may well bring an income of Rs. 15,000/- to Rs. 20,000/- per acre or even more depending upon the prevailing conditions.

Grading and Packing

Sorting and grading are desirable pre-requisites for successful marketing. Through sorting, over-ripe, damaged dull or inferior fruits are removed. The fruits sent to the market after proper grading in different lot, can fetch better price. It is a fact that fruit graded according to size or its stage of maturity brings a higher price than the fruit which is sold without any grading. Some sieves having circular holes of 8.0, 7.5 and 7.0 cm diameter can be used to distinguish fruits, the fruits of mango can be graded according to their weight as follows:

Ist grade: Fruit weight 320 g or more

2nd grade: Fruit weight 270-320 g

3rd grade: Fruit weight 200-270 g

The common practice is to pack the fruits in bamboo baskets which usually are not of any standard size. Now the wooden boxes are used for packing mangoes. The lining material may be used in the boxes. Individual fruits can be wrapped in tissue paper or ordinary paper which increases the eye appeal. The fruits intended to be shipped should be cleaned before their packing, thereafter they should be packed in suitable containers in such a way that curing occurs in the pack itself either during transit or at the market site where those are intended to be sold, such containers used for distant market should be strong and rigid. The fruits packed suitably in boxes or crates reaches its destination in a safe and sound condition and brings more profit in the long run.

Storage

To avoid the gluts in the market, the methods of proper storage of mangoes have proved useful to dispose of the fruit over extended periods. Storage at optimum low temperature has effective in increasing storage life, the treatment of fruits with wax-emulsion not only extends the storage life under cold storage and at room temperature but it also makes the fruits brighter, glossy and attractive, the fruits treated with 4 per cent wax emulsion can be kept at room temperature for 12 days and 35 days in cold storage (37°F ± 1 and 85-90% relative humidity) after packing in perforated polythene bags. Fully matured but still hard fruits of Dusehari and Langra, mango can be successfully stored for 35 45 days respectively at 7°C to 9°C temperature and relative humidity of 85-90 per cent. Mangoes meant for cold storage, must always be carefully packed in wooden crates and each individual fruit should be wrapped in tissue paper and packed in sufficient packing material to keep the fruits in position in the crate.

Whereas cold storage of mango does not offer much scope commercially quick freezing of mango slices in sugar syrup offers bright prospects for the trade. Mango slices thus preserved retain their characteristic fresh flavour for considerable time during frozen storage. Quick freezing of mango pulp and mango slices of green mangoes for preparing mango chutney or other important products can be employed profitably.

Fully developed green Langra and Dusehari mangoes can be artificially ripened by treating with 800 ppm ethral @ 1.5 g/kg of fruit, the time for ripening reduces to 4 days as compared to 8 days in untreated fruits by conventional method.

Plant Protection Measures

The mango is attacked at its various stages of development

by a number of insects and diseases. If these are not properly checked or controlled, may occur heavy losses. Some of the most important insect pests and diseases and their control measure are described below.

A. Insect-pests

Most of the mango pests have a seasonal activity and usually make serious attacks during one season or the other, a brief description of biology and control of major insect-pests is given below:

Mango mealy bug (Drosicha mangiferae)

This is a major pest of mango in India and does a lot of damage during the flowering and fruiting stage from January to April, during this time, large number of young nymphs crawl up the trees and congregate on the growing shoots and panicles. Soon after hatching, the nymphs emerge from the soil and crawl up the trees in large numbers from December to April, they suck plant juices thereby causing the tender shoot and panicles to dry up.

Nymphs should be prevented from crawling up the trunk by applying a slippery or sticky band 1 metre above the ground level by mid-December.

Slippery band

To the basal end of the stem, 15-20 cm wide sheet of alkathene is applied and its upper and lower edge is secured with 2-3 nails (2 cm), it is desirable to cover the lower end with compacted soil around the lower edge of the alkathene sheet so that nymphs are prevented from climbing up under the slippery band. In case of severe emergency, apply 50% of methyl parathion dust (Follidol 2% or BHC 10%) on the compacted soil to kill the nymphs.

Sticky band

A 5 cm wide band of Ostico or Esso fruit grease is applied on the trunk. As and when necessary, this can be repeated after scrapping off the crust. The nymphs congregating below the bands should be killed by spraying them with 200 ml of methyl parathion 50 EC in 100 litres of water. In case of the sticky band, a flame can also be used to destroy the mealy bug.

Mango hopper (Idiocerus sp. and Idioscopus sp.)

This is the most destructive insect of mango and is very active during February-March at the time of flowering. The nymphs and adults suck the sap from the tender leaves and panicles which become sticky and sooty, young fruits and dried inflorescence fall to the ground as the summer winds blow.

The insect can be controlled by spraying the trees in the end of February and again in the end of March with either 500 g Sevin or Hexavin 50 WP (Carbaryl) or 400 ml of Malathion 50 EC or 350 ml of Thiodan in 250 litres of water. Aerial spray with 550 ml of Malathion LVC per acre is also very effective.

Mango fruit fly (Dacus dorsalis):

Maggots of about half a dozen species of fruit-flies occur in various fruits like peach, plum, fig, guava and attacked fruits begin to rot and fall off. The females lay eggs just below the epidermis of fruit or some time little deeper in the pulp. After hatching the maggots starts feeding the pulp of fruit and cause brown rotten path on the fruit surface. On cutting, the wriggling maggots can be seen inside the fruits. The fruits fall and maggots come out of fruit to pupate in the soil. Its attack not only reduces yield but also affects the quality of the fruit adversely.

The maggots are found inside the fruits, the pupae in the soil and adults are active fliers, it is, thus, problematic to control this pest. However, the adults are attacked by a number of natural enemies like wasps and parasites. Affected fruits should be promptly collected and destroyed. Ploughing of the field in January-February to expose the pupae to natural enemies can reduce the population considerably.

Another method to control the incidence is to hand traps containing 100 ml emulsion of methyl eugenol 0.1% and 0.1%.

Malathion from April-June in the mango orchards. About 10 traps are sufficient for one hectare of orchard.

Mango stem-borer (Batocera rufomaculata)

The mango stem borers are well-built large long horn beetles of a dull greyish-yellow colour. The grubs inflict damage by boring galleries in the main trunk and branches, ultimately killing the tree or the branch. Wooden frass come out of the surface holes.

To control this insect remove the frass and inject 4 ml of methyl parathion 50 EC dissolved in a litre of water into the hole and plug it with mud.

Barkeating caterpillar (Indarbella guadrinolata)

The larvae of this insect are principal feeders of the bark and spun a loose brownish web of silken strands in which excretal pellets and piece of bark are entrapped. It has single generation in a year. The moths are observed during April-May. Larvae develop from May-September. Pupation occurs during February-March. The attack is more serious on old trees and neglected orchards.

For its control remove webbing and apply BHC suspension (10 g BHC 50 WP in 10 litres of water) on the bark and into the hole with wash bottle during September-October and again in January-February.

Mango shoot borer (Chulmetia transversa)

Mango shoot borer is a serious pest of mango especially in nurseries. Adults emerge in last week of March. The eggs are laid singly on the upper side of the tender leaves. Larvae on their emergence bore into midrib or leaf stalk. Later on it enters the shoot which later on dries. Full fed larvae came out for pupation. As a result of its attack the fresh growth of the plant particularly in nursery is checked. For its control remove and burn the dried shoots and spray the new growth with 700 ml of Thiodan 35 EC in 500 litres of water per acre.

Red ants (Oecophylla smargidina)

Red ants may infest some mango orchards. They are a nuisance and given protection to certain injurious coccids in their nests of leave formed on the tree. To check this pest remove the nests and burn them. Spray the trees with 500 g of BHC 50 WP in 250 litres of water.

Mango scale

The mango scale sometimes appears as a pest in certain localities. It inflects damage by sucking the sap from leaves. To control mango scale, spray the trees with 1.25 litres of Basudin 20 EC (Diazinon) or 300 ml of methyl parathion 50 EC in 500 litres of water during March and September.

B. Diseases

Mango is subject to a number of diseases at all stages of its development. Almost every part i.e., trunk, branch, leaf, petiole, flower and fruit is attacked by fungi, bacterial and algae. These manifest diseases like rot, die-back, anthracnose, scab, necrosis, blotch, and spots, some of these diseases have become a limiting factor in mango orcharding in some regions. Some major diseases and their control measures are discussed below:

Powdery mildew (Microsphaera alphitoides f. mangiferae):

Powdery mildew is one of the worst diseases of mango affecting almost every variety. The disease appears mostly during February-March and sometimes earlier due to congenial temperature and humidity in North India, a whitish powdery growth appears on the inflorescence and the floral axis. The infected floral parts show necrotic streaks and eventually drop. Small fruits may also drop because of the mildew attack on the peduncle. The branchlets and branches of the floral axis show die-back symptoms and eventually drop, leaving the main axis naked. The disease can be kept under control by spraying 0.1 per cent Karathane (500 ml of Karathane in 500 litres of water) or 0.25 per cent wettable sulphur (1.25 kg in 500 litres of water) once before flowering, again during flowering and then after fruit-set. If need be arises one more spray should be given after 10-15 days. The timing of the first spray is very important which must be given as soon as the growers observe the very young inflorescence stalks emerging out from the flowering buds. Quantity of spray suspension will depend upon the age and size of the tree.

Anthracnose (Colletotrichum gloeosporioides):

The disease mostly affects the tender parts of the mango plant. Young shoots, leaves, panicles, flowers and fruits are liable to attack. On leaves dark-brown necrotic areas appear while on the twigs black necrotic patches are observed during the season. On the rachis of the panicle (both on main and secondary rachis) very small and dark spots appears. When young shoots are infected, the attacked parts show symptoms of die-back. Fruits bearing black spots rot during storage. The spread and dissemination of the fungal pathogen is favoured under conditions of high humidity and frequent rains, which also influence the intensity of attack by the pathogen.

The diseased twigs should be pruned and burnt alongwith fallen leaves for reducing the inoculum potential. Immediately after pruning in December or January, some disinfectant solution is applied on cut ends of main branches or twigs followed by the application of Bordeaux paste, to the large cut ends of limbs, Bordeaux paint is applied, immediately thereafter spray all plants with Bordeaux mixture 2:2:250. during February, March and April and again during September-October, repeat spraying of all plants with Bordeaux mixture 2:2:250 at monthly intervals.

Leaf blight or twig die-back (Macrophoma mangiferae):

Leaf blight disease has become widespread disease. Minute light brown spots appear on large and green twigs. These spots enlarge and cover more than half of the leaf surface, the inner margin of the lesions is dark brown. The severally affected twigs die-back. Dark brown lesions appear on young and ripening fruits flowed by rotting. The measures to check the leaf blight are the same as in anthracnose expect applying additional sprays of Bordeaux mixture 2:2:250.

Stem canker (Schizophyllum commune):

Symptoms consist of discolouration and drying of the foliage of one or more branches. The most characteristic symptom of infection of fungi is the education of gum from the affected bark. The affected trees and branches may be killed in course of time. Finally, small shell like dirty white fruiting bodies of the fungus, with gills in the lower side, appear in rows on the dead main branches at very late stage.

Removal of the affected tissues, parts of branches, stem portions or lesions and protection of the exposed portions with disinfectant solution, followed by the application of Bordeaux past and within a week thereafter applying Bordeaux paint to seal the exposed wound against water damage and consequential entry of fungi, will definitely save the trees. To provide protection for the developing fruit against fruit-rot fungi, particularly if untimely rains are received, spray with 1.5 kg Copper oxychloride in 500 litres of water or Bordeaux mixture 2:2:250 at fortnightly intervals should be given.

Bacterial blight (Pseudomonas mangiferae indicae and Erwinia mangiferae indicae)s

The bacterial blight diseases has become widespread on almost all varieties of mango. It assumes serious form only in humid areas or in seasons when temperature and humidity conditions become favourable for its spread from the leaves on to the fruits in early stage of development. Leaves as well as fruits both are damaged but fruits become severally attacked and disfigured. On leaves, panicles and fruits, tiny spots appear in the initial stages; these spots gradually enlarge in area and later from a raised spot on the side of the fruit, the onset of rain at this cycle of disease, increases widespread dissemination of bacteria which are able to cause severe secondary infection under the prevalent environmental conditions, the disease may assume an epidemic form. The tissue of the fruit which has been attacked begins to show deep cracks, exudating a gummy substance which is full of bacterial cells of the pathogen, the severely affected fruits drop down and become unfit for human consumption. The bacterial ooze is spread by wind splashed rain. The spray application of Bordeaux mixture 2:2:250 immediately after every rain storm can check the disease to some extent.

Disorders in Mango

1. Alternate bearing

Alternate bearing is a very serious and an old problem in mango, it is the production of a heavy crop in one year and no crop or very little crop in the next year, alternation between good an bad bearing year's is not always regular because after a good crop year, two or more poor crop years may follow and conversely after a bad year two or more good crop years may occur. Various causes like varietal difference, growth habit, crop load, cultural practices, sex-ratio, insects-pests and diseases, etc. have been attributed to the occurrence of biennial bearing in mango. Besides, there endogenous level of growth hormones, reserve metabolits and nutrient status had also been considered responsible for the bienniality in mango. Biennial bearing is a characteristic of a variety and some workers emphasised that this is due to the genomic constitution of the particular variety.

Most of the commercial varieties of North India e.g. Dusehari, Langra and Chausa are prone to biennial bearing but varieties of South India like Totapari Red Small, Neelam and Bangalore and regular bearers.

The horticulturists since decades have worked to control this malady but so far no concrete control measures have been put forward. However, application of deblossoming, pruning, better cultural practices and exogenous plant regulator treatments have shown good results in recent years. Scientists are engaged in hybridising North Indian irregular bearing varieties with comparatively regular bearing varieties from south India. The experiments have started yielding encouraging results and as an outcome, a highly regular variety Amarpalli has been evolved by crossing "Dusehari × Neelam" by the Scientists of Indian Agricultural Research Institute, New Delhi.

Recent work to control alternate bearing has shown possibility of using an ethylene releasing compound, ethephon in inducing flowers every year. The concentration of ethephon 200 ppm coupled with 0.1 per cent urea was found effective in inducing regular flowering over the year. Five sprays in all are recommended to be made beginning from middle of September at monthly interval.

(2) Mango Malformation

Malformation is a major malady of mango in India causing heavy losses to the orchardists. This disorder is caused perhaps due to environmental factor, mites, virus or fungus (Fusarium moniliformae var. Subglutinans). Mango malformation is widely distributed in India. Maximum incidence has been reported from Punjab, Haryana and Western Uttar Pradesh, where more than 50% of the plants are affected by malformation. The incidence of malformation is, however, less in Western and Southern India. Almost all the commercial varieties of mango of North India are highly susceptible to malformation.

On seedling over three month old, swelling appear in the axil of leaves, small clustered leafy-shoots are produced at the apex on the main shoot or lateral, in the case of bearing trees the panicles are affected. The peduncles become thickened and fleshy with profuse branching, the floral branches are crowded in the form of a cone. Fertile flowers are rare and fruits are seldom formed. The whole mass turns grayish-brown and then black. A profuse development of numerous small, leafy structures occurs in place of flowers, resulting in a witch bloom appearance. Each group of the leafy structures represents a malformed floret. A few or all the inflorescence produced by a tree may be malformed, off season panicles may also be affected.

Malformation has profound influence on the sex expression of mango because malformed panicles mostly produce male flowers and hence no fruit is produced on these panicles. The fungus (Fusarium moniliformae var. Subglutinans) have been isolated from malformed panicles. Recently, floral malformation like symptoms were also induced by a plant growth regulator known as morphactin.

Different methods of checking malformation like pruning of diseased portions; use of fungicides, plant growth regulators and deblossoming have been tried with some success. To control this malady, the affected shoots should be removed every month and destroyed, one spray of 200 ppm Naphthelene acetic acid (NAA) in October (Dissolve 110 g NAA in some alcohol and make volume upto 550 litre) is effective in reducing the incidence of malformation.

(3) Fruit Drop

Fruit drop is a serious problem in mango and cause great loss to the mango growers. A tree producing several thousand panicles, yields only a few hundred fruits, most of the flowers falling down after full bloom or at later stage of development. Only 0.1 per cent flower or even less develop into mature fruit, maximum fruit drop takes place in last week of April or first week of May depends upon favourable condition. The phenomenon of fruit drop in North India has been divided into three distinct phases e.g. pin head drop, post-setting drop and May drop.

The flower drop as well as the fruit-drop is primarily due to the formation of an abscission layer at the point of attachment of the fruit with the twig. Several factors have been considered responsible for the formation of abscission layer, it has been observed that Nitrogen retards and reduces abscission. Low carbohydrates have also been found to lead to leaf, flower, bud and fruit abscission, fruit drop has been attributed to many other causes e.g. abortion of embryo, degeneration of ovules, poor soil, inadequate irrigation water, attack of insect-pest and diseases, depletion of nutrients, hormonal imbalance, etc.

Fruit drop may be controlled to some extent by the spray of 20 ppm of 2,4-D (2 g in 100 litres of water) in the last week of April or in the first week of May in Langra and Dusehari Cultivars.

(4) Black tip

Te black tip disorder of mango fruit is a very serious problem in mango orchards located in the vicinity of brick kilns. Black tip is characterized by a depressed spot of yellowing tissues at the distal end of the fruit. This spot increases in size with time and also changes colour to brown and finally black. The black-tip affected fruits almost stop further growth and after premature ripening such fruits become soft, thus these fruits never reach maturity and drop down earlier, the fumes that come out of the brick kilns as a result of burning of coal contain sulphur dioxide, ethylene and carbon monoxide. All these gases are toxic to the young developing fruits of mango.

Control of this disorder consists in

(i) shifting the site of brick kilns two km on east and west and one km on north and south of the orchard,

(ii) the operation of the existing brick-kilns should be avoided from February to the fourth week of May;

(iii) telescopic chimneys, should be 40-50 feet high, if at all, the operations of brick-kiln is necessary during the prohibitive period, and

(iv) finally the appearance of the disorder can be checked by either (a) spraying 0.6 per cent Borax, three times, i.e., before flowering, during flowering and after fruit setting alongwith Bordeaux mixture 2:2:250 or 1.5 kg of copper oxychloride per 500 litres of water.

2

Preservation Technologies

Fruit quality

Fruit quality goes back to tree stock, growing practices and weather conditions. Closer to the shipper and processor, however, are the degrees of maturity and ripeness when picked and the method of picking or harvesting.

There is a distinction between maturity and ripeness of a fruit. Maturity is the condition when the fruit is ready to eat or if picked will become ready to eat after further ripening. Ripeness is that optimum condition when colour, flavour and texture have developed to their peak.

Some fruit is picked when it are mature but not yet ripe. This is especially true of very soft fruit like cherries and peaches, which when fully ripe are so soft as to be damaged by the act of picking itself. Further, since many types of fruit continue to ripen off the tree, unless they were to be processes quickly, some would become overripe before they could be utilized if picked at peak ripeness.

From a technological point of view, fruit characterisation by species and varieties is performed on the basis of physical as well chemical properties: shape, size, texture, flavour, colour/ pigmentation, dry matter content (soluble solids content), pectic substances, acidity, vitamins, etc. these properties are directly correlated with fruit utilization. Table 2.1 shows which of the above mentioned properties have a major impact on the finished products obtained by fruit processing.

Table 2.1: Optimal use of fruits as a function of their properties

Processed Finished Products	Organoleptic (Sensory) Properties				Chemical Composition		
	Shape	Texture	Flavour	Taste	Acidity	Sugars	Pectic Sust.
Dried Fruits	++	++		++		++	
Fruit juices			++	++	++		
Marmalade			++	++			++
Jams	++	++	++	++			
Jellies	++	++	++	++			++
Fruit Paste				++		++	
When to pick							

When to Pick

The proper time to pick fruit depends upon several factors; these include variety, location, weather, ease of removal from the tree (which change with time), and purpose to which the fruit will be put.

For example, oranges change with respect to both sugar and acid as they ripen on the tree; sugar increases and acid decreases. The ratio of sugar to acid determines the taste and acceptability of the fruit and the juice. For this reasons, in some countries there are laws that prohibit picking until a certain sugar-acid ratio has been reached.

In the case of much fruit to be canned, on the other hand, fruit is picked before it is fully ripe for eating since canning will further soften the fruit.

Quality Measurements

Many quality measurements can be made before a fruit crop is picked in order to determine if proper maturity or degree of ripeness has developed.

Colour may be measured with instruments or by comparing the colour of fruit on the tree with standard picture charts.

Texture may be measured by compression by hand or by simple type of plungers.

As fruit mature on the tree its concentration of juice solids, which are mostly sugars, changes. The concentration of soluble solids in the juice can be estimated with a refractometer or a hydrometer. The refractometer measures the ability of a solution to bend or refract a light beam which is proportional to the solution's concentration. A hydrometer is a weighted spindle with a graduated neck which floats in the juice at a height related to the juice density.

The acid content of fruit changes with maturity and affects flavour, acid concentration can be measured by a simple chemical titration on the fruit juice. But for many fruits the tartness and flavour are really affected by the ratio of sugar to acid.

Percentage of soluble solids, which are largely sugars, is generally expressed in degrees Brix, which relates specific gravity of a solution to an equivalent concentration of pure sucrose.

In describing the taste of tartness of several fruits and fruit juices, the term "sugar to acid ratio" or "Brix to acid ratio" are commonly used. The higher the Brix the greater the sugar concentration in the juice; the higher the "Brix to acid ratio" the sweeter and less tart is the juice.

Harvesting and Preprocessing

Harvesting

The above and other measurements, plus experience, indicate when fruit is ready for harvesting and subsequent processing.

A large amount of the harvesting of most fruit crops is still done by hand; this labour may represent about half of the cost of growing the fruit. Therefore, mechanical harvesting is currently one of the most active fields of research for the agricultural engineer, but also requires geneticists of breed fruit of nearly equal size, that matures uniformly and that is resistant to mechanical damage.

A correct harvesting includes some simple but essential rules:

- the fruit should be picked by hand and placed carefully in the harvesting basket; all future handling has to be performed carefully in order to avoid any mechanical damage;
- the harvesting basket and the hands of the harvester should be clean;
- the fruit should be picked when it is ready to be able to be processed into a quality product depending on the treatment which it will undergo.

It is worth emphasising the fact that the proximity of the processing center to the source of supply for fresh raw materials presents major advantages; some are as follows:

- possibility to pick at the best suitable moment;
- reduction of losses by handling/transportation;
- minimises raw material transport costs;
- possibility to use simpler/cheaper receptacles for raw material transport.

Once it has left the tree, the organoleptic properties, nutritional value, safety and aesthetic appeal of the fruit deteriorates in varying degrees. The major causes of deterioration include the following:

a) growth and activity of micro-organisms;

b) Activities of the natural food enzymes;

c) Insects, parasites and rodents;

d) Temperature, both heat and cold;

e) Moisture and dryness;

f) Air and in particular oxygen;

g) Light and

h) Time.

The rapidity with which foods spoil if proper measures are not taken in indicated in Table 2.2.

Table 2.2: Useful storage life of some food products

Food products	Generalized storage life (Days) at 21°C (70°F)
Animal flesh, fish, poultry	1-2
Dried, salted, smoked meat and fish	360 and more
Fruits	1-7
Dried Fruits	360 and more
Leafy vegetables	1-2
Root crops	7-20

Source: Desrosier and Desrosier (1977)

Reception – Quality and quantity

Fruit reception at the processing center is performed mainly for following purposes:

- checking of sanitary and freshness status;
- control of varieties and fruit wholeness;
- evaluation maturity degree;
- collection of data about quantities received in connection it the source of supply: outside growers/farmers, own farm.

Variety control is needed in order to identify that the fruit belongs to an accepted variety as not all are suitable for different technological processes.

Fruit maturity degree is significant as industrial maturity is required for some processing/preservation methods while for others there is the need for an edible maturity when the fruit has full taste and flavour.

Special attention is given to size, appearance and uniformity of fruit to be processed, mainly in the form of fruit preserved with sugar suing whole/half fruits ("with fruit pieces").

Some laboratory control is also needed, even if it is not easy to precisely establish the technological qualities of fruit because of the absence of enough reliable rapid analytical methods able to show eventual deterioration.

The only reliable method for evaluating the quality is the combination of data obtained through organoleptic/taste controls and by simple analytical checks which are possible to perform in a small laboratory: percentage of soluble solids by refractometer, consistency/texture measured with simple penetrometers, etc. Some useful checks/control to be performed at reception are summarized in Table 2.3.

Temporary storage before processing

This step has to be as short as possible in order to avoid flavour losses, texture modification, weight losses and other deterioration that can take place over this period.

Table 2.3: Raw material control-Fresh fruits and vegetables at reception

1. **Checks at each delivery/raw material lot**
   - 1.1 Colour
   - 1.2 Texture
   - 1.3 Taste
   - 1.4 Flavour
   - 1.5 Appearance
   - 1.6 Refractometric extract
   - 1.7 Number per kg
   - 1.8 Variety
   - 1.9 Sanitary evaluation
2. **Checks at each ten lots (for the same raw material)**
   - 2.1 Density
   - 2.2 Water content: oven method
   - 2.3 Total sugars, reducing sugars
   - 2.4 Total acidity
3. **Audits-every six months- on five different lots**
   - 3.1 Ascorbic acid
   - 3.2 Mineral substances
   - 3.3 Tannic substances
   - 3.4 Pectic substances

The type of analysis for audits will be adapted to the specific fruits and vegetables that are received/processed.

Some basic rules for this step are as follows:

- keep products in the shade, without any possible direct contact with sunlight;
- avoid dust as much as possible;
- avoid excessive heat;
- avoid any possible contamination;

- store in a place protected from possible attack by rodents, insects, etc.

Cold storage is always s highly preferred to ambient temperature. For this reason a very good manufacturing practice is to use a cool room for each processing center; this is very useful for small and medium processing units as well.

An excellent indication of a good temporary storage is the limited weight loss before processing, which has to be below 1.0%-1.2 per cent.

Washing

Harvested fruit is washed to remove soil, micro-organisms and pesticide residues.

Fruit washing is a mandatory processing step; it would be wise to eliminate spoiled fruit before washing in order to avoid the pollution of washing tools and/or equipment and the contamination of fruit during washing.

Washing efficiency can be gauged by the total number of micro-organisms present on fruit surface before and after washing-best result are when there is a six fold reduction. The water from the final wash should be free from moulds and yeast; a small quantity of bacteria is acceptable.

Fruit washing can be carried out by immersion, by spray/ showers or by combination of these two processes which is generally the best solution: pre-washing and washing.

Some usual practices in fruit washing are:

- addition of detergents or 1.5% HCl solution in washing water to remove traces of insect-fungicides;
- use of warm water (about 50°C) in the pre-washing phase;
- shigher water pressure in spray/shower washers.

Washing must be done before the fruit is cut in order to avoid losing high nutritive value soluble substances (vitamins, minerals, sugars, etc.).

Sorting

Fruit sorting covers two main separate processing operations:

a) removal of damaged fruit and any foreign bodies (which might have been left behind after washing);

b) qualitative sorting based on organoleptic criteria and maturity stage.

Mechanical sorting for size is usually not done at the preliminary stage. The most important initial sorting is for variety and maturity.

However, for some fruit and in special processing technologies it is advisable to proceed to a manual dimensional sorting (grading).

Trimming and Peeling (skin removal)

This processing step aims at removing the parts of the fruit which are either not edible or difficult to digest especially the skin.

Up to now the industrial peeling of fruit and vegetables was performed by three procedures:

a) mechanically;

b) by using water steam;

c) chemically; this method consists in treating fruit and vegetables by dipping them in a caustic soda solution at a temperature of 90 to 100°C; the concentration of this solution as well as the dipping or immersion time varying according to each specific case.

Cutting

This step is performed according to the specific requirements of the fruit processing technology.

Heat blanching

Fruit is not usually heat blanched because of the damage from the heat and the associated sogginess and juice loss after thawing, instead, chemicals are commonly used without heat to inactivate the oxidative enzymes or to act as antioxidants and they are combined with other treatments.

Ascorbic/citric acid dip

Ascorbic acid or vitamin C minimizes fruit oxidation primarily by acting as an antioxidant and itself becoming oxidised in preference to catechol-tannin compounds, ascorbic acid is frequently used by being dissolved in water, sugar syrup or in citric acid solutions.

It has been found that increased acidity also helps retard oxidative colour changes and so ascorbic acid plus citric acid may be used together, citric acid further reacts with (chelates) metal ions thus removing these catalysts of oxidation from the system.

Sulphur dioxide treatment

Sulphur dioxide may function in several ways:

- sulphur dioxide is an enzyme poison against common oxidizing enzymes;
- it also has antioxidant properties; i.e. it is an oxygen acceptor (as is ascorbic acid);
- further SO_2 minimises non enzymatic Maillard type browning by reacting with aldehyde groups of sugars so that they are no longer free to combine with amino acids;
- sulphur dioxide also interferes with microbial growth.

In many fruit processing pre-treatments two factors must be considered:

a) sulphur dioxide must be given time to penetrate the fruit tissues;

b) SO_2 must not be used in excess because it has a characteristic unpleasant taste and odour, and international food laws limit the SO_2 content of fruit products, especially of those which are consumer oriented (e.g. except semi-processed products oriented to further industrial utilisation).

Commonly a 0.25% solution (except for semi-processed fruit products which are industry oriented and use a 6% solution) of SO_2 or its SO_2 equivalent in the form of solutions of sodium sulphite, sodium bisulphate or sodium/potassium metabisulphite are used.

Fruit slices are dipped in the solution for about two or three minutes and then removed so as not to absorb too much SO_2. Then the slices are allowed to stand for about one to two hours so that the SO_2 may penetrate throughout the tissues before processing.

Sulphur dioxide is also used in fruit juice production to minimize oxidative changes where relatively low heat treatment is employed so as not to damage delicate juice flavour.

Dry sulphuring is the technological step where fruit is exposed to fumes of SO_2 from burning sulphur or form compressed gas cylinders; this treatment could be used in the preparation of fruits (and some vegetables) prior to drying/dehydration.

Sugar Syrup

Sugar syrup addition is one of the oldest methods of minimizing oxidation. It was used long before the causative reactions were understood and remains today a common practice for this purpose.

Sugar syrup minimizes oxidation by coating the fruit and thereby preventing contact with atmospheric oxygen.

Sugar syrup also offers some protection against loss of volatile fruit esters and it contributes sweet taste to otherwise tart fruits.

It is common today to dissolve ascorbic acid and citric acid in the sugar syrup for added effect or to include sugar syrup after an SO_2 treatment.

Fresh Fruit Storage

Some fruit species and specially apples and pears can be stored in fresh state during cold season in some countries' climatic conditions.

Fruit for fresh storage have to be autumn or winter varieties and be harvested before they are fully mature, this fruit also has to he sound and without any bruising; control and sorting by quality are mandatory operations.

Sorting has to be carried out according to size and weight and also by appearance; fruit which is not up to standard for storage will be used for semi-processed product manufacturing which will be submitted further to industrial processing.

Harvested fruit has to be transported as soon as possible to storage areas. Leaving fruit in bulk in order to generate transportation is a bad practice as this reduces storage time and accelerated maturation processes during storage.

In order to store large quantities of fruit, silos have to be built.

Fruit drying and dehydration technology

The sequence of operations employed in the production of dried/dehydrated fruit is presented in section 2.4.

General technical data for fruit dehydration in tunnels are presented in Table 2.4.

Table 2.4: Technical data for fruit dehydration in tunnels

Fruits	Drying conditions		Finished product		
	Load Kg/m²	Temperature °C	Time	Moisture %	yield %
Plums	15	I. 40-50	6 H	18-20	25-35
			II. 75-80	14 H	
Apples (Rings)	10	75-55	5-6 H	20	10-12
Apricots (Halves)	10	70-60	10-15	15-20	10-15
Cherries (w. stones)	10	55-70	6-8	12-15	25
Pears (Halves and quarters)	15	70-65	15-22	18-20	10-15
Peaches	15	70-60	10-15	15-20	10-15

For fruit with a high sugar content drying temperatures have to be lower at initial stage and then increase to the maximum acceptable; for fruit with lower sugar level the temperatures are applied in a reverse order.

Some pre-treatments of fruit and vegetables for sun/solar drying are described in Table 2.5.

Technical data on some osmotically dehydrated products are presented in Table 2.6.

Moisture and shipping factors for some dried/dehydrated fruit are seen in Table 2.7.

The sequence of operations employed in the manufacture of dried/dehydrated fruits

Operation	Notes
Harvesting	Fruit for drying are harvested in a mature condition to obtain maximum yield.
Quality and quantity control	This step is needed in order to maintain finished product standards and to ensure a sound economic operation.
Grading	Maturing and size grading may be needed for individual fruit.
Preparation for drying	Small berry fruit may not require preparation. Cut fruit such as apples may require washing/cutting/coring prior to drying.
(Alkali dipping)	This treatment is applied to grapes and sometimes to prunes but not to other fruit.
Sulphuring and other treatments	Cut fruit, and light coloured grapes are exposed to the fumes of burning sulphur for 2-3 hours. The fruit takes up 1500 to 2500 ppm of sulphur dioxide, which helps to prevent darkening during drying and storage. Alternative treatment, in order to inhibit enzymes and microbial action, may be used (dipping cut fruit in solutions of sulphurous acid salts alone or in combination with ascorbic acid/citric acid).

(condt.)

Table 2.5 Some pre-treatments of fruits and vegetables for sun/solar drying

Fruit or Vegetable	Type of cut	Hot water blanching	Cold water treatment
Apples	Quarters or 1/8 pieces	-	1min., 8000 ppm SO_2
Apricots	Halved	-	3 min 4000 ppm SO_2 + 2.5% citric acid
Banana-unripe	10 mm slices	5 min	1 min., 2000 ppm SO_2
Cabbage	5 mm strips	3 min., 1% sodium bicarbonate	1 min., 8000 ppm SO_2
Carrots	pieces 3 mm X 5 mm	4 min	1 min., 8000 ppm SO_2
Green beans	pieces 2 cm long	5 min., 1% sodium bicarbonate	1 min., 8000 ppm SO_2
Mango	Pulp	-	2.5% lemon juice 2000 ppm SO_2
	5 mm slices		1 min., 2000 ppm SO_2
Okra	Whole, 6 mm or sliced lengthwise	6 min., 1% sodium bicarbonate	1 min., 8000 ppm SO_2
Peaches	Halved	-	1 min., 8000 ppm SO_2
Pears	Halved	-	1 min., 8000 ppm SO_2
Plums	Whole	-	1 min., 2% caustic soda then water wash
Potatoes	2-3 mm slices (**)	5 min	1 min., 8000 ppm SO_2
Sweet pepper	5 mm slices	-	1 min., 2000 ppm SO_2
Turnip	2-5 mm	4 min	1 min., 8000 ppm SO_2

Source: FAO, 1969a

Table 2.6: Technical data on some osmotically dehydrated products

Fruit or vegetable	Type of cut	Treatment
Banana	5 mm slices	2 hours, 80% sugar 2000 ppm SO_2 at 70°C
Carrots	10X 10 X 2 mm dices or 5 mm slices	4 hours, 60% sugar + 10% salt 4000 ppm SO_2
Mango, green	8 mm slices	2 hours, 25% salt 8000 ppm SO_2
Mango, ripe	8 mm slices	2 hours, 60% sugar 8000 ppm SO_2
Onions	2 mm slices	2 hours, 60% sugar + 10% salt 4000 ppm SO_2
Papaya	8 X 8 mm slices	4 hours, 80% sugar 2000 ppm SO_2 at 70°C
Strawberries	Whole	4 hours, 80% sugar 4000 ppm SO_2
Sweet peppers, red	6 mm dices	2 hours, 60% sugar + 10% salt 4000 ppm SO_2

Source: FAO, 1969a

Table 2.7: Moisture and shipping factors for some dried/ dehydrated fruits

Products	Form	Moisture, %
Apples	6 mm rings	20
Apricots	Caps	17-20
Banana	Cut pieces	15
Cherries	Whole	12-15
Figs	Whole	23
Guava	Quarters	6
Mango	15 mm pulp sheets	15
Peaches	Caps	15-20
Pears	Halves	23
Prunes	Whole	18-20
Raisins	Whole	17

Operation	**Notes**
Sun drying or artificial drying	Prepared and pre-treated fruit is spread on trays and dried in the sun or in factory drying tunnels employing heated air at a temperature of 68 to 74°C.
Bulk storage	The dried fruit is stored in bulk in bins (known as "sweet-boxes) for 1 to 9 months until required for packing. During this time moisture diffuses form the wetter fruit pieces to the drier ones and the fruit gradually acquires a uniform moisture content, to prevent insect infestation, periodic fumigation of the fruit may be needed.
Sorting and pre-packaging	The removal of sub-standard fruit, loose dirt, stones or other debris, as well as the removal preparation of stems from

(condt.)

Operation	Notes
	grapes and stones from dried apricots is practiced just prior to packing, the fruit may also be washed at this stage, and if it is too dry, it may be allowed to regain some moisture before packing, high moisture fruit is treated with sorbic acid, sorbates, citric acid and/or other anti-mould agents.

The moisture contents listed are considered as the best from a technical, practical and commercial point of view for delivery to the market or for shipping and safe for the shelf life needed before buying/consumption by customers/consumers.

All instructions about packing, storage and transport must be followed in order to assure delivery of a safe and high quality product to the market.

Processing of fruit bars

The fruit bar processing method developed for FAO only involves a single major operation, which it drying the fruit pulp after mixing it with suitable ingredients. It can be used to produce mango, banana, guava or mixed fruit bars.

A dual-powered dryer, working by solar energy during the day and be electric or steam power at night and on rainy days, with cross-flow movement of air and controlled temperature (from 55°C at the beginning of processing to a high of 70°C), is well suited for dehydration of the pulp to the desired moisture level of 15 to 20%.

Main raw material quantities to prepare approximately 100 kg of fruit bars are as follows (Table 2.8)

Mango fruit bar

Fully ripe mangoes are selected and washed in water at room temperature. The peeled fruit is cut into slices and assed through a helicodial pulper to extract the pulp. The required amount of sugar to adjust the Brix (the unit measure for total solids in fruits) of the mixed pulp to 25 degrees Brix is then added.

Table 2.8: Main raw material quantities to prepare approximately 100 kg of fruit bars

Type of fruit	Fruit required in kg	Pulp obtained in kg	Sugar required in kg	Yield (% of fresh fruit) approx.
Mango	720	360	33	14
Banana	600	360	30	17
Guava	406	325	60	25
Mango + banana	540+150	360	35	15
Papaya + banana	500 +140	336	54	23

Source: Amoriggi (1992), FAO (1990).

Two grams of citric acid per kilogram of pulp (or 20 ml of lime or lemon juice) are added to inhibit possible growth of micro-organisms during drying. The mixture is then heated for two minutes at 80°C and partially cooled; the heat treatment serves to imactivate the enzymes and destroy the micro-organisms.

Potassium or sodium metabisulphtie is added (two grams per kg of prepared mixture), so that the concentration of SO_2 is 1000 ppm. The mixture is then transferred to stainless steel trays which have been previously smeared with glycerine (40 ml/m^2). Each tray must be loaded with 12.5 kg of mixture per square metre.

Drying could be carried out by a dual-powered dryer for a total of 26 hours:

a) 10 hours by solar energy at about 55°C and

b) 16 hours by electric or steam power at 70°C.

At the end of the drying operation, when moisture content is between 15 and 20%, the pieces of suitable shape and size are wrapped in cellophane paper, packed in cartons and stored at ambient air temperature. Pieces of unsuitable shape and size are further cut into small pieces and used to prepare, along with peanuts and cashews, a variety of "cocktail mixtures".

Banana fruit bar

Banana varieties which give smooth pulp without serum separation must be used for this purpose, ripe, suitable fruit is selected. The hand-peeled fruits are soaked in 0.3 per cent citric acid solution for about 10 minutes (lime or lemon juice can replace citric acid). The drained fruit are pulped to obtain smooth pulp.

The rest of the procedure is the same as in the case of the mango bar.

Guava fruit bar

A mixture of pink and yellow varieties is best suited for preparing the bar. The washed fruit is hand peeled and stem and blossom ends trimmed, the peeled fruit is cut into quarters which are passed through a helicoidal extractor to separate seeds and fibrous pieces (the holes in the stainless steel screen should be between 0.8 and 1.10 mm).

To get the maximum yield of pulp, the material is passed through the extractor twice. After adjusting the refractometric solids to 25 degrees Brix, the fruit bar can be prepared by following the same procedure as for mango pulp.

Mixed fruit bar

Mango and banana pulp, as well as papaya and banana pulp, can be mixed in a calculated ratio for preparing mixed fruit bars. The rest of the procedure is the same as in the case of pure mango pulp.

Packing and storage

The dried pulp is removed from the dryer and cut into square pieces of 5 × 5 cm at a thickness weighing between 25 and 28 grams. An unit pack consist of two such blocks and weights between 50 and 56 grams.

Each block is separately wrapped in cellophane and the unit pack is filled in a printed cellophane bag of size 15 X 8 cm. Two hundreds unit packs are packed in a master carton of size 34 × 22 × 14 cm, with a net weight of about 10 kg, shelf-life is about one year at room temperature.

Fruit leathers

Fruit leather are manufactured by drying/dehydration of fruit purees into leathery sheets. The leathers are eaten as confections or cooked as a sauce. They are made from a wide variety of fruits, the more common being apple, apricot, banana, cherry, black currant, grape, peach, pear, pineapple, plum, raspberry, strawberry, kiwi, fruit, mango and papaya.

A description of procedures for mango, banana, guava and mixed fruit bars is given in this document.

Another product with good potential is ciku leather; ciku fruit is grown in Malaysia.

A standard process is carried out using ripe fruits which are washed, peeled, diced and the seeds removed. The fruit are blanched for 1 minute at 80°C and blended into puree in a food processor.

Ciku leather is prepared by mixing ciku puree with 10% sugar, 10% pre-gelatinous rice flour, 150 ppm sorbic acid an 500 ppm sodium metabisulphite ($Na_2H_2So_4$).

The mixture is cooked on a water bath at 60°C and then made into sheets 1.8 mm which on tray spread with glycerol to reduce stickiness. This is then further dried in a forced-air dehydrator at 45°C for 3.5 hr or until the surface no longer feels sticky when touched with the fingers.

The dried and cooled a leathers are cut into 12 × 12 cm squares and wrapped in polypropylene (PP) of 0.1 mm thickness.

Osmotic dehydration in fruit and vegetable processing

Introduction

Osmotic dehydration is a useful technique for the concentration of fruit and vegetables, realized by placing the solid food, whole or in pieces, in sugars or salts aqueous solutions of high osmotic pressure. It gives rise to at least two major simultaneous counter-current flows: a significant water flow out of the food into the solution and a transfer of solute from the solution into the food.

Process variables

Main process variables are

a) pre-treatments;

b) temperature;

c) nature and concentration of the dehydration solutions;

d) agitation;

e) additives.

In the light of the published literature, some general rules can be noted:

- water loss and solid gain are mainly controlled by the raw material characteristics and are certainly influenced by the possible pre-treatments;
- it is usually not worthwhile to use osmotic dehydration for more than a 50% weight reduction because of the decreases in the osmosis rate over time. Water loss mainly occurs during the first 2 hr and the maximum solid gain within 30 min.;
- the rate of mass exchanges increases with temperature but above 45°C enzymatic browning and flavour deterioration begin to take place. High temperatures, i.e. over 60°C, modify the tissue characteristics of favouring impregnation phenomena and thus the solid gain;
- the best processing temperature depends on the food; mass exchanges are favoured by suing high concentration solutions;
- phenomena which modify the tissue permeability, such as over-ripeness, pre-treatments with chemicals (SO_2), blanching or freezing, favour the solid gain compared to

water loss because impregnation phenomena are enhanced;

- the kind of sugars utilized as osmotic substances strongly affects the kinetics of water removal, the solid gain and the equilibrium water content; low molar mass saccharides (glucose, fructose, sorbitol, etc.) favour the sugar uptake;
- addition of NaCl to osmotic solutions increases the driving force for drying, Synergistic effects between sugar and salt have also been observed.

A pilot plant equipment used for detailed study of process parameters in osmotic concentration of fruits is seen in Fig. 2.1.

Applications

The effects of osmotic dehydration as a pre-treatment are mainly related to the improvement of some nutritional, organoleptic and functional properties of the product.

As osmotic dehydration is effective at ambient temperature, heat damage to colour and flavour is minimsied and the high concentration of the sugar surrounding fruit and vegetable pieces prevents discoloration.

Furthermore, through the selective enrichment in soluble solids high quality fruit and vegetables are obtained with functional properties "compatible" with different food systems. These effects are obtained with a reduced energy input over traditional drying process. The main energy-consuming step is the reconstitution of the diluted osmotic solution that could be obtained by concentration or by addition of sugar.

Various applications of the techniques a unit operation in the food area are summarised in Fig. 2.1 together with the process parameters regarded as optimal in the light of the published literature.

Drying

Air drying following osmotic dipping is commonly used in tropical countries for the production of so-called "semi-candied"

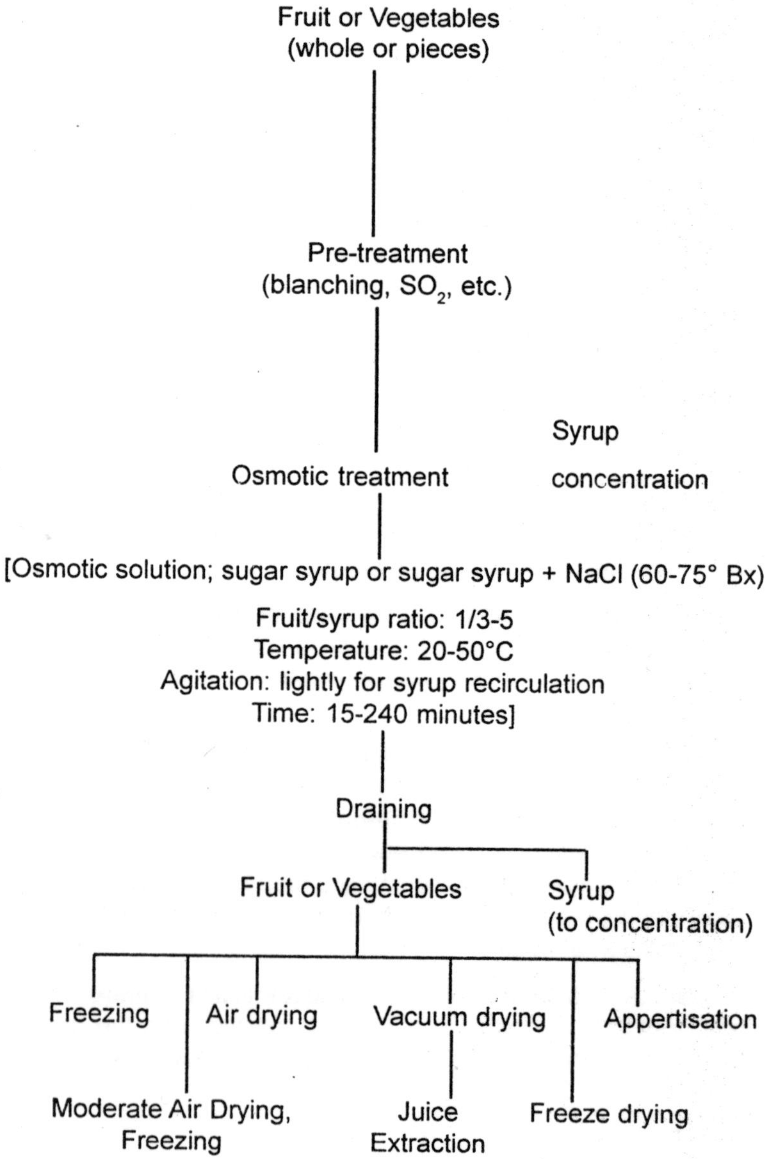

Figure 2.1 Applications of osmotic dehydration.

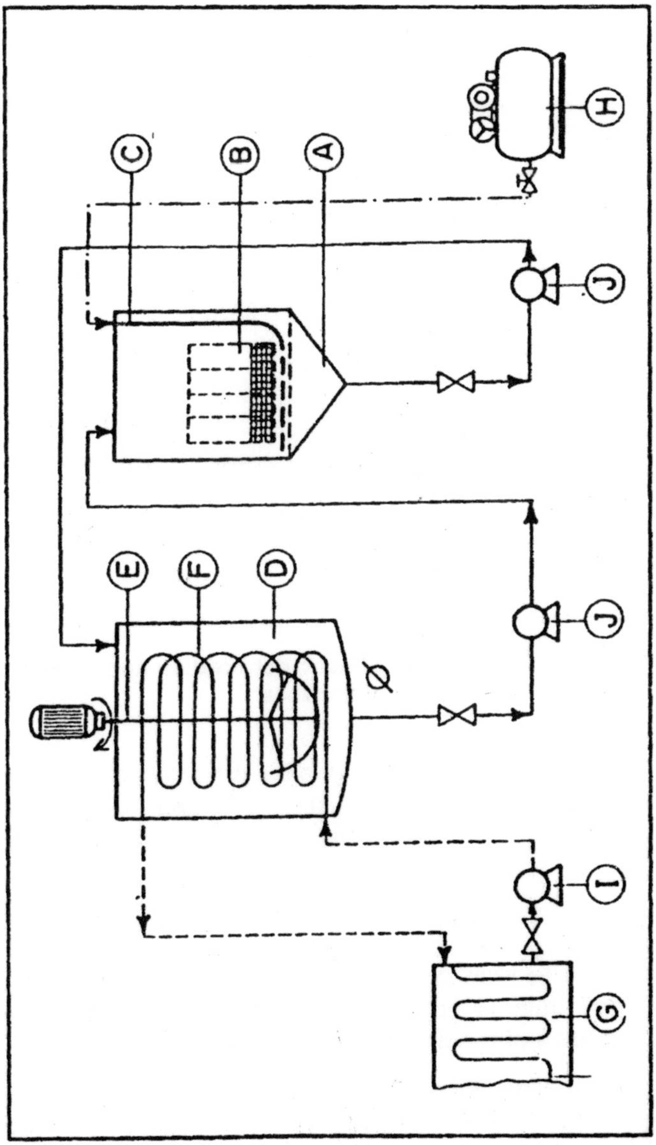

Figure 2.2 Sketch of a pilot plant used for detailed study of process parameters in osmotic concentration of fruit.

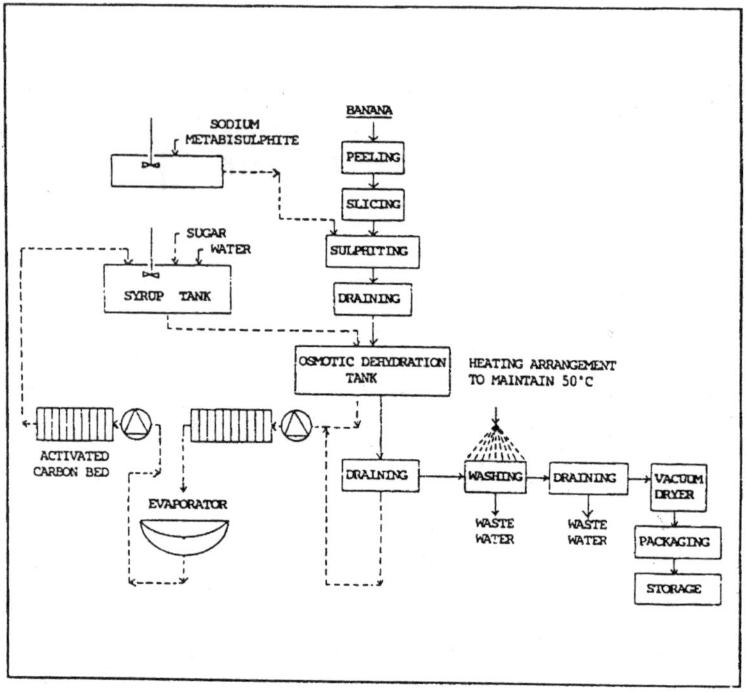

Figures 2.3 Flow diagram of osmotic dehydration and vacuum drying of bananas

dried fruits, the sugar uptake, owing to the protective action of the saccharides, limits or avoids the use of SO_2 and increases the stability of pigments during processing and subsequent storage period.

The organoleptic qualities of the end product could also be improved because some of the acids are removed from the fruit during the osmotic bath, so a blander and sweeter product than ordinary dried fruits is obtained. Owing to weight and volume reduction, loading of the dryer can be increased 2-3 times.

The combination of osmosis with solar drying has been put forward, mainly for tropical fruit. A 24 hour cycle has been suggested combining osmodehydration, performed during he night, with solar drying during the day, two-three-fold increase in the throughput of typical solar dryers is feasible, while enhancing the nutritional and organoleptic quality of the fruits.

A two-step drying process, OSMOVAC, for producing low moisture fruit products was described. The osmotic step is performed with sucrose syrup 65-75° Brix until the weight reduction reaches 30-50%.

By osmotic dehydration followed by vacuum drying puffy products with a crisp, honeycomb-like texture can be obtained at a cost comparatively lower than freeze-drying.

Commercial feasibiiity of the process on bananas has bee studied, based on the results of a semi-pilot scale operation; the process scheme is reported in Figure 2.3. Osmotically dried bananas retained more puffiness and a crisper texture than simple vacuum dried ones, and the flavour lasted longer at ambient temperature.

The combination of osmotic dehydration with freeze-drying has been proposed only at laboratory scale.

Appertisation

A combination of osmotic dehydration with appertisation has been proposed to improve canned fruit preserves. The feasibility of a process, called osmo-appertisation, to obtain high quality fruit in syrup, has been assessed on a pilot scale.

The key point of this technique is the pre-concentration of the fruits to about 20-40° Brix, that causes, together with the enhancement of the natural flavour, an increase of the resistance of the fruit to the following heat treatment, especially for colour and texture stability.

The products obtained are stable up to 12 months at ambient temperature and show a higher organoleptic quality then canned preserved alternatives.

Furthermore, because of their higher specific weight and diminished volume, the filling capacity of jars or pouches is increased.

Freezing

The frozen fruits and vegetables industry uses much energy in order to freeze the large quantity of water present in fresh products. A reduction in moisture content of the material reduces refrigeration load during freezing.

Other advantages of partially concentrating fruits and vegetables prior to freezing include savings in packaging and distribution costs and achieving higher product quality because of the marked reduction of structural collapse and dripping during thawing.

The products obtained are termed “dehydro-frozen” and the concentration step is generally carried out through conventional air drying, the additional cost of which has to be taken into account.

Osmotic dehydration could be used instead of air drying to obtain an energy saving or a quality improvement especially for fruit and vegetable sensitive to air drying.

Extraction of juices

An osmotic pre-step before juice extraction was reported to give highly aromatic fruit or vegetable juice concentrates.

Further developments

So far only applications on a pilot plant scale are reported in the literature, for further developments on a larger scale, theoretical and practical problems should be solved.

The industrial application of the process faces engineering problems related to the movement of great volumes of concentrated sugar solutions and to equipment for continuous operations. The use of highly concentrated sugar solutions creates two major problems.

The syrup’s viscosity is so great that agitation is necessary in order to decrease the resistance to the mass transfer on the solution side.

The difference in density between the solution (about 1.3 kg/

litre) and fruit and vegetables (about 0.8 kg/litre), makes the product float.

Another important aspect, so far not investigated, is the microbiological safety of the process, which should be studied thoroughly before further industrial development.

Osmoappertisation in the processing of apricots

In order to obtain an alternative to the canned fruit preserves and to maintain a high quality of the fruits, a research has been carried out on the osmoappertisation of apricots, a "combined" techniques that consists in the appertisation of the osmodehydrated apricots.

This technique could contributes also to the reduction of energy consumption, limits the cost of production and combined "convenience" (ready-to-eat, medium shelf-life) with many market outlets (retail, catering, bakery, confectionery, semi-finished products).

Apricot processing

a) Fresh apricot puree

After washing, cutting and removal of stones, apricot halves are dipped in 2% solution of sodium or potassium metabisulphite for 10 minutes, after draining, the resulting material is passed through a 0.045-in. screen pulper-finisher to produce a fresh apricot puree.

Osmoappertisation combines two unit operations: dehydration by osmosis and appertisation packaging+ pasteurization).

The fresh apricot puree obtained in this way could be further processed in different semi-processed (i.e. chemically or other wise preserved products) or finished fruit products fruit leathers, fruit bars, jams, etc.).

b) Concentrated apricot pulp.

Fresh apricot halves could also be steam blanched for 5 min., passed through a 0.045-in pulper-finisher and transformed in a puree with about 14° Brix depending on the fruit quality. This puree may be concentrated in steam jacketed kettles up to 20° Brix or in other adequate equipment e.g. a stirred vacuum evaporator) up to 28° Brix.

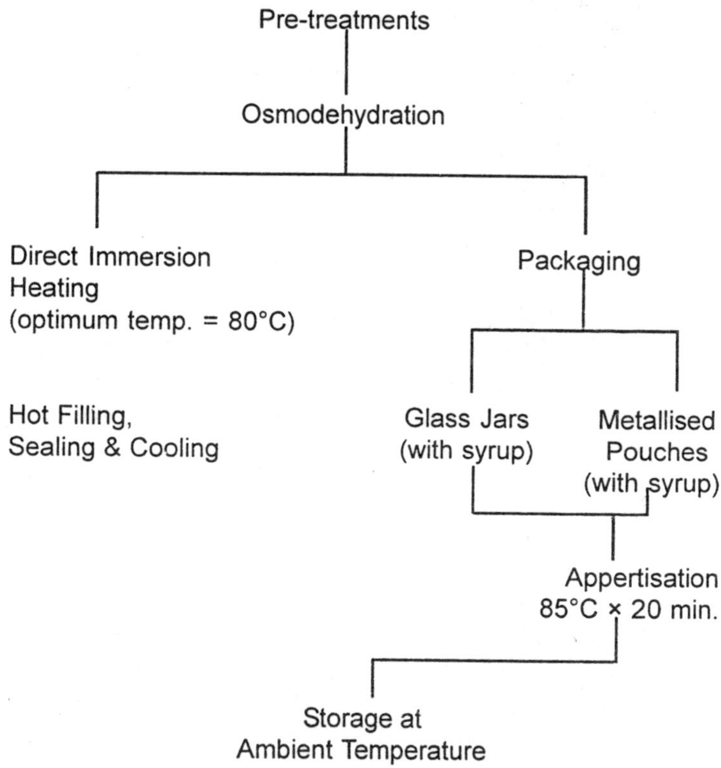

Figure 2.4 Osmoappertisation in the processing of apricots

As for fresh apricot puree, the concentrate may be further processed in various semi-processed or finished fruit products as mentioned above and as will be described below.

c. Dried apricot leather

- From fresh fruit puree by drum drying. The fresh apricot puree at about 14° Brix could be dried to 12% moisture apricot sheets, using a double-drum dryer operating at

132 degrees C with a drum clearance of 0.008 in and speed of 45 sec per revolution.

- From fruit concentrate by drum drying, the concentrate could also be dried to 12% moisture fruit sheets by the same process as described above.
- From fresh fruit puree or from apricot concentrate by sun/ solar drying or by dehydration.

a) **Trays**. – For sun/solar drying or dehydration of fruit pulp, the trays must have a solid base in order to retain the liquid contents. They may be made of metal, timber or plastic. Stainless steel or plastic trays are most suitable because they are unaffected by acid fruit pulp; they are, however, expensive.

A metal tray could be 75 × 50 cm in size and with side 5 cm high. The trays must keep level during drying; if the tray is not level the pulp will run to the lowest point, giving a layer of irregular depth which will dry unevenly. Any tray which is not mad of stainless steel or plastic must be covered inside with a sheet of heavy gauge plastic film to protect the pulp from chemical or bacteriological contamination.

Standard sun/solar trays as described can be used by covering them inside with a sheet of plastic film to create a solid base.

b) Preparation before drying/dehydration. Fresh apricot puree can be directly used for next processing steps. Fruit concentrate needs to be added to potassium metabisulphite to obtain a 0.3% concentration of SO_2 in the material.

c) **Drying/dehydration**. The apricot/fruit puree or concentrate is poured into the trays to a depth of about 1.5 cm. when stainless steel or plastic trays are used they should be coated with a thin layer of glycerine to prevent sticking.

The pulp is then sun/solar dried or tunnel/cabinet dehydrated; moisture content in the dried product should not exceed 14% and the SO_2 content should not be less than 1500 pp.

The dried product is wrapped in cellophane to prevent sticking, then put inside polythene bags and stored at best in tight fitting tins and sealed to prevent moisture transfer.

From fresh fruit puree or from apricot concentrate, with sugar addition, and then processed by sun/solar drying or by dehydration.

In some countries preference is for finished products with added sugar; and this is also interesting from a point of view of energy consumption (concentration is partially achieved by sugar dry matter) and of shelf life. The overall content in SO_2 could also be reduced as sugar is a preservation agent, the product will be close to a fruit "paste".

Reconstitution test for dried/dehydrated products

In reconstitution water is added to the product which is restored to a condition similar to that when it was fresh. This enables the food product to be cooked as if the person was using fresh fruit or vegetable.

All vegetables are cooked but many of the dried fruits can be used for eating after they have been soaked in water. The following reconstitution test is used to find out the quality of the dried product.

Reconstitution test

1. Weigh out a sample of 35 grams from the bulked and packed final product of the previous day's production.
2. Put the sample into a small container (beaker) and add 275 ml of cold water (and 3.5 g salt).
3. Cover the container (with a watch-glass) and bring the water to the boil.
4. Boil GENTLY for 30 minutes.
5. Turn out the sample onto a white dish.

6. At least two people should then examine the sample for palatability, toughness, flavour and presence or absence of bad flavours. The testes should record their results independently.
7. The liquid left in the container should be examined for traces of sand/soil and other foreign matter.

This test can be used also to examine dried products after they have been stored for some time. Evaluation of rehydration ratio may be performed according to the following calculations.

Rehydration ratio

If weight of the dried sample is 10 g (Wd) and the weight of the sample after rehydration is 60 g (Wr), rehydration ratio is:

$$\frac{W_r}{W_d} = \frac{60}{10} = \frac{6}{1}, \text{ or 6 to 1.}$$

Rehydration coefficient

The weight of rehydrated sample is 60 g (Wr); the weight of dried sample is 10 g (Wd) and its moisture is 5% (Wu); raw material before drying had 87% water (A); rehydration coefficient is:

$$\frac{W_r}{\dfrac{W_d - W_u \times 100}{100 - A}} = \frac{60 \times (100-87)}{10-[10 \times 0.05]} = \frac{780}{9.5} = 82.1.$$

A simpler test for eating quality can be carried out without weighting and measuring, the material is placed in a cooking pot with water (and a little salt). The pot is then covered and boiled as described above.

Except for a few products which are eaten in the dry state, most dried fruit and all dried vegetables are prepared by asking and cooking, often this preparation is carried out incorrectly and dried products get a bad reputation.

Good quality dried products, after cooking and if properly treated should be similar to cooked fresh produce. In order to get good results, the following methods are recommended:

Quick method

Cold water, ten times the weight of the dry product, is added to the dried product. The container is covered, brought to the boil and simmered GENTLY until the product is tender. The cooking time may be 15 to 45 minutes after the boiling point has been reached.

Slow method

This gives better results then the quick method. Cold water is added to the dry food and is left to soak for 1 to 2 hours before cooking, the product is then cooked in the same water as that in which it was soaked. The actual cooking time will probably be shorter than that for the quick method.

Other points to remember are:

- if too much water is added the cooked product will have little flavour. However, if too little water is added the product may dry and burn, this can be avoided by adding small quantities of water during cooking;
- always cook with a lid on the container.
- salt, if required, should be added when the cooking is almost complete;
- partly used packages of dry products should be reclosed tightly or kept in containers with good fitting lids.

The composition of some dried fruits is seen in Table 2.9.

Handling, sorting, packing and storage of dried and dehydrated fruit and vegetables.

It is not easy to assess when drying had been completed. In absence of instrumentation, the characteristics of the various products after drying/dehydration can only be assessed by experience. Although this cannot be conveyed adequately on paper, some general indications can be given.

Table 2.9: Composition ofs some dried fruits

Fruit	Moisture content %	Sugar as monosac-charides, %	Other carboh-ydrates	Vitamin C mg/100 g
Raisins	21.5	64	7	0.0
Dates	12.5	55	7	0.0
Prunes	20.0	45	15	0.0
Apricots	15.0	45	24	4.8
Peaches	15.5	55	14	8.0

Fruit products

When a handful of fruit is squeezed tightly together in the hand and then released, the individual pieces should drop apart readily and no moisture be left behind on the hand. It should not be possible to separate the skin by rubbing unpeeled fruit and the fruit center should no longer reveal any moist area. Banana should be leathery and not too tough to eat in their dry state.

Vegetable products

Onions should be dried until they are crisp whereas tomatoes should be leathery.

In general, the lower the moisture content, the better the keeping quality will be, but over-dried products generally have an inferior quality. Also the loss in weight from excessive drying cannot be tolerated in a commercial operation designed to run profitably.

It is, however, essential to dry up to an optimum/safe moisture level, related to the type of the product and his designed shelf life, and to avoid running the risk of the products becoming spoiled due to excess water content.

When drying is completed, the material should be sorted either on trays or on a table in order to remove pieces of poor quality and colour and any foreign matter.

Very fine material should be separated from the bulk of the material by using a sieve (12 or 16 mesh per inch). Bad quality products which show poor colour need to be removed from the bulk of finished product.

After selection and grading, dried products should be packed immediately, preferably in polythene bags which must be folded and closed/tied tightly. However, plastic bags are easily damaged and therefore they must be packed into cartons or jute sacks before they are transported.

Deterioration of dried fruit during storage

Dried fruit must be considered as a relatively perishable commodity in the same category as cereals, pulses and similar stored products. It is subject to deterioration resulting from mould growth, insect and mite infestation and physical and chemical changes.

Mould growth

When the moisture content of dried fruit is allowed to exceed the maximum permissible level for safe storage then mould growth may occur. Table 2.4 indicates the moisture levels applicable to various types of fruit, and it can be seen that the safe moisture levels for dried fruit are much higher than those for other similar commodities.

At the present time, suitable field moisture meters for use with dried fruit are not readily available, and moisture determinations can only be satisfactorily carried out where laboratory facilities are available.

Various species of drought resisting fungi may develop on dried fruit when the moisture content is just above the safe level, and a number of osmophilic yeasts are quite commonly associated with spoilage in dried fruit.

Many of the yeasts bring about fermentation with the production of lactic acid or alcohol, and yeasts are frequently present in wart-like crystalline growths which occur in fruit which has become "sugared". In very moist fruit mucoraceous fungi may predominate and are visible as white fluffy growths on and within the fruit.

Mite infestation

Severe mite infestations are often associated with the growth of osmophilic yeasts in fermenting dried fruit products. Many of these mites are unable to complete their development in the absence of yeast. They have been reported as occurring on dried fruit, and particularly figs and prunes in Mediterranean countries. Such infestations are difficult to eradicate and affect consumer acceptance of the contaminated products.

Insect infestation

Insect infestations may begin in the field before harvest, may continue during bulk storage after drying, and unless measures are taken to prevent it, may occur in the finished packaged product during storage prior to distribution and consumption.

Regular treatments of the stack of dried fruit with a suitable insecticide will be necessary as a routine to combat light insect infestations. Pyrethrins synergised with piper only butoxide are commonly used as a surface spray or as an aerosol fog for this purpose. Heavy infestations will require that the fruit be fumigated.

Equipment for "dry sulphuring of fruit before dehydration/ drying

SO_2 generator

(1) SO_2 outlet pipe

(2) Sulphur feeding door

(3) Plate for sulphur burning

(4) Small door

(5) Burner for gas

(6) Metallic sieve

Sulphuring installation

(1) Exhaust pipe

(2) SO_2 pipe

(3) SO_2 generator

(4) SO_2 distributor

(5) SO_2 distribution pipes

(6) Sulphuring cells

(7) SO_2 flow regulator

(8) Pipe for removing SO_2 from sulphuring cells

(9) Electrical fan

(10) Exhaust pipe for removing SO_2 from sulphuring installation

(11) Hole for SO_2 coming from cells

Solar dryer with air heater-tunnel type; community or business level

1. Air heaters

   1.1 Cover: Transparent 3 mm. plexiglass plate or plastic sheet

   1.2 Absorber-bottom-corrugated black painted iron sheets-intermediary-black painted iron sieve

   1.3 Insulation: none

   1.4 Frames: metallic black painted corner/angle ironR

II. Drying tunnel or room

   2.1 Cover: transparent plastic sheets

   2.2 Frames: metallic black painted angle iron

2.3 Insulation: for back only on the outside

2.4 Back wall: wood plate, painted black on inside

2.5 Front wall: transparent plastic sheets

2.6 Side doors: - frames = wood

-transparent plastic sheets

2.7 Dimensions of drying tunnel/room

- L = 22 feet
- W = 18 feet
- H = 5 feet

2.8 One range of trolleys

III. Trays

3.1 Frames: wood, black painted

3.2 Bottom: nylon mesh or wood slats

3.3 Dimensions: - 1 = 3 feet

- W = 2.4 feet

IV. Trolleys

4.1 Metal platform with wheels

4.2 Number of trays per trolley: 15

4.3Distance between trays: 3"

4.4 Total height of trolley: 3 × 15 = 45 inch + 4" (wheel) = 49 inch

V. Capacity calculation; number of trolleys and trays

5.1 Hypothesis: 300 kg fresh apricots received per day

2 days solar drying

5.2 Tunnel/dryer capacity: 2 X 300 = 600 kg fresh apricots

5.3 Number of trolleys and trays calculation:

-number of trays/trolley = 15

- kg fresh apricots per tray = 6 kg
- kg fresh apricots per trolley: 6 X 15 = 90 kg
- number of trolleys needed in drying room; 600: 90 = 7
- number of trolleys in sulphuring cells = 2
- number of trolleys in "wet preparation section" = 3
- number of trolleys in dry section (after tunnel) = 2
- total number of trolleys needed = 14
- total number of trays needed : 14 X 15 = 200

VI. Sulphuring cell

6.1 Capacity: 2 trolleys

6.2 Dimensions: 1 = 5 feet; w = 3.5 feet; H = 55 inch

6.3 One sulphuring pipe inside the cell, diameter = 15 cm

VII. SO_2 generator: diameter = 45 cm; h = 70 cm

VIII. Air heater/heat collector

8.1 Dimensions: L = 5 M; H = 30 cm; H1= 15 cm; H2 = 20 cm

8.2 Bottom/corrugated black painted iron sheets

8.3 Intermediate heat absorber: iron black painted metallic plate/sieve with holes of about 3 cm in diameter fixation: at mid-distance between cover and bottom of the heat collector

8.4 Cover: transparent 3 mm plexiglas plate (or transparent plastic sheets)

The calculation used in this dryer is based on a real situation in a developing country, within the framework of FAO projects availability of building materials was confirmed.

For the orientation of the dryer geographical position of the available drying yard and local wind direction were taken into consideration.

Technology of semi-processed fruit products

The semi-processed fruit products are manufactured in order to be delivered to industry processing centres (in the fruit producing country itself or in importing countries) where they will be further manufactured in consumer oriented finished products: jams, jellies, syrups, fruits in syrup, etc.

In the practice of semi-processed fruit products and for the purpose of this document the following categories are defined:

a) fruit "pulps": semi-processed products, not refined, obtained by mechanical treatment (or, less often, by thermal treatment) of fruit followed by their preservation. Either whole fruit, halves or big pieces are used which enables easy identification of the species. "Pulps" can be classified in boiled or non boiled (raw).

b) Fruit "purees-marks": semi-processed products obtained by thermal and mechanical treatment or, very rare, raw and then refined, operations by which all non-edible parts (cores, peels, etc.) are removed. "Purees-marks" are classified in boiled (the more usual case) and non boiled raw).

c) Semi-processed juices: products obtained by cold pressure or very rare by other treatments (diffusion, extraction, etc.) followed by the preservation.

Technical processes for preservation of semi-processed fruit products

Preservation can be achieved by chemical means, by freezing or by pasteurization. The choice of preservation process for each individual case is a function of the semi-processed product type and the shelf life needed.

Chemical Preservation

In many countries, in practice, this is carried out with sulphur dioxide, sodium benzoate, formic acid and, on a small scale, with sorbic acid and sorbates.

Preservation with sulphur dioxide is a widespread process because of its advantages: universal antiseptic action and very economic application. The drawbacks of SO_2 are: SO_2 turn firms the texture of some fruit species (pomaces), desulphiting is not always complete and recolouring of red fruits is not always complete after desulphitation.

Practical preservation dosage levels with SO_2 for about 12 months is 0.18-0.20% SO_2 (with respect to the product to be preserved).

This level could be reduced to 0.09% SO_2 for 3 months and to 0.12% SO_2 for 6 months preservation.

The preservation with sulphur dioxide is in use mainly for "pulps" (Table 2.10) and for "purees-marks" (Table 2.11) .

Chemical preservation can be performed from a practical point of view by the utilisation of 6% SO_2 water solutions or by direct introduction of sulphur dioxide gas in the product (for "purees-marks"). The preparation of 6% SO_2 solutions is done by bubbling the gas from cylinders in cold water; from a 50 kg SO_2 compressed gas cylinder results 830 litre of 6% SO_2 solution.

These SO_2 solutions have to be stored in cool places, in closed receptacles and with periodic concentration control/check by titration or by density measurements -approximate results – (see Table 2.12).

Preservation with sodium benzoate has the following advantages:

It does not firm up the texture and does not modify fruit colour. The disadvantages are: it is not a universal antiseptic, its action needs an acid medium and the removal is partial. Sodium benzoate is in use for "pulps" and for "purees-marks" but less for fruit juices.

Practical dosage level for 12 months preservation is 0.18-0.20% sodium benzoate, depending on the product to be preserved. Sodium benzoate is used as a solution in warm water; the dissolution water level has to be at maximum 10% reported to semi-processed product weight.

Formic acid preservation is performed mainly for semi-processed fruit juices at a dosage level of 0.2% pure formic acid

9100%). Formic acid is an antiseptic effective against yeasts, does not influence colour of products and is easily removed by boiling.

Formic acid would be diluted with water in order to insure a homogeneous distribution in the product to be preserved; water has to be at maximum 5% of the product weight. Because of a potential effect of pectic substance degradation, formic acid is less in use for "pulps" and "purees-marks" preservation.

Sorbic acid used as potassium sorbate (easily water soluble) can be used for preservation of fruit semi-processed products at a dosage level of 0.1% maximum. Advantages of sorbates are: they are completely harmless and without any influence on the organoleptic properties of semi-processed fruit products.

Preservation by pasteurization

As fruit has a low pH, preservation of semi-processed fruit products could also be performed by pasteurization (heat treatment step at maximum temperature of 100°C), the length of this step varying with the size of the receptacles.

The advantages of this type of treatment are: hygienic process, which assure a long term preservation; the disadvantages are: need for air tight receptacles, and pectic substances could begin to deteriorate if the thermal treatment is too long.

Figure 2.5 shows a technological line for the preparation of semi-processed "puree-marks".

Thermal preservation of fruit semi-processed products could also be done by a "self-pasteurization": very hot semi-processed products are filled into receptacles (e.g. metal cans) which are sealed and then inverted in order to sterilise the air which goes through the hot fruit mass.

Preservation by freezing

This is done on an industrial scale in some countries and can be done with or without sugar addition. The advantages of this process are: absence of added substances; very good preservation of quality of fruit constituents (pectic substances, vitamins, etc.)

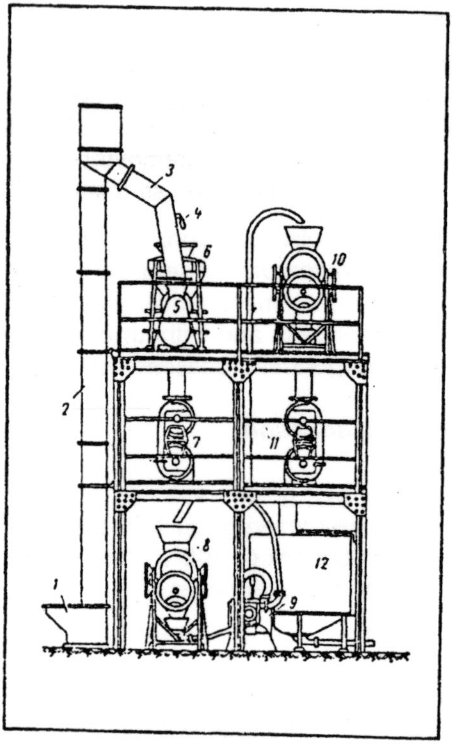

Figure 2.5 Technological line for semi-processed fruit products 1. Washing tank, 2. Vertical transporter, 3. Transport tubes, 4. Regulating plates, 5. Crushing machine, 6. Grating machine, 7. Preheating equipment, 8. Pulper, 9. Centrifugal pump, 10. Finisher, 11. Storage tank

From the storage tank 11, the product is transferred by pump to a mixing tank (mix with SO_2)

and good preservation of organoleptic properties (flavour, taste, colour). Freezing is done at about –20 to –30°C and storage at –10 to –18°C.

Freezing is applied mainly to semi-processed fruit products aimed at very high quality and high cost finished products.

Technological flow-sheet for semi-processed fruit "pulps"; chemical preservation

Sorting is needed in order to remove sub-standard fruit (with moulds, with diseases, etc.) and all foreign bodies.

Washing is obligatory in order to remove all impurities which cannot be eliminated at the processing step in finished products.

Coring and **Cutting**, mainly for pomace fruits, has as main objective a better utilisation of preservation "space: in receptacles and is not mandatory; this will be defined by customer/supplier agreements/standards. This operation is preferably performed by mechanical means.

Preservation is carried out with the 6% SO_2 solution which is added to the prepared fruits (placed in bulk in receptacles) in the quantity needed to obtain the preservation dosage level, for a better/homogeneous preservative distribution, the initial 6% SO_2 solution could be diluted with water; however, the diluted solution (which will be filled in receptacles) ahs to be at a dosage level of less than 10% of the semi-processed product weight.

For some soft fruit, especially strawberries, preservation is done with a mix of 6% SO_2 solution and calcium bisulphate solution (containing also 6% SO_2).

Preparation of calcium bisulphate solution is done by the introduction of 30 kg of CaO in 1 m^3 SO_2 solution and mixing up to clarification. The resulting solution is mixed with the initial 6% SO_2 solution, generally in a 1:1 ratio, but the ratio can be adapted to the fresh fruit texture. Firming of soft fruit texture by this treatment is based on the formation of calcium pectate with pectic substances from fruit tissues.

In the case of sodium benzoate, formic acid or potassium sorbate, the dosage levels to be used are as indicated above with the rule that it is not allowed to add more that 10% liquid in receptacles on the prepared fruits.

Preservation by pasteurization or "self-pasteurization" will need as additional steps: (a) boiling with a minimum water addition (maximum 10%); (b) filling of receptacles; (c) hermetic closing followed by (d) pasteurization or "self-pasteurization".

Some general technical data for the preparation of chemical preserved semi-processed fruit "pulps" are seen in Table 2.10.

Table 2.10: General technical processing data for semi-processed fruit "pulps"

Fruit species	Preliminary operations	Preservation means
Apples, pears, quinces	Sorting, washing, coring, cutting	Sulphur dioxide
Prunes, peaches, wax	Sorting, washing, stone	Sulphur dioxide or
Cherries, apricots	removal (pitting)	sodium benzoate
Cherries	Sorting, washing	Sulphur dioxide or sodium benzoate, sometimes with calcium bisulphate addition
Strawberries	Sorting, washing	Sulphur dioxide in mix with calcium bisulphate
Wild berries	Sorting, washing	Sulphur dioxide or sodium benzoate; in some cases with calcium bisulphate addition

Technological flow-sheet for semi-processed "puree-marks"

The general technological flow-sheet includes the following operations:

Sorting and **Washing** are obligatory and are carried out in a similar manner as for "pulps".

Heat Treatment / Boiling is needed in order to soften the fruit tissues before refining. For some fruits as strawberry and wild berries, this step is not done and fruits are refined "raw" in order to preserve their flavour.

Pulping is performed with specific equipment- refiners or pulpers- which eliminate seeds, pits and other non edible parts (peels, cores, etc.).

Preservation is carried out by chemical means, by freezing or by pasteurization.

The general technical/processing data for the manufacture of "puree-marks" are seen in Table 2.11.

Table 2.11: General technical processing data for semi-processed: purees-marks"

Fruit species	Preliminary operations	Preservation means
Apples, pears, quinces	Sorting, washing, boiling	Sulphur dioxide; in less
	Refining	frequent cases formic acid or sodium benzoate
Prunes, peaches, wax	Sorting, washing, boiling,	Sulphur dioxide, formic acid
Cherries, apricots,	refining	or sodium benzoate; freezing with or
Cherries		without sugar; self-pasteurization
Strawberry, wild berries	Sorting, washing, refining	Chemical preservation, freezing or self-pasteurization

Fruit sugar preserves technology; jams, jellies, marmalade, fruit paste

As a overall rule of thumb, a sugar concentration of about 60% in finished or processed fruit products generally insures their preservation. Preservation is not only determined by the osmotic pressure of sugar solutions but also by the water activity values in the liquid phase, which can be lowered by sugar addition; and by evaporation down to 0.848 aw; this value however does not protect products from mould and osmophile yeast attack.

Maximum saccharose concentration that can be achieved in the liquid phase of the product is 67.89%; however higher total sugar quantities (up to 70-72%) found in products are explained by an increased reducing sugar solubility resulting from saccharose inversion.

Table 2.12 Correlation between density and concentration for SO_2 solutions

Density at 15°C	Concentration of solutions % SO_2
1.0168	3.00
1.181	3.25
1.194	3.50
1.206	3.75
1.221	4.00
1.248	4.25
1.261	4.50
1.275	4.75
1.289	5.00
1.302	5.25
1.315	5.50
1.340	5.75
1.353	6.25
1.365	6.50
1.377	6.75

Jams

The preservation of fruit by jam making is a familiar process carried out on a small scale by housewives in many parts of the world. Factory jam making has become a highly complex operation, where strict quality control procedures are employed to ensure a uniform product, but the manufacturing operations employed are in essence the same as those employed in the house.

Fresh or pre-cooked fruit is boiled with a solution of cane or beet sugar until sufficient water has been evaporated to give a mixture which will set to a gel on cooling and which contains 32-34% water.

Gel formation is dependent on the presence in the fruit of the carbohydrate pectin, which at a pH of 3.2 – 3.4 and in the presence of a high concentration of sugar, has the property of forming a viscous semi-solid.

During jam boiling, all micro-organisms are destroyed within the product, and if it is filled hot into clean receptacles which are subsequently sealed, and then inverted so that the hot jam contacts the lid surface, spoilage by micro-organisms will not take place during storage.

The composition of jam made from stone fruit and berry fruit is shown in Table 2.13. About 30% of the vitamin C present in fresh fruit is destroyed during the jam-making process, but that which remains in the finished product is stable during storage.

Table 2.13 Composition of some fruit jams

Type of Jam	Moisture content %	Sugar (as invert Sugar, %)	Vitamin C mg/100 g
Jam made from berry fruits: strawberry, raspberry, etc.	29.8	69.0	10-25
Jam made from Stone fruits: Apricot, peach, etc.	29.6	69.3	10-35

Source: FAO/WFP, 1970.

The high moisture content of jam (equivalent to an equilibrium relative humidity of about 82%) makes it susceptible to mould damage once the receptacle has been opened and exposed from some time to the air. No problems of microbiological spoilage are likely to arise in the canned product during storage.

Marmalade

This sugar preserve is defined as "semisolid or gel-like product prepared from fruit ingredients together with one or more sweetening ingredients and may contains suitable food acids and food pectins; the ingredients are concentrated by cooking to such appoint that the TSS—Total Soluble solids—of the finished marmalade is not below 65%".

Fruit paste

Fruit paste is a product obtained in the same way as special non-gelified fruit marmalade but with a lower water content- about 25% TSS in fruit paste.

Lowering water content could be achieved by continuing boiling of the product or by drying the product by natural or artificial drying. An example of paste without sugar is the sun dried apricot or prune paste.

General procedure for the preparation of jams, jellies and marmalade

a) Boil the pulp or the juice (with water when necessary)

b) Add the pectin* to the batch while stirring very vigorously

*Pectin which ahs previously been mixed with 5 times its weight in sugar taken from the recipe)

c) Boil for about 2 minutes to assure a complete dissolution

d) Add the sugar while keeping the batch boiling

e) Boil down quickly to desired Brix

f) Add the acid (usually citric acid) and remove the froth

g) Fill hot into the (previously cleaned) jars and close

h) Invert the jars for three minutes to pasteurize the cover

Note: the pectin in solution can also be added at the end of the step (e) and has to be prepared as follows: use a strong blender. For one liter of water add slowly into the blender 25 g of protein mixed with 100g of sugar taken from the recipe.

Basic recipes

The following recipes must be considered only as guidelines because the composition of the fruit can vary; also the taste of the consumers varies concerning the consistency, the sweetness and acidity.

Before starting to make jam it is important to know the yield to settle the question on containers. The calculation is made as follows:

$$\frac{\text{Total Soluble Solids content of all the raw ingredients}}{\text{Percentage of Total Soluble Solids in the final product}} \times 100$$

In these basic recipes it is assumed that the fruits are poor in pectin content.

Recipe 1. Fruit: sugar = 50: 50; desired Brix in the finished product is 68.s

	Soluble Solids
10 kg of fruit at 10% TSS	1.000 kg
10 kg of sugar	10.000 kg
60 g of pectin (grade 200)	0.060 kg
55 g of citric acid	0.055 kg
	11.115 kg

$$\text{Yield} = \frac{11.115 \times 100}{68} = 16.4 \text{ kg}$$

Recipe 2. Fruit: sugar = 45: 55; desired Brix in the finished product is 68.

	Soluble Solids
10 kg of fruit at 10% TSS	1.000 kg
2.5 litre of water	-
12.2 kg of sugar	12.2000 kg
65 g of pectin grade 200	0.060 kg
60 g of citric acid	0.060 kg
	13.325 kg

$$\text{Yield} = \frac{13.325 \times 100}{68} = 19.6 \text{ kg}$$

Recipe 3. Fruit: sugar 40: 60; desired Brix in the finished product is 68.

	Soluble Solids
10 kg of fruit at 10% TSS	1.000 kg
3.3 litre of water	-
15 kg of sugar	15.000 kg
85 g of pectin grade 200	0.085 kg
80 g of citric acid	0.080 kg
	16.165 kg

$$\text{Yield} = \frac{16.165 \times 100}{68} = 23.8 \text{ kg}$$

Various factors must be taken into account:

1. **Size of the container:** the quantity of pectin indicated in the recipes is valid for containers of 1 kg or less.

If container capacity is between:	Increase pectin by:
1 kg and 2.5 kg	5%
2.5 kg and 5.0 kg	10%
5.0 kg and 10.0 kg	20%
10.0 kg and 20.0 kg	30%

2. **Finishing point:** the quantity of pectin is given for a final Brix – Total Soluble Solids (TSS) of 68%.

   If the final Brix is 66 increase the pectin by 5%

   If the final Brix is 65 increase the pectin by 10%

   If the final Brix is 64 increase the pectin by 15%

   If the final Brix is 62 increase the pectin by 20%

   If the final Brix is 60 increase the pectin by 30%

3. Acidic taste. If the product is too acid, replace the citric acid by tartaric acid (63% of the amount of citric acid).

4. Formation of clots: If batch clots, it is probably due to the pH being too low or the or TSS being too high; correct accordingly.
5. Formation of liquid at the surface: if liquid forms on the surface, it is probably due to too low a pH or too low pectin content.
6. Crystallisation:
   a) if liquid forms on the surfaces, then the pH is too low; reduce the acid content;
   b) if liquid does not form on the surface, then TSS or pH is too high.
7. Formation of mould: the TSS is probably below 68 deg. Brix. The filling may have been done at a low temperature. If the containers are large, wait until they are cold before closing.
8. Wrong batch: dilute the jam with water to 30% TSS; cook briefly. Add this diluted jam to a new batch but in a ratio not exceeding 10%.

Processing of pineapple-papaya jam

The fruit should be prepared as per previous instructions.

For pineapples, the ends are removed and discarded; the cores and outer parts of the fruits are also removed. The fruit cylinders obtained are pulped through a special extractor (Fitzpatrick communiting machine) equipped with a 0.40 in. screen sieve, the pulp thus obtained is used for making jam.

The papaya are prepared by hand-peeling the fruit; the fruit is then halved and the seeds removed. It is then pulped in the communiting machine using a 0.40 in. screen sieve.

When ginger root is used as flavouring, it is peeled and macerated in a Kenwood blender to a very fine consistency.

A typical formula for a pineapple-papaya jam (50:50 ratio) with ginger flavouring is given as follows:

Pineapple pulp	25.0
Papaya pulp	25.0 pounds
Cane sugar	50.0
Apple pectin (150 grade)	6.0 ounces
Citric acid	6.4
Fresh ground ginger	7.5

Processing is carried out in the following way:

The weighted fruit pulp is placed in a stainless steel steam-jacketed kettle and heated to about 110°F under constant stirring.

When the product reaches this temperature, the heat is turned off. The pectin (mixed in about ten times its weight with some of the weighed sugar), is then mixed into the fruit pulp, stirring constantly in order to prevent the pectin from clotting.

When the pectin has dissolved, the remainder of the sugar is added and dissolved completely in the mixture. The heat is then turned on and the jam mixture is stirred constantly until it starts boiling vigorously. During the remainder of the cooking, the product is stirred occasionally. Near the finishing point (approximately 221°F), the citric acid and the ginger (if it is used) are also added.

Determination of the finishing point is done by removing samples at intervals, cooling, and reading the soluble solids by means of a refractometer equipped with a Brix scale. After the jam reaches the proper Total Soluble Solids content, the heat is turned off and the surface scum/foam is removed.

The jam then is quickly put into receptacles which have been cleaned and sterilized with boiling in water for 30 minutes. The filling operation is done rapidly in order to prevent the temperature of the jam from falling below 190°F.

After filling, sterilized lids (boiled for 30 minutes in water) are placed on the receptacles and they are then sealed.

After this operation the receptacles are inverted for about 3 minutes to insure that the lids are sterilized. The receptacles are then placed upright, at this stage it is not necessary to do any further processing, therefore the receptacles are cooled in running cold water until they reach a temperature slightly above room temperature. They are then dried in air and labeled.

Evaluation of finished products.

During production at medium/large scale, it is recommended that quality controls be performed during manufacturing.

After ten weeks of storage at room temperature it is recommended that an examination of finished products be performed. The receptacles are opened and contents carefully emptied on to enamel trays without disturbing the formation of the jam.

The empty cans (if metal cans were used) are then inspected for signs of corrosion. Factors other than flavour include colour, appearance, syrup separation, firmness and spreading quality, for flavour, jam is tested on pieces of bread. Samples are taken for measurement of pH (with a glass electrode pH meter) and Total Soluble Solids (with refractometer equipped with a Brix scale).

This evaluation enables to have a quality check during product shelf life and to obtain data needed for necessary improvements of future productions.

For pineapple-papaya jam, product made with 30% pineapple and 70% papaya with added ginger has the highest score for flavour. The use of plain tin cans causes corrosion problems which is not the case when acid resistant lacquer cans are used.

Pineapple jam making

1. Boil 40 lb. Of pulp and 12 lb. Of water.
2. Add 225 g of pectin to the batch while stirring rapidly.
3. Boil for about 90 sec to assure complete dissolution.
4. Add 60 lb. Of sugar gradually if possible in several portions, while keeping the batch boiling.
5. Boil down quickly to 69 deg. Brix (223 deg. F).
6. Take off steam, remove foam.

7. Add 300 cc citric acid solution 50%.
8. Fill hot (180 deg. F).
9. Invert receptacles for 3 minutes.

Check each batch for Brix 68-70 deg.; acidity/pH = 3.2 +/-0.2.

Evaluate: absence of defects; colour; flavour; consistency.

Various fruit: sugar ratios can be manufactured; some basic recipes are as follows:

Ratio 50:50	Ratio 45:55	Ration 40:60	
Fruit	55 lb	49.5 lb	444 lb
Water	—	11 lb	13.2 lb
Sugar	55 lb	60.5 lb	66 lb
Pectin (150 grade)	225 g	237.5 g	250 g
Citric acid (50% sol.)	300 cc	320 cc	335 cc

Gelified sugar fruit preserves

Technology of fruit jellies

Jellies are gelified products obtained by boiling fruit juices with sugar, with or without the addition of pectin and food acids. Jellies are usually manufactured from juices obtained from a single fruit species only, obtained by boiling in order to extract as much soluble pectin as possible.

Jellies have to be clear, shiny, transparent and with a colour specific to the fruit from which they are obtained. Once the product is removed from the glass receptacles where it was packed, jellies must kept their shape and gelification and not flow, without being sticky or of a too hard consistency.

Technological flow-sheet for jellies manufacturing covers two categories of operations: those to obtain gelifying juices and those related to the manufacturing of jelly itself.

a) Production of gelifying juices:

Washing and **Sorting** are carried out in usual conditions;

Cutting is applied eventually only to pomaces (apples, quinces) and are limited to cutting in halves or quarters;

Boiling is Performed With Water Addition With 50-100% water, needed fro pectin extraction. The boiling time is 30-60 min., it should not be longer so as to avoid pectin degradation; at the same time boiling must not be too violent.

Juice Separation is carried out by a simple drain through metallic sieve or cloths; in these cases the yield is lower and the residue can be used for marmalade production. In bigger productions it juice separation by hydraulic press is preferred, yield being in these cases greater.

Juice Clarification is strictly necessary in order to obtain clear jellies. This step can be achieved by sedimentation during 24 hours or by filtration.

b) Manufacturing of jellies

Basic Recipe Setting is done starting with equal parts in weight of sugar and juice (for example 1000 g juice and 1000 g sugar). As final jelly has to contain about 60% added sugar, weight of finished product must be of about 1600 g, by evaporation of about 400 g water.

Boiling is carried out as following; juice is boiled up to removal of about half of the water that has to be evaporated, then the calculated sugar quantity is added gradually; the remainder of the water is evaporated until a concentration in soluble substances (refractometric extract) of 65-67% is reached, in which is incorporated also the sugar from juice.

During boiling it is necessary to remove foam/scum formed, product acidity must be brought to about 1% (malic acid) corresponding to pH >3. Any acid addition is performed always at the end of boiling.

For juices rich in pectin, gelification will occur without pectin addition. If at the trial boiling test the gelification has not occurred. Because of pectin absence, in this case 1-2% powder pectin will be added by operating as indicated: pectin is mixed with 10-20 fold sugar quantity and is introduced directly in the partially evaporated juice and then boiling is conducted rapidly up to final point, evaluation of final point is done not only by refractometry but also by gelifying test.

A rapid test for evaluation of juice pectin content is possible by mixing a small sample of juice with an equal volume of 96% alcohol; the apparition of a compact gelatinous precipitate indicates a sufficient pectin content for gelification.

Boiling of jellies is performed in small batches (25-75 kg) in order to avoid excessively long boiling time which brings about pectin degradation.

Cooling is optional and is carried out up to 85 deg. C, in double wall baths with water circulation.

Filling is performed at a temperature not below 85 deg. C in receptacles (glass jars, etc.), which must be maintained still about 24 hours to allow cooling and product gelification.

Receptacle Closing is done after product gelification.

Usual jelly types are: quinces, strawberries, cherries, wild berries, alone or in mixes with apples.

Grading of marmalades

Three categories can be defined:

- fine marmalade, manufactured from one fruit;
- superior marmalade, obtained from a mix of fruit in which 30% are "noble" species (cherries, strawberries, apricots, etc.) and 70% from other species;
- marmalade from fruit mixes; apples, pears, plums, quinces, ungrafted apricots and wax cherries may be used, with the optional addition of "superior" fruit which was rejected at sorting but which was sound.

The content in total soluble substances (refractometric extract) of marmalades must be 64% minimum; the acidity must be between 0.5% and 1.8% expressed as malic acid.

Basic Recipe Setting For a normal composition-marmalade without pectin addition - the following is a basic recipe:

100 kg semi-processed fruit product	
(10% refractometric extract)	10 kg soluble substances
55 kg sugar	5 kg soluble substances
155 kg	65 kg soluble substances
55 kg water to be evaporated	
100 kg marmalade with 65% refractometric extract	

This marmalade satisfies many standards and at same time has a good shelf-life since it contains less then 35% water. Semi-processed fruit product must have a minimum 8% refractometric extract; in this case the recipe should use 125 kg of raw material, with 80 kg water to be evaporate.

The use of semi-processed fruit products with a low refractometric extract presents the following drawbacks:

a) higher water quantity to be evaporated;

b) longer boiling items with negative impact of pectin degradation;

c) loss of flavour and

d) lower equipment efficiency.

Pectin addition in marmalade manufacture produces the following advantages;

a) improvement of gelification,

b) economy in fruit;

c) shorter boiling time; this maintains taste and flavour and produces higher equipment efficiency.

Pectin addition makes it possible to obtain the "fine" type of marmalade from "noble" fruits which do not contain enough pectin (cherries, peaches, apricots, etc.). In marmalades from fruit mixes, low pectin content can be compensated by addition of semi-processed fruit products which are in this component (for example apples).

When pectin is to be added, the above recipe should be modified as follows;

80 kg semi-processed fruit product (10% refractometric extract)	8 kg soluble substances
55 kg sugar	55 kg soluble substances
10 kg pectin extract (10% R.E.)	1 kg soluble substances
145 kg	64 kg soluble substances
45 kg water to be evaporated	
100 kg marmalade with 64% refractometric extract	

Pectin can be added as pectin extract with about 105 refractometric extract (R.E.) in the recommended proportion or in the form of a powder considered with 100% dry matter (e.g. 100% soluble substances) in a quantity of about 1%.

In some countries it is usual to add 5-12% of corn syrup (calculated to finished product weight) to replace the corresponding quantity of sugar (100 parts corn syrup can replace 80 parts sugar). Corn syrup has to be liquefied by heating before use. Corn syrup addition reduces the too sweet taste of marmalade, avoids sugar crystallisation and gives a special shine to finished products.

Marmalade manufacturing follows the technological line drawing in Fig. 2.6 and covers the following steps:

"Mark" Preparation can be achieved from fresh fruits (as indicated in the section related to semi-processed fruit products) or starting from chemical preserved semi-processed fruit products: "marks" or "pulps". In the latter case, pulps will be processed in marks which then will be desulphitated.

Desulphitation is carried out by boiling at atmospheric pressure, under vacuum in specialized equipment or under pressure in special retorts built in acid-resistant material. In any case, the desulphitation must be carried out before sugar addition because sugar will bound to the sulphur dioxide. The desulphitation operation must be conducted so as to be, if possible, fully completed; the finished product must contain less than 0.005% free SO_2.

The technological flow for marmalade production according to Fig. 2.6.1 is the following: fresh fruit after sorting on control belt (1) is washed in a washing machine (2) is brought to the continuous boiling equipment (3) then to the pulper (4); the semi-finished mark is passed on to the storage tank (6). Pulps are boiled and desulphited in continuous boiling equipment (3), then are brought to pulper (4) and to the storage tank (6).

Boiling aims at evaporating the required water quantity, to facilitate the formation of pectin-sugar-acid gel and to partially invert sugar (about 40% from total sugar). The boiling operation can be carried out in open kettles or in evaporators under vacuum.

In the latter case, the warm "mark" from storage tank (6) is aspirated in a concentrator (7) in a vacuum and submitted to a partial boiling up to removal of half of water quantity which needs to be evaporated; the calculated sugar quantity is then added by aspiration, keeping the boiling on.

After this the pectin extract or powder pectin which has previously been dissolved in warm water, is added; when the final concentration is reached, as indicated by refractometric control, the required quantity of acid is added. Sugar is added in proportion of 55% in finished product, pectic extract (10% refractometric extract) at a level of about 10-15% and the acid (citric, tartaric, lactic) in a quantity needed to obtain a finished product acidity of about 1%.

Boiling at atmospheric pressure affects not only the appearance but also the nutritional value of the products, mainly if these contain proteins, as some albuminoids coagulate even at 60°C.

Food products for which flavour is an essential property as for example fruit juices, etc., are also affected by the action of heat. Heat treatment has an impact on vitamin losses, mainly of vitamin C, in the presence of oxygen as is the case to concentration in open vessels.

Sugars are generally less damaged by heat at temperature below 100°C; as the boiling point is increasing above 100°C, a risk of partial sugar caramelization exists.

In the study of heat effects on products submitted to concentration operation, it is necessary to take into account not only the evaporation surface temperature but also the distribution of the temperature in the whole liquid mass.

The length of the heating period also has a major influence because in many cases it is preferable to concentrate the liquid at a relatively high temperature in a short time avoiding the drawbacks of lower temperatures acting during a long time.

In order to maintain the food value and organoleptic properties, it is necessary that concentration take place at a low temperature which can be achieved by concentration under partial vacuum, taking into account that boiling point decreases when the residual pressure decreases, respectively with the increase of vacuum degree.

Advantage of concentration under partial vacuum are the following:

- lowering of boiling point;
- the total time needed for concentration of food products under a residual pressure of about 200 mm Hg is about half as compared to the that of concentration by boiling at atmospheric pressure;
- by lowering the concentration temperature and time, organoleptic properties and of nutritional value are maintained better particularly as far as the vitamins are concerned;
- when products are concentrated in a vacuum, it is possible to recover volatile aromatic substances by suing adequate installations.

Technical procedures of concentration by vaporisation can be classified in:

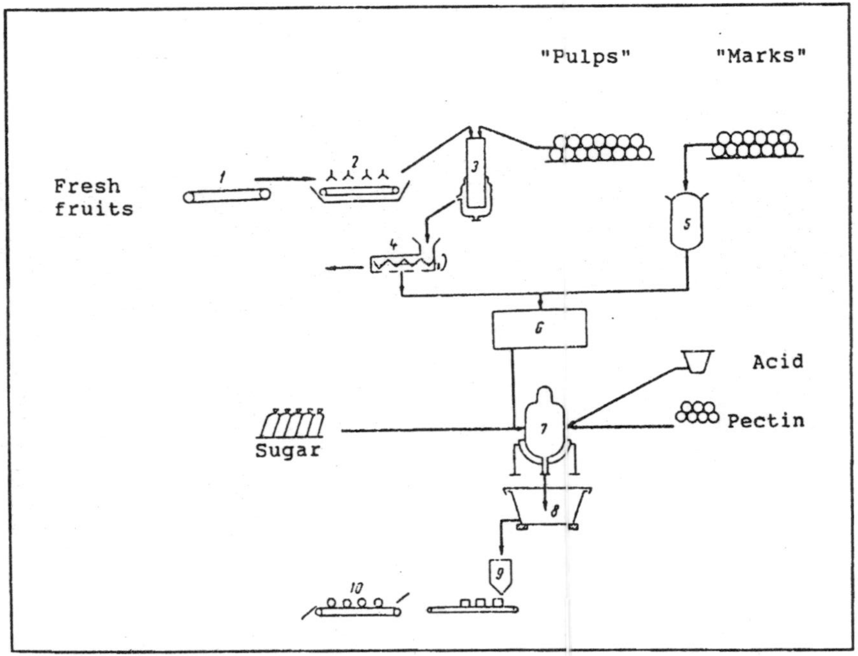

Fig. 2.6: Technological line for marmalade production
1. Control belt, 2. Washing machine, 3. Continuous cooking equipment, 4. Pulper, 5. Desulphiting equipment 6. Tank, 7. Vacuum (evaporator) pan, 8. Cooling and/or storage tank, 9. Filling machine, 10. Labelling

a) concentration at atmospheric pressure: continuous or discontinuous;

b) concentration under partial vacuum: discontinuous (in vacuum equipment with simple or multiple effect) or continuous (in vacuum installations with continuous action or in thin film vaporization installations).

Even if open kettle equipment sis less expensive than evaporators in a vacuum, it is necessary to take into account that boiling under vacuum has the following advantages:

a) low boiling temperature (60-70°C) , depending the degree of the vacuum; this give the fruit better taste and flavour-keeping qualities;

b) easy feeding with raw and auxiliary materials;

c) shorter boiling time;

d) better working conditions (vapour elimination in condensed water and not in open air).

There are small size evaporators under vacuum which can be well suited to the needs of medium size operations in developing countries.

Cooling of marmalade to about 50-60°C can even be done in a vacuum evaporator by closing the hearting steam and maintaining vacuum degree or by discharge in storage tanks (8).

Filling in receptacles (boxes, jars, glasses, etc.) is done preferably with filling machines (9) followed by labeling (10). Small packages can be closed warm or after complete cooling; big packages (boxes, etc.) must be closed only after cooling, e.g. 24 hours after processing.

Storage of marmalade must be done in dry rooms (air relative humidity at about 75%), well ventilated, medium cool places (temperature 10-20 degrees C), disinfected and away from direct sunlight and heat. These measures are necessary because marmalade is a hygroscopic product and, by water absorption, favourable conditions for mould development are created.

Technology of special fruit jams

Special fruit jams are products similar to marmalades but in which fruit partially keep their shape (whole, halves, etc.). Special fruit jams are obtained by boiling fruit with sugar, with or without pectin addition, with acid addition followed by n concentration by evaporation.

Special fruit jams present a pronounced gelification at their cooling and can be considered as fruits included in a pectin-sugar-acid gel.

High quality special fruit jams are obtained only from fresh fruit or possibly frozen and from only one fruit species.

Special fruit jams are classified in:

a) non-pasteurized (min. 68% refractometric extract) and

b) pasteurized (min. 65% refractometric extract); minimum acidity, expressed in malic acid, is 0.5%.

Basic Recipe Setting is done taking into account following elements: - maintenance, as much as possible, of fruit shape, because this is specific to these finished products;

- added sugar, in relation to finished product, must be at 60-65%; this high percentage is needed in order to obtain a rapid and strong gelification and to facilitate conservation of fruit shape;
- a satisfactory gelification cannot generally be obtained without pectin addition, at a level of 1-2%, or respectively 10-20% pectic extract (10% refractometric extract);
- partial (about 40%) inversion of added sugar is necessary.

The basic recipe is: 80 kg fruit + 100 kg sugar + 1.6-2.0 kg pectin powder and 1 kg citric or tartaric acid; this will yield about 165 kg of special fruit jam with 60% added sugar; water quantity to be evaporated is about 18 kg. If the finished product has to contain 65% added sugar, the boiling has to be continued up to evaporation of about 30 kg water, the resulting finished product quantity will be about 153 kg.

Technological flow sheet for manufacturing of special fruit jams is as follows:

Fruit Preparation: sorting, washing, peeling and coring (for apples, pears, quinces), or removal of quetches and stones/pits (for plums, peaches, apricots, cherries) or of short tails (for strawberries and wild berries). Pomace fruits are then cut in slices or quarters.

Boiling With Sugar is the most important operation in production of special fruit jams and has as objective to evaporate water until gel formation and partial inversion of sugar. Boiling has to be conducted in such a way as to avoid fruit disintegration, but fruits must be well penetrated with sugar.

By **boiling** an equilibrium is reached, by osmosis, between sugar solution and cellular juice. The initial concentration gap between sugar syrup and cellular juice is very high and if the equilibration process is forced, juice comes out of cells and fruit loses its shape and may even disintegrate.

The boiling process accelerates the equilibration, intensity of which increases with temperature and boiling time.

Pectin addition shortens boiling and thus delays the equilibration; for this reason there are different methods for special fruit jams preparation:

- maintaining fruit in sugar, at ambient temperature, over 8-24 hours; fruit to sugar ratio is that indicated in recipe. After this sugar impregnation, fruits and resulting sugar syrup are brought together to boil; toward the end of boiling, pectin, dissolved in warm water, and necessary acid quantity are added.
- preparation of a very concentrated sugar syrup (at least 75%), in which fruit is introduced in order to be boiled.

The rest of the operations are similar to those described in the previous method.

- soft fruit (strawberries, wild berries) can be mixed with sugar directly in evaporating open kettles, without added water and then heated gradually up to boiling, which is continued as in previous method.

Boiling is preferably carried out in small open kettles (50-100 kg) in order to avoid too long a boiling and fruit disintegration.

Gelification corresponds generally to the reaching of a concentration of 65% soluble extract, respectively 68% refractometric extract. Practical test for gelification is done as for jellies and marmalades.

Cooling is a technological step strictly necessary in order to avoid fruit rising to the surface in preservation receptacles. Cooling is done in a double bottomed water bath in which water circulates at about 80°C.

Filling of receptacles (jars, boxes, glasses, etc.) is carried out and it is necessary to assure at this stage that the finished product is homogeneous (equal quantities of fruits and gel).

Pasteurization is only applied to special fruit jams with 65% refractometric extract packed in jars or boxes and is performed at about 100°C for about 20 min.

Gelification is carried out during product cooling and intensifies during storage.

Storage must follow the same conditions as for marmalades.

Non-gelified sugar fruit preserves

Technology of fruit jams

Fruit jams are products obtained by boiling of fruits (whole, halves, etc.) with sugar syrup until the reaching a viscous consistency. Jams can be defined as fruits included in a concentrated syrup.

Jams are only prepared from fresh fruits; the usual product range covers the following species: strawberries, cherries, apricots, wild berries, peaches, plums, raisin, quinces, rose petals, etc.; manufacturing of jams from fruit mixes is not an accepted practice. Standards indicate that fruit jams have to conform with following conditions:

- fruit or fruit pieces content 45-55%;
- soluble substances, refractometric degree min. 72%;

- acidity (expressed in malic acid) min. 0.7%.

Basic Recipe Setting is presented below as an indication:

100 kg fruits

150 kg sugar

250 kg

---

35 kg water to be evaporated

---

215 kg jam at about 72% refractometric extract

Fruit Preparation is similar to special fruit jams with the difference that stone/seed removal is mandatory for all species.

Boiling Fruits With Sugar can be achieved by the same three methods described above for special fruit jams. By boiling a sugar content equilibration is foreseen and the operation must be conducted in such a way that texture, flavour and colour of fruits be preserved. Foam/scum has to be removed during boiling.

Generally boiling in concentrated sugar syrup (at least 75%) after a previous diffusion during 2-4 hours is in practical use. Boiling must to be carried out in small portions (about 15 kg) in order to avoid fruit disintegration.

For some fruit species, boiling has to be conducted in many phases/steps with "stops" to enable sugar diffusion. At the end of boiling, vanillin at a ratio of 125 g for 100 kg jam may be added for some fruits (white cherries, raisin, etc.). At the same time, it is also possible to add citric or tartaric acid in order to avoid the "sugaring" defect.

Cooling of jams, necessary in order to avoid fruit rising to the surface, is carried out as for special fruit jams.

Filling of receptacles and Storage for jams are preformed in same way as for special fruit jams.

Technology of special non gelified fruit marmalades

Special non gelified fruit marmalades are products resulting from fruit without stones or seeds, sieved or squashed, concentrated by boiling, without sugar added and non gelified. Their consistency results from a low water content (about 35%) and a high percentage of insoluble substances (5-10%). Sugar the from fruits acts as a preserving agent.

Plum special non gelified fruit marmalade is the product representative of this category. Other fruit is used very rarely, because they have a reduced sugar content as compared to plums; though there are some countries producing special non gelified fruit marmalade from pears or sweet apples.

For plums, the finished product in this category must contain minimum 55-60% soluble substances (refractometric extract), rising up to 70% for a high quality product.

Basic Recipe Setting for plums is done in relation with sugar content of fruits; when this is higher, the product quality is better and the yield is higher. Thus, if plums, with 18% refractometric extract are used, 300-350 kg of fruits are needed for 100 kg finished product.

At the same time, concentration of sugar by boiling, also increases by three fold acidity and astringency of this special plum non gelified marmalade; for this reason it is recommended to use only sweet and completely mature plums.

Washing is performed in usual conditions.

Pre-boiling of fruits can be carried out in water or vapour, preferably with continuous running and has as its objective the softening of tissues.

De-Stoning is performed in a pulper.

Boiling of the sieved mass is done in double bottom open kettles with a big evaporation surface or in vacuum evaporators.

Boiling in open kettles enables production of a more tasty slightly caramelized, product; boiling in vacuum evaporators has the technological advantages indicated in marmalade production.

At the end of boiling and once of necessary concentration is reached, the product is poured directly into receptacles (drums, etc.) and left to cool in order to form a hard surface layer (crust).

Storage of well closed receptacles is carried out as for marmalade.

Special non gelified fruit marmalade can also be prepared from chemically preserved semi-processed fruit products, but the quality is lower than that obtained from fresh fruits.

Sometimes dried prunes in a mix with preserved semi-processed products can be used for plum special non gelified marmalade preparation.

In some countries plum finished products in this category are sweetened by the addition of maximum 30% sugar, calculated in relation to the finished product.

Technology of fruit pastes

These products are obtained in a similar way to marmalades and special non gelified marmalades, but have a lower water content (about 25%). Reduction of water content can be achieved by continuing the boiling of the product or by natural or artificial drying.

A typical example of fruit paste without sugar added is the apricot paste – "pistil", etc. – which is a concentrated special non gelified fruit marmalade poured in thin layers and sun dried.

An example of fruit paste with sugar added is quince paste which is a marmalade concentrated by evaporation. Sugar content must be 65%; soluble substances content, 70-75% refractometric extract and acidity at least 0.5% expressed as malic acid. Packing is done usually in polyethylene sheets and then in boxes or tins; storage conditions are similar to those for marmalade.

Technology of fruit syrups

Fruit syrups are products obtained by dissolving sugar in juices obtained from direct pressing of fruits. Sugar dissolving can be done at room temperature or by heating.

Syrups have to contain 68% soluble substances (refractometric extract) and minimum 1 g/100 ml malic acid. Up to a maximum 10% of sugar can be replaced by corn syrup. Syrups must be manufactured form the juice of only one fruit species.

Juice Preparation is carried out at room temperature as described above.

Sugar Dissolving in Fruit juice can be performed by one of the following methods:

a) Boiling in open kettles, done by using the basic recipe:

350-400 kg fruit juice;

650-660 kg sugar;

max. 10 kg citric or tartaric acid.

The juice is brought to boiling and the sugar is dissolved; the total time has to be as short as possible in order to avoid flavour loss and a too high sugar inversion degree (optimum inversion degree is 40%). Acid is added preferably towards the end of boiling.

During all boiling processes it is necessary to remove foam/ scum. In order to avoid caramelization, the syrup has to be cooled rapidly, and this can be carried out in baths with double bottoms through which are circulated water.

One alternative to this method is to boil syrup in closed vessels to avoid flavour losses.

b) Boiling in a vacuum. The basic recipe is the same as above. Sugar and fruit juice are mixed previously in a pre-heating kettle and then transported to vacuum equipment.

Boiling is performed at 50°C and at the end the temperature is raised slowly up to 65-70°C. the syrup can be called directly in vacuum equipment by closing the steam inlet and by increasing the vacuum. In this boiling method it is possible to incorporate a flavour recuperation device.

c) A continuous process for syrup preparation can be carried out by dissolving components with heat while passing them through a horizontal cylinder with a screw inside.

In the methods where sugar is dissolved by heat, it is also possible to use chemically preserved juices.

In this case it is necessary to first perform the desulphitation of juices preserved with SO_2. This can be performed by boiling juice with optional water addition (and before any sugar addition). High quality syrups are obtained however from fresh juices.

d) Sugar can also be dissolved at room temperature by using continuous flow percolators. These are similar to those used for salt solution preparation in vegetable canning processes. The juice goes over a sugar layer and is concentrated progressively until saturation (about 65%). The syrup is then passed through a filtration section in the bottom of the percolator.

Syrup filtration is needed in order to clarify crystals; the filtration of syrup is done in warm conditions through cloth.

Filling of syrup in bottles is done in aseptic conditions as much as possible in order to avoid syrup infection with osmophile yeasts.

Syrup preservation is assured by the high sugar content with respect to a low water activity [unclear].

Storage takes place in well ventilated storage rooms; avoiding sunlight at 10-15°C.

The usual product range is; strawberries, cherries, wild berries, citrus fruits.

Technology of "fruit in syrup" products

This type of product is represented by fruit (whole, halves or pieces) covered by a sugar solution and preserved by pasteurization. In these products sugar does not have preservation effect but only a sweetening role.

Technological general flow-sheet covers the following steps:

Sorting is necessary in order to choose mature fruit, whole, unblemished, undamaged and with a specific texture. Fruit of good quality but with a texture not compatible with this type of finished product are used for the production of semi-processed products, marmalades, etc. This step is done manually on a sorting belt.

Washing is performed in equipment with fan and sprays.

Cleaning covers removal of leaves, etc., skin removal by one of the desired methods for some fruits and coring/pitting for others.

Cutting is applied only to pomace fruits and is performed preferably by mechanical means.

Preliminary Heat Treatment depends very much upon the fruit types and can be as different as a light blanching up to a real boiling; this step is aimed toward softening of tissues for hard fruits, elimination of waxy pruin later (plums, etc.) or enzyme inactivation for pomace fruits.

This treatment has to be reduced to the minimum necessary in order to avoid sugar losses. Some fruit (for example apricots, black cherries, grapes, etc.) does not undergo preliminary heat treatment.

Cooling is carried out in water (as cold as possible) and should not be too long to avoid soluble substances loss.

Receptacle Filling Fruit is introduced manually or sometimes mechanically (filling tables, etc.) in receptacles and then sugar syrup is added.

Sugar Syrup Preparation is performed by dissolving crystal sugar in hot water (90-100°C). After the sugar has been dissolved, the syrup is boiled briefly; removal of impurities and coagulated substances is then performed by foaming/scumming. An addition of about 0.3% citric acid helps syrup clarification, followed by filtration through cloth.

Preheating/Emptying of open receptacles has as its objective to eliminate air from fruit tissues and this step is largely replaced today by receptacle closing under vacuum. Pre-heating may be done in steam or in water in such a way that syrup temperature reached 80-90°C and is maintained for 10-15 min.

Hermetic Sealing is performed according to the type of receptacle and of cover/cap.

Pasteurization is carried out at 100°C and may be performed in continuous installations or in normal water baths. In some countries fruits in syrup are pasteurized at 80-90°C; this contributes to a greater flavour retention.

Cooling should be intensive in order to avoid discolouration and colour modifications and to reduce corrosion in metal cans.

Refractometric extract is to be measures 30 days after manufacturing. In order to establish exact concentration of sugar syrup to be added in each individual case it is possible to use the following formula:

$$C = 1.5 \times [(2 \times E - F)]$$

C = added syrup concentration;

E = refractometric extract needed in finished products, according to Table 2.14.

F = fruit refractometric extract.

Hot syrup is put into receptacles with a minimum temperature of 80°C in order to enable a corresponding vacuum after cooling.

It is possible to add in the syrup 0.3-0.5% citric or tartaric acid for fruit with a low acidity. Adding ascorbic acid in proportion of 0.8% assures colour maintenance and taste improvement based on its reducing action.

Avoidance of excessively soft texture in finished products may be achieved for soft fruit (strawberries, apricots, etc.) by dipping fruit in a solution of calcium chloride (5% $CaCl2$ in water).

Finished product defects and production "accidents" for "Fruit in syrup" and the means of preventing them

- Change of colour in red fruit (red cherries, plums, etc.) to violet; to avoid this it is necessary to use glass jars or vanished/lacquered tinplate;
- Colour change to red for pears and quinces (pink shade) could arise in products which are over-pasteurized and insufficiently cooled;
- Change of colour of whole peaches peeled by chemical means is due to an incomplete inactivation of oxidative enzymes; to avoid this it is necessary to boil fruit after

chemical peeling followed by washing with 0.5% citric or tartaric acid solutions or by adding ascorbic acid in syrup;

- Softening of strawberries tissues can be prevented by a pre-treatment with warm syrup and also by addition of calcium salt.

Some technical data for processing are seen in Table 2.14.

Table 2.14 Technical data for "Fruits in Syrup"

Type of Fruit/product Name	Size/shape	Minimum fruit content, %	Soluble substances (in syrup), RE** at 20°C minimum
Apricots	Halves	55	25
Strawberries	Whole	47	25
Cherries	Whole	53	22
Quinces	Slices, 30 mm	50	26
Apples	Halves or quarters	47	25
Pears	Halves or quarters	57	22
Plums	Whole	45	25
Melon	Pieces	55	26
Wax cherries	Whole	53	27
Wild cherries	Whole	47	27
Pineapples	Slices	55	26
Mangoes	Pieces	50	25
Papaya	Pieces	55	27
Fruit mixes	According to the Conditions indicated Above, for each fruit	50	25

** RE = Refractometric extract.

Fruit Juice Technologies

Fruit juices are products for direct consumption and are obtained by the extraction of cellular juice from fruit, this operation can be done by pressing or by diffusion.

Table 2.15: Quality defects in fruit products preserved with sugar and means to prevent them

Defects	Products	Means of prevention
"Syruping" **Causes**: Synergies with partial exudation of liquid phase (sugar syrup) due to: too low pH; not enough pectin or with low jellying power; gel aging; mechanical damage.	Jellified products	- Avoid pH values below 2.8 by reduction of added acid. -Use of fruits rich in pectin or add good quality pectin at 1-2%. - Avoid mechanical "bumps" during jellifying phase, handling and transport.
Crystallization of Sugars ("sugaring") **Causes:** Sucrose or glucose crystallization from inversion due to: too much sugar added; too high or too low inversion degree; impurities in sugar initiate crystallization; too low storage temperatures.	All sugar preserved products	-Follow sugar quantities as per standards or recipes, keep an optional inversion degree (30-40%) from total sugar); for this, do accelerate boiling and review acid added quantity. -Storage must not be at temperatures below 10°C. - The replacement of about 10% of sugar with corn syrup could prevent "sugaring". - Use only clean sugar and always filter syrup before filling.
Moulding and fermentation **Causes:** Water activity values obtained do not assure inhibition of mould and osmophile yeasts development. Surface water absorption due to products hygroscopicity.	All products	-Handling and filling of products in as sterile as possible conditions. - Washing and disinfection of recipients; treatment of corks and capsules for bottles. - Keep air relative humidity at about 70-75% in storage areas.
Causes: Too low sugar and too high water content in fruits, due to an insufficient equilibrium.	Jams	-Conduct boiling to obtain sugar and water content uniform in fruits and syrup or gel.

Defects	Products	Means of prevention
Fruit lose integrity Causes: Forces equilibrium of sugar content in fruits and syrup, due to a too intense or too long boiling.	Jams	- Pre-treat fruits with sugar before boiling. - Avoid boiling too a long time. - Pre-treat fruit with calcium hydroxide or chlorure (1-1.5%).

For the purpose of this document, the technology of fruit juice processing will cover two finished product categories:

- juices without pulp ("clarified" or "not clarifies");
- juices with pulp ("nectars").

We will also define as

a) "natural juices" products obtained from one fruit; and

b) "mixed juices" products obtained from the mix of two or three juices from different fruit species or by adding sugar.

Juices obtained by removal of a major part of their water content by vacuum evaporation or fractional freezing will be defined as "concentrated juices".

Technological steps for processing of fruit juices without pulp

Fruit juices must be prepared from sound, mature fruit only.

Soft fruit varieties such as grapes, tomatoes and peaches should only be transported in clean boxes which are free from mould and bits of rotten fruit.

Washing: fruit must be thoroughly washed. Generally, fruit will be submitted to a pre-washing before sorting and a washing step just after sorting.

Sorting: removal of partially or completely decayed fruit is the most important operation in the preparation of fruit for production of frits quality fruit juices; sorting is carried out on moving inspection belts or sorting tables.

Crushing/Grinding/Disintegrations Step is applied in different ways and depends on fruit types:

Crushing for grapes and berries;

Grinding for apples, pears;

Disintegration for tomatoes, peaches, mangoes, apricots.

This processing step will need specific equipment which differs from one type of operation to another.

Enzyme Treatment of crushed fruit mass is applied to some fruits by adding 2-8% pectolitic enzymes at about 50°C for 30 minutes.

This optional step has the following advantages: extraction yield will be improved, the juice colour is better fixed and finished product taste is improved.

However, for fruit which is naturally rich in pectic substances, this treatment makes the resulting "exhausted" material useless for industrial pectin production.

Heating of crushed fruit mass before juice extraction is an optional step used for some fruit in order to facilitate pressing and colour fixing; at same time, protein coagulation takes place.

Pressing to extract juice.

Diffusion is an alternative step for juice extraction and can be carried out discontinuously or in batteries at water temperature of about 80-85°C.

Juice Clarifying can be performed by centrifugation or by enzyme treatment, contribution achieves a separation of particles in suspension in the juice and can be considered as a pre-clarifying step. This operation is carried out in centrifugal separators with a speed of 6000 to 6500 RPM.

Enzyme clarifying is based on pectic substance hydrolysis; this will decrease the juices' viscosity and facilitate their filtration. The treatment is the addition of pectolitic enzyme preparations in a quantity of 0.5 to 2 g/l and will last 2 to 6 hours at room temperature, or less than 2 hours at 50°C, a temperature that must not be exceeded.

The control of this operation is done by checking the decrease in juice viscosity, sometimes, the enzyme clarifying is completed with the step called "sticking" by the addition of 5-8 g/hl of food grade gelatine which generates a flocculation of particles in suspension by the action of tannins.

Filtration of clarified juice can be carried out with Kieselgur and bentonite as filtration additive in press-filters (equipment).

De-Tartarisation is applied only to raisin juice and is aimed to eliminate potassium bitartrate from solution. This step can be performed by the addition of 1% calcium lactate or 0.4% calcium carbonate.

Pasteurization of juice can be done for temporary preservation (pre-pasteurization) and in this case this operation is carried out with continuous equipment (heat exchangers, etc.); warm juice is stored in drums or large size receptacles (20-30 kg). Pasteurization conditions are at 75°C in continuous stream.

Pasteurization of bottled juice is then carried out just before delivery to the market; this is performed in water baths at 75°C until the point where the juice reaches 68°C. in cases when the final pasteurization is done without pre-pasteurization and temporary storage, modern methods use a rapid pasteurization followed by aseptic filling in receptacles.

Rapid pasteurization conditions are as follows: temperature about 80°C, over 10-60 sec., followed by cooling; all operations are carried out in continuous stream.

Preservation under CO_2 pressure may be done at a concentration of 1.5% CO_2 under a pressure of 7 kg/cm^2. At the distribution step. Proceed at CO_2 decompression and the juice is then submitted to a sterilising filtration and aseptic filling in receptacles.

Preservation by freezing is carried out at about –30°C, after a preliminary de-aeration; storage is at –15 to –20°C.

Production of concentrated juices by evaporation is performed under vacuum (less than 100 mm Hg residual pressure) up to a concentration of 65-70% total sugar which assures preservation without further pasteurization. Modern evaporation installations recover flavours from juices which are then reincorporated in concentrated juices.

Additional operation for juice manufacturing are the vacuum de-aeration and mixing with other fruit juices or with sugar.

For the production of non clarified juices the centrifugation is the only specific step, enzyme clarifying and subsequent filtration being eliminated.

The optimum sugar/acid ratio for the majority of fruit, mainly for pomaces, is 10/1 to 15/1.

Fruit which is rich in carotenoids (apricots, peaches, etc.) is only processed as juices with pulp ("nectars").

Technological steps for processing of specific fruit juices without pulp are seen in Table 2.16.

Figure 2.7 describes a general technological line for the production of fruit juices without pulp.

Technological flow-sheet for fruit juices with pulp ("Nectars")

This process is divided at industrial scale in two categories of operations:

a) processing for obtaining juices;

b) juice conditioning for preservation.

a) Operations in the first category are differ according to the type of fruit which to be processed.

Pomaces (apples, pears) are washed and stored and then crushed in a colloid mill; fruit puree is then passed through a screw type heating equipment where direct steam is used as a source of heat. Warm fruit mass is treated in a pulper with a 2 mm screen and then through an extractor similar with the equipment used for tomato juice.

Stone fruits (apricots, peaches, cherries, etc.) after washing and sorting are submitted to steam in a continuous heater, then the warm fruit mass is passed through a pulper and then an extractor (as mentioned above). Berries (strawberry, wild berries, etc.) are washed, sorted and then crushed, preheated and then introduced in extractor.

Table 2.16: Technological steps for processing of specific fruit juices without pulp

Type of Juice	Preliminary processing	Mixing with other Juices	Usual Preservation
Apples	Grinding, pressing, Centrifugation, Enzyme clarifying, Filtration	It is not usual	-Pasteurization -under CO2 -Sterilization filtration -Concentration by evaporations
Pears	As for apples	Apple juice (1:1)	-Pasteurization
Raisins	Debunching, optimal heating at about 60°C, pressing, detartration, optional enzyme clarifying, filtration.	Mix of juices of different varieties	As for apples
Quinces	As for apples, with "sticking" after enzyme clarifying	Apple juice	-Pasteurization
Cherries	partial crushing, optional heating (65°C), centrifugation, filtration	Mix with sugar (5-10%) or with apple juice	-Pasteurization
Prunes	Crushing, enzyme treatment, diffusion at 85°C (ratio prunes/ water 2/1), pressing, mix of liquids, filtration	Mix with 5% sugar	-Pasteurization

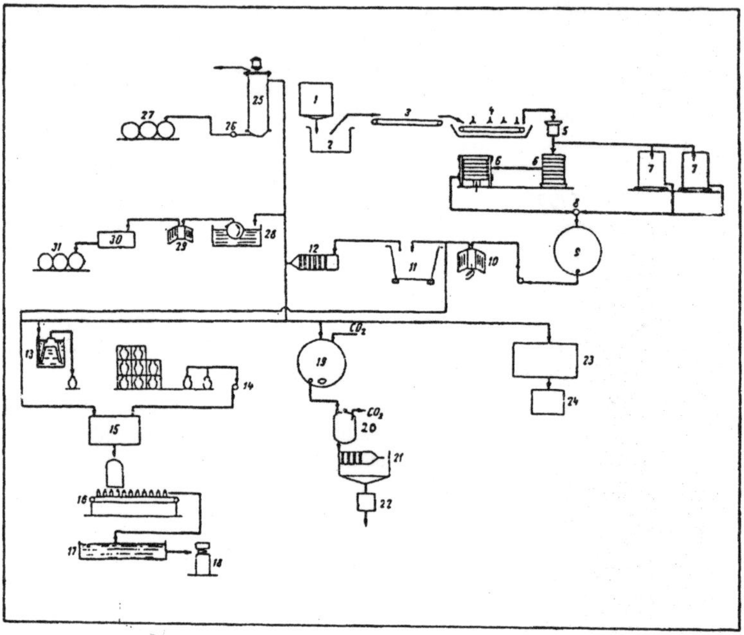

1. Fruit storage/bin, 2. Preliminary washing, 3. Sorting on belt, 4. Washing, 5. Fruit crusher, 6. Hydraulic press, 7. Diffusion battery, 8. Pump, 9. Collecting tank, 10. Centrifuge, 11. Enzymatic treatment, 12. Filter-press, 13. Pasteurizer, 14. Pump, 15. Collecting tank, 16. Filling machine, 17. Bottle pasteurizer, 18. Labelling, 19. Tank or treatment with CO_2, 20.Table 2.16: Technological steps for processing of specific fruit juices without pulp, 21. Filter (Sterile), 22. Filling tank, 23. Freezer, 24. Storage for frozen juice, 25. Thin layer vacuum evaporator, 26. Pump, 27. Storage tanks, 28. Refrigerated rotating drums, 29. Centrifuge, 30. Collecting tank, 31. Storage tanks

Figure 2.7.1 General technological flow-sheet Fruit Juices w/o pulp

In order to avoid browning and undesirable taste modifications it is usual to add about 0.05% ascorbic acid.

b) Second category type of operations are similar for all fruit species, partial elimination of cellulose is achieved with a continuous centrifugal separator; the resulting juice is then processed in order to adjust sugar and acid content for viscosity.

Sugar (about 8-10%) is added as a syrup (in water or in the juice of same fruit obtained by pressure). Acidity is adjusted with citric or tartaric acid. The adjusted juice is then de-aerated under vacuum at about 40°C. This step aims at avoiding oxidative reactions and vitamin C loss reduction.

An important subsequent step is an intensive homogenisation (under pressure at 150-180 A) in order to obtain particles with dimensions below 100. The homogenized juice obtained is then continuously pasteurized in plate heat exchanger equipment at a temperature of about 130°C, cooled down to about 90°C and aseptically packed in receptacles.

The principal characteristics of fruit "nectars" are uniformity and stability of the content provided by the advanced disintegration of fruits, stability can be obtained by increasing product viscosity by adding pectin for fruit which is deficient in this component. In order to avoid "separation", intensive homogenisation is carried out as described above.

Fruit "nectars" contain all the important components of the original fruit and to a large extent maintain their taste and flavour. The sugar/acidity (as citric acid) ratio is to a large extent determined by the type of fruit and the correction applied; for example, this ratio is 30 for apricots, 40 for peaches, 160 for pares, etc.

Banana and plantain processing technologies

Traditional processing

Products: Uses and Dietary Significance

Most of the world's bananas are eaten either raw, in the ripe state, or as a cooked vegetable, and only a very small proportion are processed in order to obtain a storable product. This is true

A general technological flow-sheet for fruit juice processing is presented below:

Temporary Storage
(Slices, bins, boxes)
↓
PRE-WASHING
↓
SORTING
↓
WASHING
↓
CRUSHING-GRINDING
↓
HEATING
(optional)
↓
ENZYME TREATMENT
(optional)
↓
JUICE EXTRACTION
(Pressing; diffusion)
↓
JUICE
↓
INTERMEDIARY STORAGE
↓
CENTRIFUGATION
↓
ENZYME CLARIFYING
↓
FILTRATION
↓
PASTEURIZATION
↓
FILLING OR STORAGE
(in sterile tanks or bulk receptacles)
↓
(COLLECTOR TANK)
↓
BOTTLE FILLING
↓
PASTEURIZATION
↓
COOLING
↓
LABELLING
↓
STORAGE

both at a traditional village level with both desert and cooking bananas and when considering the international trade in dessert bananas.

In general, preserved products do not contribute significantly to the diet; however, in sole localized areas the products are important in periods when food are scarce.

Probably the most widespread and important product is flour preparation from unripe banana and plantains by sun-drying. In Uganda, dried slices known as "mutere" are prepared for storage from green bananas, the dried slices being either used directly for cooking or after grinding into a flour. "Mutere" is used chiefly as a famine reserve and does not feature largely in the diet under normal conditions.

In Gabon, plantains are sometimes made into dried slices which can be stored and used on long journeys, and plantains are used in Cameroon to prepare dried pieces which are stored and ground as needed into flour for use in cooking a paste known as "fufu". Dried green banana slices are also used in parts of south and Central America and West Indies for preparing flour.

The other nutritionally important is beer which is a major product in Uganda, Rwanda and Burundi where green banana utilization is particularly high.

Preservation Methods and Processes

Drying. Both ripe and unripe bananas and plantains are normally peeled and sliced before drying, although banana figs are sometimes prepare from whole ripe fruit. Sun during is the most widespread technique where the climate is suitable but frying in ovens or over fires is also practiced. In West Africa, plantains are often soaked and sometimes parboiled before drying, the slices of unripe fruit are normally spread out on bamboo frameworks; or a cemented area; or on a mat; or on a sweet-bare patch of earth; or on a roof; or sometimes on stones outcrops or sheets of corrugated iron.

Oven-drying of ripe bananas is practised in Polynesia as a mean of preserving the fruits, which are then wrapped in leaves and bound tightly to store until needed. In East Africa a method has been reported that involves drying the peeled bananas on a frame placed over a fire for 24 hr before drying in the sun, to accelerate the process.

Product Stability and Storage Problems

There is little experimental data on the storage life of the traditionally made banana and plantain products.

Potential for Sealing up of Traditional Processes to Industrial Level

Many banana products are now produced on an industrial scale, including the traditional banana figs and flour, and the processing techniques are described below. One of the main problems encountered has been the susceptibility of banana products to flavour deterioration and discoloration and in the past many products reaching the market have been of poor quality.

A great deal of research has been directed to overcoming these problems although however good the resultant products are they cannot compare in flavour and other characteristics with the fresh banana fruit. Indeed, an important constraint on the large-scale development of banana processing is the lack of demand for banana products since the fresh fruit is available throughout the year in most parts of the tropical world.

The production of beer from banana and plantains has not been scaled up to an industrial level, and while an important product in localized areas of tropical Africa, the market is rapidly declining in flavour of European-type brews produced locally.

Industrial Processing

Products and Uses

The main commercial products made from bananas are canned or frozen puree, dried figs, banana powder, flour, flakes, chips (crisps), canned slices and jams.

Banana products can be divided roughly into two types- those for direct consumption, such as figs, and those for use in food manufacturing industry, for example purees and powder.

Banana figs, or fingers as they are sometimes known, are usually whole, peeled fruit carefully dried so as to retain their shape, although sometimes the fruit is sliced or halved to facilitate drying, banana and plantain chips (crisps) are thinly sliced pieces of fruit fried in oil and eaten as a snack like potato chips (crisps).

The main use of canned slices is in tropical fruit salads. Banana flakes are used as a flavouring or in breakfast cereals. Banana puree find use mainly in the production of baby foods. Banana flour is said to be highly digestible and is used in baby and invalid foods, but can also be used in the preparation of bread and beverages.

Banana powder is used chiefly in the baking industry for the preparation and fillings for cakes and biscuits and is also used for invalid and baby foods.

Processing Technology

In general, to obtain a good-quality product from ripe-bananas the fruit is harvested green and ripened artificially under controlled conditions at the processing factory. After ripening, the banana hands are washed to remove dirt and any spray residues, and peeled. Peeling is almost always done by hand using stainless steel knives, although a mechanical peeler for ripe bananas has been developed, capable of peeling 450 kg of fruit per hour (Banana Bulletin, 1974).

The peeling of unripe bananas and plantains is facilitated by immersing the fruit in hot water. For example, immersion in water at 70-75°C for 5 min. has been suggested as an aid for peeling green bananas for flour production, while the peeling of green bananas for freezing has been facilitated by immersion in water at 93°C for 30 min.

Banana Figs

Fully ripe fruits with a sugar content of about 19.5% are used and are treated with sulphurous acid after peeling, then dried as soon as possible afterwards. Various drying systems have been described using temperatures between 50 and 82°C for 10 to 24 hr to give a moisture content ranging from 8 to 18% and a yield of dried figs of 12 to 17% of the fresh banana on the stem.

One factory in Australia uses a solar heat collector on the roof to augment the heat used for drying bananas. Bananas can also be dried by osmotic dehydration, using a technique which involves drawing water from 1/4 –in. Thick banana by placing them in a sugar solution of 67 to 70 deg. Brix for 8 to 10 hr, followed by vacuum-drying at 65 to 70°C, at a vacuum of 10 mm hg for 5 hr. The moisture content of the final products is 2.5% or less, much lower than that achieved by other methods.

Banana Puree

Banana puree is obtained by pulping peeled, ripe bananas and then preserving the pulp by one of three methods: canning aseptically, acidification followed by normal canning, or quick-freezing.

The bulk of the world's puree is processed by the aseptic canning technique. Peeled, ripe fruits are conveyed to a pump which forces them through a plate with 1/4 –in. Holes, then onto a homogeniser, followed by a centrifugal de-aerator, and into a receiving tank with 29-in. Vacuum, where the removal of air helps prevent discoloration by oxidation.

The puree is the passed through a series of scraped surface heat exchangers where it is sterilized by steam, partially cooled, and finally brought to filling temperature. The sterilised puree is then packed aseptically into steam-sterilised cans which are closed in a steam atmosphere.

Banana Slices

Several methods for canning of banana sliced in syrup are used. Best-quality slices are obtained from fruit at an early stage of ripeness. The slices are processed in a syrup of 25 deg. Brix with pH about 4.2, and in some processes calcium chloride (0.2%) or calcium lactate (0.5%) are added as firming agents.

A method for producing an intermediate-moisture banana product for sale in flexible laminate pouches has been developed.

Banana slices are blanched and equilibrated in a solution containing glycerol (42.5%), sucrose (14.85%), potassium sorbate (0.45%), and potassium metabisulphite (0.2%) and 90 deg. C for 3 min. to give a moisture content of 30.2%.

Banana Powder

In the manufacture of banana powder, fully ripe banana pulp is converted into a paste by passing through a chopper followed by a colloid mill. A 1 to 2% sodium metabisulphite solution is added to improve the colour of the final product. Spray-or drum-drying may be used, the latter being favoured as all the solids are recovered.

A typical spray dryer can produce 70 kg powder per hour to give yields of 8 to 11% of the fresh fruit, while drum-drying gives a final yield of about 13% of the fresh fruit, in the latter method the moisture content is reduced to 8 to 12% and then further decreased to 2% by drying in a tunnel or cabinet dryer at 60°C.

Banana Flour

Production of flour has been carried out by peeling and slicing green fruit, exposure to sulphur dioxide gas, then drying in a counter-current tunnel dryer for 7 to 8 hr, with an inlet temperature of 75°C and outlet temperature of 45°C, to a moisture content of 8%, and finally milling.

Banana Chips (crisps)

Typically, unripe peeled bananas are thinly sliced, immersed in a sodium or potassium metabisulphite solution, fried in hydrogenated oil at 180 to 200°C, and dusted with salt and an antioxidant.

Alternatively, slices may be dried before frying and the antioxidant and salt added with the oil. Similar processes for producing plantain chips have been developed.

Banana Beverages

In a typical process, peeled ripe fruit is cut into pieces, blanched for 2 min., in steam, pulped and pectolytic enzyme added at a concentration of 2 g enzyme per 1 kg pulp, then held at 60 to 65°C and 2.7 to 5.5 pH for 30 min.

In a simpler method, lime is used to eliminate the pectin, calcium oxide (0.5%) is added to the pulp and after standing for 15 min. this is neutralised giving a held of up to 88% of a clear, attractive juice. In another process banana pulp is acidified, and steam-blanched in a 28-in Hg vacuum which ensures disintegration and enzyme inactivation, the pulp is then conveyed to a screw press, the resulting puree diluted in the ratio 1:3 with water, and the pH adjusted by further addition of citric acid to 4.2 to 4.3, which yields an attractive drink when this is centrifuged and sweetened.

JAM

A small amount of jam is made commercially by boiling equal quantities of fruit and sugar together with water and lemon juice, lime juice or citric acid, until setting point is reached.

Product Stability and Spoilage Problems

All dried banana products are very hygroscopic and susceptible to flavour deterioration and discolouration, but this can be overcome to some extent by storing in moisture-proof containers and sulphiting the fruit before drying to inactivate the oxidases.

The dried products are also liable to attack by insects and moulds if not stored in dry conditions, although disinfestations after drying by heating for 1 hr to 80°C or by fumigation with methyl bromide ensures protection against attack. Banana powder is said to be stored for up to a year commercially and flakes have been stored in vacuum-sealed cans with no deterioration in moisture, colour for flavour for 12 months.

Banana chips tend to have a poor storage life and to become soft and rancid. However, chips treated with an antioxidant have been stored satisfactorily at room temperature in hermetically sealed containers up to 6 months with no development of rancidity.

Quality Control Methods

In general a good quality product is obtained if fruit is harvested at the correct stage of maturity and, where appropriate, ripened under controlled conditions. For example, in the case of banana figs, the fruits should be fully mature (sugar content of 19.5% for above) or the final product is liable to be tough and lacking in flavour. However, if over-ripe fruit is used, the figs tend to be sticky and dark in colour, so the fruit must be fully yellow but still firm.

For banana flour, which is prepared from unripe bananas, the fruit is harvested at three-quarters the full-ripe state and is processed within 24 hr, prior to the onset of ripening. If less mature fruit is used, the flour tastes slightly astringent and bitter due to the tannin content, bananas harvested between 85 and 95 days after the emergence of the inflorescence, with a pulp-to-peel ratio of about 1.7, were considered to be most suitable for the deep-fat flying.

Other criteria suggested for assessing maturity were beta-carotene and reducing sugar content, both of which increase with increasing maturity and pH which decreases as the fruit ripens, and these should b, respectively, about 2000 ug/100 g, less than 1.5% and 5.8 or above. Browning was found to occur if the sugar content was higher than 1.5%. The determination of crude fat in processed chips is also considered to be a necessary quality control measure.

It is important to remove all impurities prior to processing of products, and this is dome by washing to remove dirt and spray residues and control on the processing line so that substandard fruit can be removed.

Preparation Methods for Fresh Bananas and Plantains

The main ways of preparing fresh bananas for consumption are boiling or steaming, roasting or baking and frying. Boiling followed by pounding into "fufu" is also widely adopted in certain areas of the tropics.

Boiling or Steaming

Plantains and bananas are often prepared simply by boiling in water, either in their peel or after peeling, and either ripe or unripe; if unripe, the fruit is scraped thoroughly after peeling to remove all traces of fibrous material. The boiled fruit is eaten alone or more usually accompanied by a sauce. This preparation technique is widely used in West Africa.

Roasting or Baking

Unpeeled or peeled fruit, either ripe or unripe, is roasted simply by placing in the ashes of a fire or in an oven. This method is widely used in West Africa, East Africa and the South Pacific islands. For example, ripe plantains are placed unpeeled in an oven and when partly brown and tender, removed and peeled, then replaced in the oven and roasted evenly.

Frying

Ripe or unripe plantains or bananas are often peeled, sliced and cooked in oil, particularly in West Africa and in parts of South America and the West Indies. Similar products are also made in East Africa. Typically, ripe plantains are peeled, cut into slices or split lengthways, and fried in palm oil or with groundnut oil, the pieces being served wither hot with a sauce or with fried eggs, or cold as a snack.

Pounding

Pounding is a process, used particularly in West Africa, for preparing most perishable staple food crops including plantains, cassava, yams and cocoyams to obtain a paste or dough known as "fufu" (also spelled "foofoo", "foufou"). The plantains are peeled or boiled and peeled after boiling and pounded in a wooden mortar, the resulting paste normally being eaten with soup or a spiced sauce of meat and vegetables, but sometimes after wrapping in leaves and steaming.

MANGO AND GUAVA PROCESSING TECHNOLOGIES

Mango Processing Technologies

Mangoes are processed at two stages of maturity. Green fruit is used to make chutney, pickles, curries and dehydrated products. The green fruit should be freshly picked from the tree. Fruit that is bruised, damaged, or that has prematurely fallen to the ground should not be used. Ripe mangoes are processed as canned and frozen slices, puree, juices, nectar and various dried products. Mangoes are processed into many other products for home use and by cottage industry.

The mango processing presents many problems as far as industrialization and market expansion is concerned. The trees are alternate bearing and the fruit has a short storage life; these factors make it difficulty to process the crop in a continuous and regular way. The large number of varieties with their various attributes and deficiencies affects the quality and uniformity of processed products.

The lack of simple, reliable methods for determining the stage of maturity of varieties of processing also affects the quality of the finished products. Many of the processed products require peeled or peeled and sliced fruit. The lack of mechanised equipment of the peeling of ripe mangoes is a serious bottleneck for increasing the production of these products.

A significant problem in developing mechanised equipment is the large number of varieties available and their different sizes and shapes. The cost of processed mango products is also too expensive for the general population in the areas where most mangoes are grown. There is, however, a considerable export potential to developed countries but in these countries the processed mango products must compete with established processed fruits of high quality and relatively low cost.

Green mango processing

Pickles

The optimum stage of maturity should be determined for each variety used to make pickles.

There are two classification of pickles–salt pickles and oil pickles, they are processed from whole and sliced fruit with and without stones. Salt is used in most pickles.

The many kinds of pickles vary mainly in the proportions and kinds of spices used in their preparation, one basic recipe for the study of the preparation and storage of pickles in oil is as follows:

Mango pieces	250 g
Salt	60 g
Mustard powder	30 g
Chili powder	20 g
Turmeric powder	2 to 4 g
Fenugreek seeds	2 to 4 g
Bengal gram seeds	2 to 4 g
Gingelly oil	20 to 30 g

The ingredients are mixed together and filled into wide-mouthed bottles of 0.5 kg capacity. Three days later the contents are thoroughly mixed and refilled into the bottles. Extra oil is added to form a 1-2 cm layer over the pickles.

Chutney

The product is prepared from peeled, sliced or grated unripe or semi-ripe fruit by cooking the shredded fruit with salt over medium heat for 5 to 7 minutes, mixed and then sugar, species and vinegar are added. Cook over moderate heat until the product resembles a thick puree, and remaining ingredients and simmer another 5 min. cool and preserve in sterilized jars.

Spices usually include cumin seeds, ground cloves, cinnamon, chili powder, ginger and nutmeg. Other ingredients such as dried fruits, onions, garlic and nuts may be added.

Drying/dehydration

Immature fruit is peeled and sliced for sun-drying, the dried mango slices can be powdered to make a product called amchoo. The use of blanching, sulphuring and mechanical dehydration gives a product with better colour, nutrition, storability and fewer microbiological problems.

Ripe mango processing

Puree

Mangoes are processed into puree for re-manufacturing into products such as nectar, juice, squash, jam, jelly and dehydrated products. The puree can be preserved by chemical means, or frozen, or canned and stored in barrels. This allows a supply of raw materials during the remainder of the year when fresh mangoes are not available.

It also provides a more economical means of storage compared with the cost of storing the finished products, except for those which are dehydrated, and provides for more orderly processing during peak availability of fresh mangoes.

Mangoes can be processed into puree from whole or peeled fruit. Because of the time and cost of peeling, this step is best avoided but with some varieties it may be necessary to avoid off-flavours which may be present in the skin. The most common way of removing the skin is hand-peeling with knives but this is time-consuming and expensive. Steam and lye-peeling have been accomplished for some varieties.

Several methods have been devised to remove the pulp from the fresh ripe mangoes without hand-peeling. A simplified method is as follows: the whole mangoes were exposed to atmospheric steam for 2 to 21/2 min in a loosely covered chamber, then transferred to a stainless steel tank.

The steam-softened skins allowed the fruit to be pulped by a power stirrer fitted with a saw-toothed propeller blade mounted 12.7 to 15.2 cm below a regular propeller blade. The pulp is removed from the seeds by a continuous centrifuge designed for use in passion fruit extraction, the pulp material is then passed through a paddle pulper fritted with a 0.084 cm screen to remove fibre and small pieces of pulp.

Mango puree can be frozen, canned or stored in barrels for later processing. In all these cases, heating is necessary to preserve the quality of the mango puree. In one process, puree is pumped through a plate heat exchanger and heated to 90°C for 1 min and cooled to 35°C before being filled into 30 lb tins with polyethylene liners and frozen at –23.5°C.

In an other process, pulp is acidified to pH 3.5, pasteurized at 90°C, and hot-filled into 6 kg high-density bulk polyethylene containers that have been previously sterilized with boiling water. The containers are then sealed and cooled in water. This makes it possible to avoid the high cost of cans.

Wooden barrels may be used to store mango pulp in the manufacture of jams and squashes. The pulp is acidified with 0.5 to 1.0% citric acid, heated to boiling, cooled, and SO_2 is added at a level of 1000 to 1500 ppm in the pulp. The pulp is then filled into barrels for future use.

Slices

Mango slices can be preserved by canning or freezing, and recent studies have shown the feasibility of pasteurized-refrigerated and dehydro-canned slices. The quality of the processed product in all of these procedures will be dependent upon selection of a suitable variety along with food processing procedures. Thermal process canning of mango in syrup is the most widely used preservation method.

Beverages

The commercial beverages are juice, nectar and squash. Mango nectar and juice contain mango puree, sugar, water and citric acid in various proportions depending on local taste, government standards of identity, pH control, and fruit composition of the variety used. Mango squash in addition to the above may contain SO_2 or sodium benzoate as a preservative. Other food grade additives such as ascorbic acid, food colouring, or thickens may be used in mango beverages.

A short description of finished products found in literature is as follows:

Mango juice: prepared by mixing equal quantities of pulp (puree) and water together and adjusting the total soluble solids (TSS) and acidity to taste (12 to 15% TSS and 0.4 to 0.5% acidity as citric acid);

Mango nectar containing 25% puree can be prepared using the following procedure (Table 2.17).

Table 2.17: Mango Nectar Making Procedure

Nectar components	Brix of puree		
	15°	17°	20°
Puree	100	100	100
Sugar	45	43	40
Water	255	257	260

Commercial processing conditions may require the use of a preservative.

The pH is adjusted to approximately 3.5 by adding citric acid as a 50% solution.

The time of heat processing will vary with filling temperature, can size and viscosity of the juice or nectar.

Mango squash may be prepared according to flow-sheet described below; the finished product may contain 25% juice, 45% TSS and 1.2 to 1.5% acidity and may be preserved with sulphur dioxide (350 ppm) or sodium benzoate (1000 ppm) in glass bottles.

Mango Squash Simplified Flow-sheet

Ingredients

Mango pulp	900	900
Sugar	900	1100
Citric acid	18	15
Water	900	900

Mangoes are washed, stored, peeled with stainless steel knives.

The pulp is prepared by using a pulper with fine sieve (0.025-in);

Sugar is mixed with water and citric acid = syrup;

The pulp is added to the syrup and mixed well;

The mixture is strained trough cloth;

The squash is heated at 85°C and bottles are filled and closed.

For additional heat treatment bottles may need to be maintained at a product temperature of 80°C for 30 minutes if the product is to be processed without preservatives. The bottles are then left to cool in water and stored at room temperature.

Two negative points must be avoided: presence of air bubbles (which is a source of quick deterioration) and separation of squash solids (giving an undesirable appearance). The means to avoid these two phenomena are described in the fruit juices section.

A type of "squash type" beverage may also be manufactured with 1/3 pulp + 1/3 water + 1/3 sugar and pH adjusted to 3.7 by addition of citric acid. Using different sieve sizes affects the quality and reduces air bubbles to a certain extent but homogenisation and de-aeration of puree or squash seem to be important in order to avoid separation and air bubbles.

The squash quality is evaluated on the basis of the following characteristics: pH, titrable acidity, soluble solids, ascorbic acid (by 2,6 dichlorophenol indophenol method), specific gravity.

Dried/Dehydrated

Ripe mangoes are dried in the form of pieces, powders, and flakes. Drying procedures such as sun-drying, tunnel dehydration, vacuum-drying, osmotic dehydration may be used. Packages and stored properly, dried mango products are stable and nutritious.

One described process involves as pre-treatment dipping mango slices for 198 hr (ratio 1:1) in a solution containing 40° Brix sugar, 3000 ppm SO_2, 0.2% ascorbic acid and 1% citric acid; this method is described as producing the best dehydrated product. Drying is described using an electric cabinet through flow dryer operated at 60°C. The product showed no browning after 1 year of storage.

Drum-drying of mango puree is described as an efficient, economical process for producing dried mango powder and flakes. Its major drawback is that the severity of heat pre-processing can produce undesirable cooked flavours and aromas in the dried product. The drum-dried products are also extremely hydroscopic and the use of in-package desiccant is recommended during storage.

Canning

This preservation technology is described in various technological flow-sheets in this bulletin.

Mango bar or "fruit leather" is presented in various flow-sheets.

GUAVA PROCESSING TECHNOLOGIES

Guava Puree

Guava puree is used in the manufacture of guava nectar, various juice drink blends and in the preparation of guava jam. The washed sound fruit is first passed through a chopper or slicer to break up the fruit and this material is fed into a pulper. The pulper will remove the seeds and fibrous species of tissue and force the remainder of the product through a perforated stainless steel screen. The holes in the screen should be between 0.033 and 0.045 in. the machine should be fed at a constant rate to ensure efficient operation.

The pureed material coming from the pulper is next passed through a finisher. The finisher is equipped with a screen containing holes of approximately 0.020 in. the finisher will remove the stone cells from the fruit and provide the optimum consistency to the product.

Perhaps the best way to preserve the guava puree is by freezing and the material passing through the finisher can be packaged and frozen with no further treatment. It is not necessary to heat the product to inactivate enzymes or for other purposes. The material can be frozen in a number of types of cartons and cans; however, a fibre box with a plastic bag inside is commonly used and is probably the less expensive.

It is also possible to can and heat process the guava puree and this can be accomplished by heating the puree to 195°F in an open double bottom kettle, filling into cans, closing the cans, inverting the cans for a few seconds, followed by cooling. Cans should be cooled rapidly to approximately 100°F before they are cased and stacked into warehouses.

Guava Juice and Concentrate

Guava juice can be used in the manufacture of a clear guava jelly or in various drinks. A clear juice may be prepared from guava puree that is depectinised enzymatically. About 0.1% pectin-degrading enzyme is mixed into the puree at room temperature; heating of the product at approximately 120°F will greatly speed the action of the enzyme. After 1 hr, clear juice is separated from the red pulp by centrifuging or by pressing in a hydraulic juice press. A batch-type or continuous-flow centrifuge can be used on the depectinised puree with no further treatment.

The clear juice after centrifuge or after press (and subsequent filtration) can be preserved by freezing or by pasteurization in hermetically sealed cans.

For shipment to overseas markets it may be advantageous to concentrate either the puree or the juice.

RECENT TRENDS IN FRUIT AND VEGETABLE PROCESSING

New Products

The number and variety of fruit and vegetable products available to the consumer has increased substantially in recent years. The fruit and vegetable industry has undoubtedly benefited from the increased recognition and emphasis on the importance of these products in a healthy diet.

Traditional processing and preservation technologies such as heating, freezing and drying together with the more recent commercial introduction of chilling continue to provide the consumer with increased choice. This has been achieved by new heating (e.g. UHT, microwave, ohmic) and freezing (e.g. cryogenic) techniques combined with new packaging materials and technologies (e.g. aseptic, modified atmosphere packaging).

The overall trend in new fruit and vegetable products is "Added value", thus providing increased convenience to the consumer by having much greater variety of ready prepared fruit and vegetable products. These may comprise complete meals or individual components. The suitability of products and packages for microwave re-heating has been an important factor with respect to added convenience.

The major trends in the development of fruit and vegetable heat processed products in recent years are shown in Table 2.18.

Table 2.18: Fruit and Vegetable Product Trends

Heat processed products

1. Canned fruits and vegetables
   - combination of vegetables in sauces and vegetable recipe dishes. Exotic fruits.
2. Glass packed fruits and vegetables
   - "Condiverde"/"antipasti" products based on vegetables in oil.
   - high quality fruit packs.
3. Retortable plastics
   - Basic vegetables or vegetable meals
   - Fruit in jelly
4. Aseptic cartons
   - Ready made jelly
5. Rosti meals
   - Potato based products in retort pouches
6. Fruit juices
   - New combinations of juices and freshly squeezed products
7. Crisps
   - Thick and crunch skin-on crisps. Kettle or pan fried chips. Lower fat crisps.

New product development in the fruit and vegetable sector is most important in meeting the continued challenge of providing the consumer with choice and high quality products.

A Fresh Look at Dried Fruit

New fruit varieties and advance in drying technologies are putting a fresh twist on dried fruit applications. Fruits that have been introduced to the drying process include cranberries, blueberries, cherries, apples, raspberries and strawberries- not to mention the traditional mainstays of raisins, dates, apricots, peaches, prunes and figs.

Perceived as a "value-added" ingredient, dried fruit adds flavour, colour, texture and diversity with little alteration to an existing formula. The growing interest in ethnic cuisines in U.S.A. and the change to a more healthy way of eating, has also moved dried fruit considerably closer to the mainstream.

Found primarily in the baking industry, dried fruit is coming into its own in various food products, including entrees, side dishes and condiments. Compotes, chutneys, rice and grain dishes, stuffings, sauces, breads, muffins, cookies, deserts, cereals and snacks are all food categories encompassing dried fruit.

Since some dried fruit is sugar infused (osmotic drying), food processors can decrease the amount of sugar in formula- this is especially the case in baked products. Processors are making adjustments in moisture content of the dried fruit so that a varied range is available for different applications. An added bonus is dried fruits' shelf stability (a shelf life of at least 12 months). Dried fruit is more widely available in different forms, including whole dried, cut, dices and powders.

Citric Acid and its Use in Fruit and Vegetable Processing

Citric Acid may be considered as "Nature's acidulant"

It is found in the tissues of almost all plants and animals, as well as many yeasts and moulds.

Commercially citric acid is manufactured under controlled fermentation conditions that produce citric acid as a metabolic intermediate from naturally-occurring yeasts, mould and nutrients. The recovery process of citric acid is through crystallisation from aqueous solutions.

Citric acid is widely used in carbonated and still beverages, to impart a fresh-fruit "tanginess". Citric acid provides uniform acidity, and its light fruity character blends well and enhances fruit juices, resulting in improved palatability, the amount of citric acid used depends on the particular desired flavour (e.g., High-acid: lemonade; Medium-acid: orange, punch, cherry; Low-acid: strawberry, black cherry, grape).

Sodium citrate is often added to beverages to mellow the tart taste of high acid concentrations. It provides a cool, distinctive smooth taste and masks and y bitter aftertaste of artificial sweeteners. In addition, it serves as a buffer to stabilize the pH at the desired level. The high water solubility of citric acid (181 g/ 100 ml) makes it an ideal additive for fountain fruit syrups and beverages concentrates as a flavour enhancer and microbial growth inhibitor (preferably at pH < 4.6).

In processed fruits and vegetables, citric acid performs the following functions:

a) It reduces heat-processing requirements by lowering pH: inhibition of microbial growth is a function of pH and heat treatment, higher heat exposure and lower pH result in greater inhibition. Thus the use of citric acid to bring pH below 4.6 can reduce the heating requirements. In canned vegetables, citric acid usage is greatest in tomatoes, onions and pimentos. For tomato packs, the National Canners Association recommends a pH of 4.1 to 4.3. In general, 0.1% citric acid will reduce the pH of canned tomatoes by 0.2 pH units.

b) Optimize flavour: citric acid is added to canned fruits to provide for adequate tartness. Recommended usage level is generally less then 0.15%.

c) Supplement antioxidant potential: citric acid is used in conjunction with antioxidants such as ascorbic and erythorbic acids, to inhibit colour and flavour deterioration caused by metal-catalysed enzymatic oxidation. Recommended usage levels are generally 0.1% to 0.3% with the antioxidant at 100 to 200 ppm.

d) Inactivate undesirable enzymes: oxidative browning in most fruits and vegetables is catalysed by the naturally present polyphenol oxidase. The enzymatic activity is strongly dependent on pH.

Addition of citric acid to reduce pH below 3 will result in inactivation of this enzyme and prevention of browning reactions.

CHERRY AND APRICOT OILS ARE SAFE FOR FOOD USE

The oils obtained by cold pressing the kernels of the cherry (Prunus cerasus) and the apricot (Prunus armeniaca) have been declared acceptable for food use by the UK Ministry of Agriculture, Fisheries & Food's Advisory Committee on Novel Foods and Processes (ACNDP).

In its assessments of the safety in use of the cherry and apricot kernel oils, the ACNFP consider specifications that included data on fatty acid composition, the presence of natural antioxidants and the content of cyanide, mycotoxins and heavy metals.

The Committee says that it gave particular consideration to the possible presence in the oils of the cyanogenic glucoside amygdalin, from which cyanide is released by enzymic action when the kernels of cherry and apricot are crushed. Amygdalin was found to be absent from the cherry and apricot kernel oils.

The ACNFP is satisfied that there are no food safety reasons why the use of cherry and apricot kernel should not be acceptable provided there is compliance with the specifications shown in Table 2.19.

The oils are obtained by the mechanical mincing and cold pressing of kernels extracted from cleaned cherry or apricot stones. After filtering, the oils are stored and are to be sold in a raw, unrefined state. The cherry and apricot kernel oils are high unsaturated and are expected to be used as speciality oils for salad dressings, baking and shallow frying applications.

Table 2.19: Specification of Purity for Cherry and Apricot Kernel Oils as Determined by UK ACNFP

	Cherry	Apricot
Contaminants limits:		
Heavy metals (total)	0.5 mg/kg	0.5 mg/kg
Aflatoxins (total)	4.0 g/kg	4.0 g/kg
Cyanide	0.15 mg/kg	0.15 mg/kg
Pesticide residues	0.01 mg/kg	0.01 mg/kg
Tocopherols:		
Alpha/delta/gamma (mg/kg)	356-886	569-899

The Use of Fruit Juices In Confectionery Products

During the last decade, the concept of fruit juices has gained immensely on consumer popularity, the majority of new non-alcoholic and alcoholic fruit drink products ere a combination of syrups, fruit juices and flavours.

The confectionery industry followed suit and new products incorporated fruit juices as part of their confectionery formulations and processes. Fruit juice concentrates of high solids are often used instead of normal or single-fold juices.

Juice concentrates are made of pure fruit juices. The process starts with pressing fruits and obtaining pure fruit juice; this is stabilized by heat treatment which inactivates enzymes and micro-organisms. The next processing step is concentration under vacuum up to 40-65° Brix or 4-7 fold. The concentrates are then blended for standardisation and stored.

These fruit juice concentrates are often further stabilized by the addition of sodium benzoate and potassium sorbate and are usually stored away from light and are refrigerated or frozen.

Depectinised fruit juices are also used to prevent foaming in confectionery processes and are essential for use in clear beverage products. Fruit juice concentrates which are depectinised, and have added preservatives are called stabilised, clarified, fruit juice concentrates.

Fruit juices are used in confectionery products in conjunction with natural and artificial flavours which provided intense flavour impact and are cost-effective for a confectionery product.

The traditional concern in using fruit juice concentrates in confectionery applications has been the effect of the natural acids on the finished product, particularly the formation of invert sugar during processing.

This is a logical concern since concentrates contain differing amounts and types of acids. For example: apple, cherry, strawberry and other berries contain primarily malic acid. grapes mainly contain tartaric acid. Cranberry is high in quinic acid. Citrus fruits and pineapple contain differing amounts of citric acid. The concentrates, when used, are normally buffered to a pH of 5-7 with sodium hydroxide.

In formulating products with fruit juice concentrates, the solids of the concentrate are considered as mostly reducing sugars and a reduction in corn syrup is made to compensate for equivalent amount of reducing sugar being added in the concentrate.

The exact replacement can be determined by measuring the D.L. of the concentrate to be added. In formulations when small amounts of concentrate are used (less than 1%), no adjustment is made since the reducing sugar contribution of the concentrate is not significant.

Fruit juice concentrates can also be used to provide a source of natural colour, in particular red colour. Grape, raspberry, cherry, strawberry and cranberry concentrates in small amounts are very effective in colouring cream centers.

The inclusion of fruit juices in confectionery products is now left up to the imagination of the manufacturer. These products must, of course, hold up to the standards of flavour integrity, and product excellence, during the shelf-life of these products.

3

Mango Processing Unit - Mango Juice in Bags "Hot Fill" Procedure

a) Main production equipment

i. Scalder/washing machine model 1 106
ii. Destoner model 1 602
iii. Thermobreak model CC05
iv. Refiner
v. Reception tank
vi. Transfer pump
vii. Mixing tank with shaking
viii. Transfer pump
ix. Tubular pasteurizer
x. Bag filling machine model E 104
xi. Cooling tunnel

b) Packaging materials

i. Special bags, capacity from 5 kg to 25 kg, with adequate

valve system for filling and closing' adapted to bag filling machine model E 104.

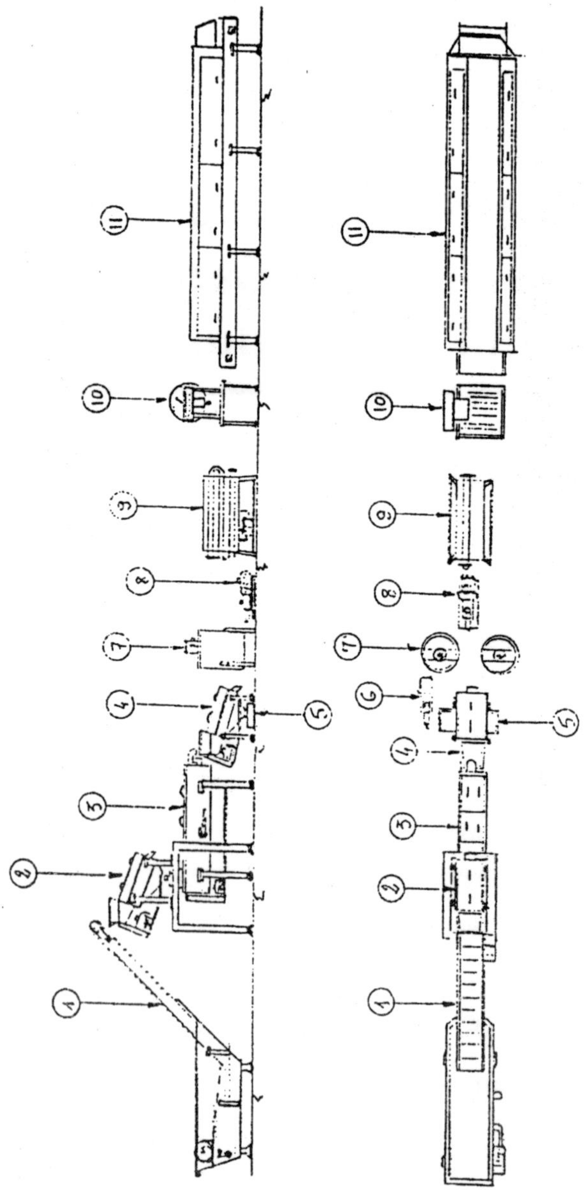

Figure 3.7.3. Mango processing unit-Mango juice in bags "Hot Fill" process

4

Fruit and Vegetable Processing Flow Sheets (Simple Processing)

PROCESSING MANGO BARS

PROCESSING OF MANGO BARS

↓

RECEPTION

↓

WASHING

↓

SORTING

↓

PEELING

↓

CUTTING

↓

JUICE EXTRACTION

$K_2S_2O_5$

MIXING----------------------------SUGAR

LEMON JUICE

↓

↓

HEATING

↓

JUICE POURED INTO TRAYS

↓

DRYING

↓

CUTTING

↓

PACKING

↓

LABELLING

Ripe fruit is used; the mangoes are washed, peeled and cut into pieces with a stainless steel knife. Pulp extraction is carried out with a hand-driven or electrical juice extractor.

Sugar, lemon juice (or citric acid) and potassium metabisulphite are then added to the pulp so that mixture contains 25% TSS (total soluble solids) as determined by a refractometer.

The composition of ingredients is as follows:

- sugar : 10 to 15% of the weight of the pulp;
- lemon juice: 2 spoons per kg of pulp;
- potassium metabisulphite ($K_2S_2O_5$): 2 g per kg of pulp.

The pulp thus prepared is heated for two minutes at 70-80°C. it is then poured into aluminium trays coated with glycerine (this facilitates the removal of the dried pulp). The prepared pulp should be placed on trays at the rate of 15 kg per square metre.

The trays are brought to a sun or solar dryer. The drying is completed when the product has the consistency of leather (about 15% moisture content). The yield ratio between raw material and finished product is about 12:1. Two or three layers of dried product are piled one on top of the other and cut into small squares (4 X 4 cm). Each square is wrapped in cellophane paper, packed in cellophane bags then labeled and stored in a dry place.

PROCESSING OF DRIED MANGO SLICES

RECEPTION
↓
WASHING
↓
SORTING
↓
PEELING
↓
CUTTING
↓
SOAKING
↓
DRYING
↓
PACKING
↓
LABELING
↓
STORAGE

Half-ripe fruits, without fibres, are used.

The mangoes are washed, peeled and cut into 6-8 mm thick slices with a stainless steel knife. To obtain finished products with good quality and long storage life, the mango slices are soaked for 18 hours in a solution containing:

- boiling water: 1 litre;
- sugar : up to 40 Brix (7-800 g);
- potassium metabisulphite: 3 g/litre of water;
- lemon juice: 2 spoons/litre of water.

The slices thus prepared are drained and placed on glycerine coated aluminium trays, which are placed in a sun or solar dryer.

The drying is completed when the product has a moisture content of 15%. The dried slices (150 g) are packed in cellophane bags, labelled and stored in a dry place.

Mango Bars and Mango Slices

Storage life : about 9 months.

Remark : without preservative (potassium metabisulphite),

The storage life of the products is relatively short.

PROCESSING OF MANGO JUICE

Reception
↓
Washing
↓
Sorting
↓
Peeling
↓
Juice extraction
Lemon Juice
↓
Mixing------------------------------Water, Sugar, Lemon juice
↓
Bottling
↓
Capping
↓
Pasteurization
↓

↓
Cooling
↓
Washing
↓
Labeling
↓
Storage

Fully ripe fruit is used. The mangoes are washed, peeled and cut into slices with a stainless steel knife. Pulp extraction is carried out with a hand-driven or electrical juice extractor.

Boiling water, lemon juice and sugar are added to the pulp so that the mixture contains 12% TSS (total soluble solids) as determined by a refractometer and pH of 3.5 to 3.8. The composition of ingredients is as follows:

- boiling water: 1 litre/kg of pulp;
- sugar: 200 g/kg of pulp;
- lemon juice: 2 spoons/kg of pulp.

Bottles are filled and capped with a manual capper. Pasteurization times is related to the size of bottles.

Size of bottles In litre	Pre-heating	Pasteurization time in minutes
0.33	Yes	20
0.50	Yes	25
0.75	Yes	30

Allow the bottles to cool in the same container till the following morning then wash, label and store them.

Storage time: about 12 months

PROCESSING OF MANGO JAM

Reception
↓
Washing
↓
Sorting
↓
Peeling
↓
Cutting
↓
Cooking 1st step
↓
Cooking 2nd step
↓
Bottling while hot
↓
Closing
↓
Pasteurization
↓
Cooling
↓
Washing
↓
Labelling
↓
Storage

Both ripe and under-ripe fruit is used.

The mangoes are washed, peeled and cut into small slices with a stainless steel knife. The amount of sugar required represents 60% of the weight of the mangoes prepared.

The cooking is done in two stages.

1st Step consists in adding 70% of the amount of sugar calculated, plus 2 spoons of lemon juice per kg of mango. Stir well during the entire cooking until 55° Brix of solids by refractometer is reached.

2nd Step consists in adding the remaining 30% of the sugar plus 2 spoons of lemon juice per kg of mangoes. Stir well during the entire cooking, unit 67-68° Brix of solids by refractometer is reached.

The jars are filled while the mixture is hot ("hot-fill" process). During the operation the jam must be stirred with the handle of a wooden spoon in order to eliminate the air that has entered the jars. The jars are closed with screw-tops. Jars cooling, washing and labelling are the last stages before storage.

5

Fruits/Vegetables Processing (Drying/Dehydration)

PROCESSING FLOW-SHEET FOR DRIED/DEHYDRATED PLUMS (PRUNES)

Reception

↓

Temporary storage

↓

Washing

↓

Size & Maturity Sorting

↓

Drying/dehydration

↓

Size Grading

↓

Temporary Storage

↓

Size Grading

↓

↓

Sorting

↓

Reprocessing of dried prunes

↓

Packaging

↓

Storage

↓

Shipping

The lowest acceptable degree Brix for raw materials is 21 with an average at 24° Bx and a maximum at 30° Bx.

Mechanical drying installation (tunnel) can handle up to 8-11 t/day raw material.

Initial air temperature is 55°C and final air temperature is 72-75°C.

Plums are dried down to 23-24% moisture in the first step.

After storage, commercial practice is to re-process the prunes by immersion in warm water (80°C), containing 2% sodium sorbate, during 10 min and thus rehydrating products up to 26-28% or to 30-32% moisture; this treatment provides a ready-to-eat product which is very appreciated.

PROCESSING FLOW-SHEET FOR DRIED/DEHYDRATED APPLES

Reception

↓

Temporary storage

↓

Size grading

↓

↓
Washing
↓
Peeling and coring
↓
Control
↓
Slicing sulphuring
↓
Drying/dehydration
↓
Temporary storage
↓
Resulphuring/treatment
↓
Packaging
↓
Storage
↓
Shipping

- After peeling and coring/slicing dip slices in salted water (2% NaCl) before further treatment in order to prevent browning due to contact of tissues with oxygen from air.
- Apples should be cut into in 8 slices (= cut each quarter in two slices). Peeling is optional and depends upon customer specification or consumer preference.
- Sulphuring can be performed by two alternative methods:
  a) Wet sulphuring: dipping slices for 10 minutes in a solution containing:

     0.5% Potassium metabisulphite ($K_2S_2O_5$) + 0.2% Citric acid.

b) Dry sulphuring: keeping slices (on drying trays, in sulphuring cells) exposed to fumes of burning Sulphur

2 g Sulphur for each kg of apple; sulphuring time; 30-40 minutes.

Resulphuring has to be performed by exposing dried apple in bulk to fumes of burning sulphur in order to avoid insect infestation.

PROCESSING FLOW-SHEETS FOR DRIED/DEHYDRATED LEEKS

Reception

↓

Temporary storage

↓

Sorting

↓

Washing

↓

Separation*

↓

Cutting

↓

Blanching

↓

Drying/dehydration

↓

Sorting/sieving

↓

Control

↓

Packaging

↓

↓

Storage

↓

Shipping

It is necessary to separate the white parts of the vegetables from the green ones by cutting manually.

The following step-cutting operation-is then done separately for each colour.

Sorting and sieving steps require elimination of "fines" and a control of adequate separation by colour.

PROCESSING FLOW-SHEET FOR DRIED/DEHYDRATION POTATOES

Reception

↓

Temporary storage

↓

Washing

↓

Rectification

↓

Peeling

↓

Control & rectification

↓

Cutting

↓

Blanching* & treatment

↓

Drying/dehydration **

↓

↓
Sorting
↓
Sieving
↓
Control
↓
Packaging
↓
Storage
↓
Shipping

- Temporary storage in good conditions is done in darkness, at low temperatures (if possible at 10°C or down to 5°C). Potato peeling could be performed preferably by mechanical or chemical means. After each main peeling step, a manual rectification must be added in order to obtain good final results.
- After cutting, slices or pieces must be immediately dipped in 0.5% solution sodium metabisulphite for 1 minute and then kept in 2% NaCl water solution until next processing step to avoid contact of tissues with oxygen from air.
- Slices optional size could be evaluated at 5-6 mm.

* Optimal blanching time is 2-5 min according to variety.

- Treatment after blanching is dipping in water containing 8000 ppm SO_2 (12 g $K_2S_2O_5$ to each litre of after).

** Optimal dehydration temperature is 65°C.

An alternative treatment is with slices soaked in a 10-fold weight solution of 5% (w/w) sodium chloride (salt) + 1% $K_2S_2O_5$ for 16-18h, at ambient temperature (around 20°C) and then dried.

6

Juices, Fruits in Syrup, Sauces, Jams, Pulps and Nectars, Canned Products Processing

FLOW-SHEET FOR ORANGE JUICE PROCESSING

Oranges

↓

Sorting

↓

Sound ripe oranges

↓

Soaking and washing

↓

Sorting

↓

Juice extraction

↓

Sieving and finishing

↓

↓

Blending and mixing tanks --------Sugar syrup

↓

Pasteurization

↓---------------------Sterilised cans

↓

Filling

↓

Can closing

↓

Cooling

↓

Labelling and packaging

↓

Marketing

Fruit to be used for juice production should be from a well run cultivation, freshly picked and well ripened.

The fruit is first sorted to remove rotten and other unfit items. It then passes through a soak tank of disinfectant and water and then to a brush-washer where rapidly revolving brushes and sprays wash the fruit very vigorously and thoroughly, the brush-washed fruit is again sorted and conveyed to the juice extractor, or halved and juiced.

The pulpy juice flows into the mesh screen finisher for the removal of seeds, heavy pulp and skin portions. The finished juice passes on to the blending, mixing and heating tanks where the requisite amount of sugar syrup is added, if sweetened juice is to be produced. Blended juice is pasteurized and filled into sterilized cans. Filled cans are sealed, cooled, labeled and packaged for marketing.

FLOW-SHEET FOR PROCESSING MANGO JUICE

Mangoes
(mature and unripe)
↓
Ripening
↓
Sorting of sound ripe fruit
↓
Soaking and washing
↓
Peeling
↓
Steaming
↓
Pulping and finishing
↓
Blending and mixing tanks——Sugar syrup
↓
Pasteurization
↓
Sterilized cans
↓
Filling
↓
Sealing
↓
Cooling
↓
Labeling
↓
Packaging

Fruit to be used for juice production should be factory ripened, fully mature, unripe mangoes are harvested and shifted to the cannery where they are allowed to ripen in a closed atmosphere. Usually it takes about three to four days to ripen the fruit.

Fruit is then sorted and sound ripe mangoes are passed to a soak tank of antiseptic and water, and then to a brush washer where rapidly revolving brushes and sprays wash the mangoes. The washed fruit is conveyed to the preparation tables where it is hand peeled. In some cases, the washed unpeeled fruit is steamed and pulped, but for a quality product it should be peeled.

The peeled mangoes are steamed and pulped. The coarse pulp thus obtained is sieved with the help of a finisher and conveyed to the blending, mixing and heating tanks where the requisite quantity of sugar syrup is added. The juice is then pasteurized, filled into the steam-sterilised cans and sealed. The sealed cans are water-cooled, labeled and packaged for sale.

FLOW-SHEET FOR PROCESSING OF PINEAPPLE JUICE

Small Pineapples

↓

Sorting

↓

Removing the crown

↓

Soaking and washing

↓

Peeling

↓-------Cores and eradicated meat

Shredding and crushing

↓

Juice extraction ------------Juice drippings

↓

Finishing

↓

Blending and mixing ------------- Sugar syrup

↓

Pasteurization

↓ ---------------------- Sterilized cans

Filling

↓

Can closing

↓

Cooling

↓

Labelling

↓

Packaging

Canned pineapple juice is now third to canned tomato juice and orange juice in terms of volume (world production). It is an excellent juice for canning, since it retains its fresh flavour and aroma remarkably well and is of an acidity and sugar content such that it is properly balanced in flavour.

Pineapple juice is a by-product obtained during the canning of pineapple slices or rings in syrup. The principal raw materials from which pineapple juice is prepared are the shredded meat obtained from the inner portion of the peels left after the peeling of the pineapple, the small pineapple that is too small for canning, the trimmed cores and the juice drippings from the crushed pineapple.

Small pineapples are peeled. The peeled, small pineapple cores and eradicated meat are shredded; the juice is extracted and then passed through a finisher. The juice thus obtained is blended with sugar syrup, pasteurized and filled into sterilized cans. The cans are sealed hot ("hot-sea" process), cooled, labeled and packaged.

FLOW SHEET FOR PROCESSING OF MANGO SLICES IN SYRUP

Mangoes
(mature and unripe)
↓
Ripening
↓
Sorting
↓
Canning variety mangoes
↓
Soaking and washing
↓
Hand peeling
↓
Slicing
↓-----Stones----------Steamed/pulp
Grading
↓----------------------Sterilised cans
Filling
↓
Hot syruping
↓
Exhausting
↓
Sealing (Can closing)
↓
Processing
↓
Cooling
↓

↓

Labelling

↓

Packaging

↓

Marketing

Fully mature, unripe mangoes are ripened in the cannery to optimum canning ripeness. Mangoes high in flavour, with more flesh and low in fibre are always recommended for canning.

Sound ripe mangoes are soaked in antiseptic and water, brush washed and then conveyed to the preparation tables and hand peeled. "Cheeks" of the peeled mangoes are sliced off and longitudinally cut into two or three slices. Side cuts are packed separately. Slices are then conveyed to the filling tables where they are graded for size, colour and maturity and filled into sterile cans. Filled cans are syruped, steam exhausted, sealed, processed in boiling water, cooled, labelled and packaged.

Stones with the left over flesh are steamed and pulped and the pulp thus obtained is packed as such or converted into mango juice or nectar.

FLOW-SHEET FOR PROCESSING OF PINEAPPLE RINGS IN SYRUP

Pineapples

↓

Grading for size and ripeness

↓

Removing the crown

↓

Washing

Peeling and coring

↓------Cores and eradicated meat

↓

Slicing--------------------Broken pieces

↓

Punching

↓--------------------Juice production

Trimming

↓

Sorting

↓----------------------Sterilised cans

Filling

↓

Syruping

↓

Exhausting

↓

Can closing

↓

Processing

↓

Cooling

↓

Labelling

↓

Packaging

↓

Marketing

Pineapples are harvested when they have reached full maturity in order to obtain maximum flavour and quality, usually the fruit is harvested when 20 to 25 per cent of bracts have turned orange in colour, and then transferred to the cannery in the shortest possible time. Fruit weighing 1.5-2.0 kg are the best suited for canning as rings.

Fruit in size graded and the crown removed. It is then washed thoroughly and prepared, which includes peeling, coring, slicing and punching, slices are then graded for size, colour and maturity. Slices should be free from peels and eyes. Each can is filled with slices of the same size and colour. The filled cans are syruped hot, exhausted, sealed, processed, cooled, labeled and packaged.

SIMPLIFIED TECHNOLOGICAL FLOW-SHEET FOR FRUIT JAMS PROCESSING

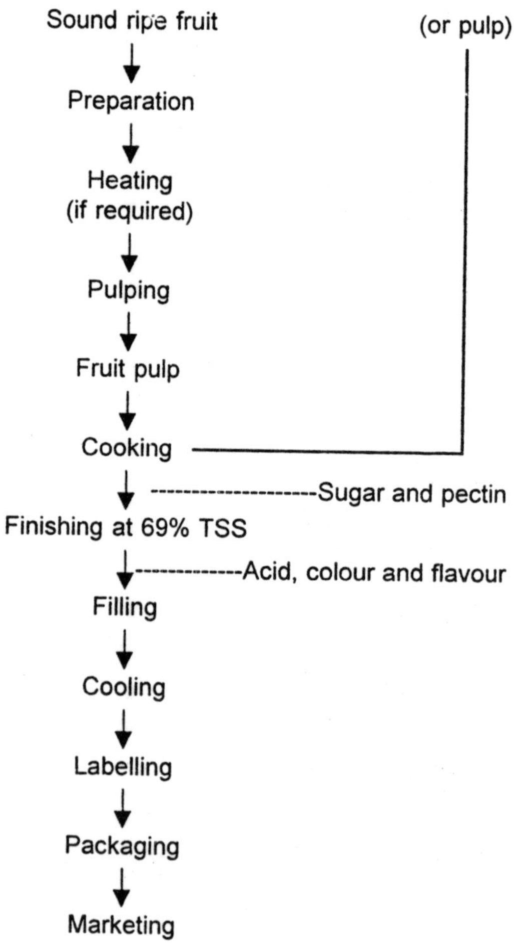

Jams may be made from practically all varieties of fruit. Various combinations of different varieties of fruit can be often be made to advantage, pineapple being one of the best for blending purposes because of its pronounced flavour and acidity.

Sound fruit is sorted, washed in running water or, preferably, brush-washed and prepared, the mode of preparation varies with the nature of the fruit. For example, mangoes are peeled, steamed and pulped; apples are peeled, cored, sliced, heated with water and pulped; plums are scalded and pulped; peaches are peeled and pulped; apricots are halved, steamed and pulped; berries are heated with water and pulped or cooked as such.

Fruit pulp is cooked with the requisite quantities of sugar and pectin, and finished to 69% Total Soluble Solids (TSS). Permitted food colours and the requisite amounts of citric acid and flavouring are added at this stage. The product is packed in cans or glass jars, and cooled, followed by labeling and packaging.

PROCESSING FLOW-SHEETS FOR MANUFACTURING JAMS FROM BERRIES

Washing

↓

Sorting

↓

Paring

↓

Refining

↓

Sugar + water or syrup------- Premix

↓

Citric acid + Pectin---------Concentration

↓

Pasteurization

↓

↓
Filling
↓
Closing
↓
Cooling
↓
Jams in Glass Jars
↓
Cans
↓
Plastic jars

FLOW-SHEET FOR MANGO AND GUAVA PROCESSING-PULPS AND NECTARS

Fresh mango/guava
↓
Pitting-Crushing
↓
Thermic treatment
↓
Refining
↓

Branch 1:
Acidity rectification
↓
Tubular pasteurization
|

Branch 2:
Mixing tanks
↓
Deaeration
↓
Homogenization
↓

↓
↓
↓
Filling/closing
↓
Closing
↓
Pulp in 20 kg bags

↓
Flash pasteurization
↓
Filling/Closing
↓
Closing
↓
Nectars in cans
Jars
Bottles
Cartons

TECHNOLOGICAL FLOW-SHEET FOR PINEAPPLE CANNING

Receiving
↓
Washing
↓
Size-grading
↓
Peeling & Coring
↓
Trimming
↓
Slicing
↓
Quality grading
↓
Cubing
↓
Can filling
↓

Exhausting

↓

Vacuum syruping

↓

Double seaming

↓

Heat treatment

↓

Cooling

↓

Labelling

↓

Warehousing

Coring is a major limiting factor in the recovery of the fruit and in the whole processing operation. Trimming should be mainly to remove the deep "eyes".

Sugar syrup concentration is adapted to the type of finished products:

45-55° Brix for "Fancy" slices

30-35° Brix for "Choice" slices

20-25° Brix for standard slices

Removal of air is performed in continuous steam exhauster equipment for 7-9 min at 185-212°F or discontinuously in boiling water.

Heat treatment is carried out in continuous rotary cookers at 212°F for 10-20 min.

Cooling is be done in rotary coolers in water for 10 min.

FLOW-SHEET FOR THE PROCESSING OF PASSION FRUIT

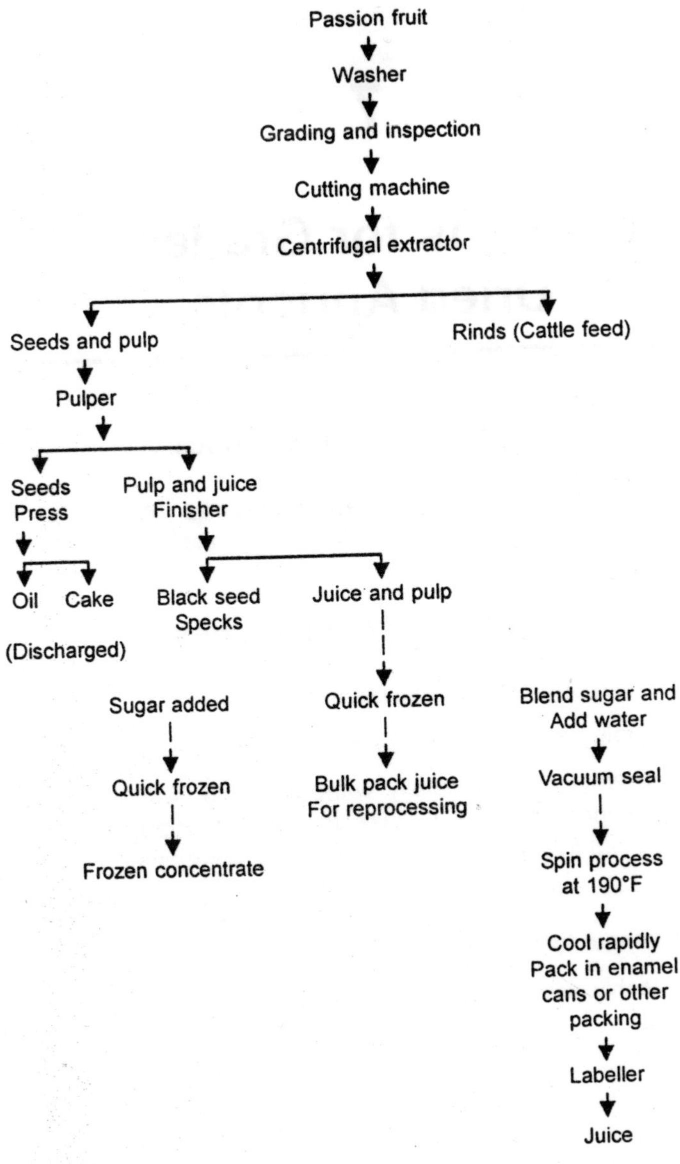

7

Standards for Grades of Dried Apricots

DEFINITION OF THE PRODUCT

These standards refer to apricots dried (naturally) or dehydrated, obtained from mature fruits, botanical name: Prunus Armeniaca L.

GENERAL QUALITY REQUIREMENTS

In all categories, dried apricots must be:

— Whole (with or without kernel) or halves;

— Healthy and especially without mould, without visible evidence of attack by insects or by other parasites and without living insects in any stage of development;

— Clean, without any visible foreign matter;

— Without foreign smell* and / or flavour;

— Fleshly, with an elastic and flexible pulp.

The moisture content must not be over 20%. However, at the request of customer, moisture content could be in the range of 20-25% or 25-30%, with the reserve of special processing treatment utilisation (for assuring shelf-life) and mentions in the section "Marks".

The manufacturing and state of dried apricots should be such to enable them to support transport and handling and assure their arrival in good conditions to the delivery point.

GRADING

The dried apricots are graded as follows:

Extra Category

Dried apricots shipped under this category must be of superior quality. If the product is whole, it must be without kernel. The colour has to be characteristic to the product and homogenous (colour "Apricot") without any part which are black, discoloured or with texture defects. The halves must have a clean/net cutting (by knife).

Category I

Dried apricots shipped under this category must be of good quality. If the product is whole, must be without kernel. The colour has to be characteristic to the apricots. Tolerance: slight appearance or colour defects (discoloured) and small cuttings of skin but with the condition that all these defects have no impact on product appearance, quality or shelf life.

Category II

This category covers dried apricots which cannot be classified in superior categories but are according to the minimum requirements defined in General Quality. If the product is whole, it could be with kernel. Appearance and colour defects (spots, brown parts but without darkening of fruits) and slight damages of the skin are accepted with the condition that the finished products keeps its characteristics.

SIZE GRADING

The size grading is determined by the number of fruits per pound:

Category	Wholes	Halves
Very big	Less than 50	Less than 100
Big	50-65	100-130
Medium	66-75	131-150
Small	76-90	151-180
Very small	More than 90	More than 180

The size grading is mandatory for dried apricots in category "Extra" and "Category I" and has to be mentioned in section "Marks".

TOLERANCES

Category Extra

Five per cent in weight of fruits not answering to the quality specifications for this category but in conformity with those of "Category I".

Category I

Ten per cent in weight of fruits not answering to the quality requirements for this category but being in conformity with those of "Category II".

A maximum 0.5% in number of fruits having traces of mould or fermentation or containing dead insects or other parasites is also tolerated.

Category II

Fifteen per cent in weight of fruits not answering to the quality specifications for this category but being in conformity with the minimum requirements defined in general quality requirements. A maximum 1% number of fruits with moulds or fermentation or containing dead insects or other parasites is also tolerated.

The presence of any living insect or parasite is NOT tolerated, in any of their biological cycles.

In all categories, a tolerance is accepted for size grading-10% in weight of fruits in each pack-in conformity with size from immediately superior and / or inferior size grade identified.

Tolerance in moisture level. – It is accepted a variation of 1% more or less as compared to the level indicated in section "Marks".

HOMOGENEITY

The content of each shipping or consumer pack must be homogenous and must contain only dried apricots of same origin, quality and size. The visible part of the pack must be representative of all the content.

PACKING

The content of each shipping or consumer pack must be protected against any external or internal deterioration/damages. The packing and material must be new, clean, free from any foreign body, according to the specifications, in line with consumer requirements.

MARKS

All packages of dried apricots must bear:

— Indication as to contents and their origin: (country of origin name) Dried Apricots;

— Indication as to the category: Extra, I or II;

— Indication as to size grade: very big, big, medium, small or very small and type: wholes or halves;

— The packer's mark as specified by local authorities;

These indications must be made clearly and legibly by means of indelible ink or branded outside the package in letters of 2 cm height;

— Indication as to the moisture content, if above 20%, i.e. "Moisture content 20-25%" or "Moisture content 25-30%";

— Indication as to the net weight of the package.

8

Recipe Guidelines: Dried Fruit and Vegetables

RECIPE GUIDELINES—FRUIT PRESERVES WITHOUT SUCROSE

1. Strawberry Jam with Rsunett and Sorbitol

Ingredients:

Strawberries	500 g
Sunett	0.75 g
Sorbitol (powder)	250 g
Gelling agent	

Method: Prepare the fruit as usual. Add the sorbitol powder and the gelling agent and bring to the boil while stirring continuously. Dissolve the Sunett in some water and add it to the other ingredients. Add the additional ingredients which are usually added in producing jams. Let the ingredients boil for approximately 1 minute while stirring constantly. Fill into the prepared jars.

Calorific value: ca. 480 KJ/100 g (ca. 115 kcal/100g)

2. Berry jam with Rsunett, cyclamate and sorbitol

Ingredients:

Red currant	100g
Black currant	100g

Blackberry	100g
Sorbitol	150 g
Jelling agent	to suit
Sunett	0.45 g
Cyclamate	0.45 g

Method: Prepare the jam in the usual way

Calorific value: ca. 480 KJ/100 g (ca. 115 kcal/100 g)

3. Red currant jam with Rsunett and Sorbitol

Ingredients:

Red currants 450 g

Sunett	0.9 g
Sorbitol	450 g
Gelling agent	

Method: Prepare the fruit as usual. Add the sorbitol and the gelling agent and bring to the boil while stirring continuously. Dissolve the Sunett in some water and add it to the other ingredients. Add the additional ingredients which are usually added in producing jams. Let the ingredients boil for between 2 and 4 minutes while stirring constantly. Fill into the prepared jars.

Calorific value: ca. 897 KJ/100 g (ca. 215 kcal/100 g)

DRIED PLUM (PRUNE) PUREE

1. Ingredients	Weight/measures
Soft pitted prunes	3 lbs.
Sugar	½ cup
Light corn syrup	1 cup
Boiling water	2 ½ cups

II. Method

This puree may be made in any commercial-size processor with a 1-gallon capacity work bowl. Lacking a large processor, follow the instructions in the Note at the end of the recipe. Puree keeps well, refrigerated, for 6 to 8 weeks. Use directly from the refrigerator. Freeze for longer storage, thaw before using.

Place first three ingredients in work bowl fitted with the metal blade. Start motor and pour boiling water through feed tube. Process about 2 minute, until mixture is completely smooth. Stop motor occasionally to scrape side of work bowl. Cool completely; cover and refrigerate.

Note: To make puree without a processor, combine all ingredients in large saucepan. Bring to boil, cover pan, and stew prunes slowly until fruit is very tender. Mash well with large wooden spatula, pressing prunes along side of saucepan. Alternatively, grinding this mixture through the finest blade of a meat grinder. You may multiply this recipe any number of times.

RECIPES

Apricot Fruit Preserves

1. 1 kg apricot halves (without stones)

   0.6 kg sugar

   5 g citric acid

Add 420 g sugar to prepared fruits and bring to boil; boil gently during 15 min

Add the remaining 180 g sugar and 5 g citric acid

Continue boiling gently up to required refractometric extract

2. 1 kg apricot halves prepared as above

   1.5 kg sugar

   For all sugar to the fruit; mix gently with a spoon

   Leave the mix overnight

3. Dip apricot halves for 7 min in a solution containing:

   2% sodium metabisulphite

   and

   0.5% citric acid

Obtain fruit pulp by available means/equipment: a) through a sieve in traditional preparation; b) with a simple juice/pulp extractor in small scale operation; c) with a pulper in other cases).

Basic recipe is 1 kg fruit pulp + 0.6 kg sugar.

Methods for drying some vegetables and fruits

1. Garlic

The cloves are separated and the outer skins removed by hand. The skins of individual cloves are not removed. The cloves are cut into pieces not more than 5 mm cube. No blanching nor other treatment are applied.

The product is spread evenly on drying trays. Dry until brittle. The final moisture content should be about 5%. The yield is about 5:1. After completing drying, separate dry skin by winnowing.

The dry product may be ground into powder which should then be protected against moisture pick-up as it is very hygroscopic.

2. Beetroot

After washing, peeling and trimming the material is cut into slices about 2-3 mm thick. Only steam blanching could be used as water blanchnig will wash out the colour. The slices are immersed in a solution containing 8000 ppm SO2 for 1 minute.

The prepared material is placed on drying tray sand dried to a moisture content of about 6%. Shade drying might also be dried. Overall shrinkage ratio is about 12:1.

3. Turnip

The material is peeled after cutting off tops and roots then cut into slices 2 to 5 mm thick. The slices are submerged for 4 to 6 minutes in boiling water. slices are dipped for 1 minute in a solution of metabisulphite containing 8000 ppm sulphur dioxide.

After treatments, material is spread thinly and evenly on standard trays and dried to a moisture content of 6%. Shrinkage ratio is 28:1.

Turnips are white fleshed, and Swede Turnip yellow or orange fleshed. The latter will produce a dried product of better quality.

4. Sweet Pepper

The raw material is washed thoroughly and broken up. Cores and interlocular partitions are removed by hand, defective parts are cut out with knives. The prepared flesh is held under water or a weak solution of sodium metabisulphite (2000 ppm SO_2) before being hand cut into strips about 5 mm wide.

The cut pieces are dipped for 1 minute in a solution of 2000 ppm SO_2 (3 g sodium metabisulphite per litre).

The material is spread in a thin layer on trays and shade dried until crisp or to a moisture content of about 7%. Average shrinkage ratio is about 25:1; drying ratio is about 13:1.

For finishing, pick out any burnt or discoloured pieces; put the material on a sieve of suitable mesh to remove small pieces and "fines". Both green and red peppers may be used for drying.

5. Banana

Both fully ripe and unripe fruits can be dried, but since they are used for different purposes they must not be mixed together.

The fruit is washed, peeled and diced into transverse slices 10 mm thick or lengthwise.

Unripe fruits are blanched in boiling water for a few minutes and then peeled. The ripe fruits are not blanched.

The prepared material is dipped for 1 minute in a solution containing 2000 ppm sulphur dioxide.

The slices are dried on standard trays which have been coated with a very thin glycerine layer to avoid sticking. The final moisture content should be around 12%.

The dried slices prepared from unripe banana may be converted into flour which can be used alone or in combination with other flours.

Dried bananas produced from ripe fruit are usually consumed in the dry state, like dates.

GLOSSARY

Shrinkage ratio: the ratio of unprepared raw material to dry finished product.

Drying ratio: the ratio of prepared raw material to dry product.

Ppm: parts per million

Carrot Dehydration

As an alternative to described method, a double blanch processing was found to give significant increases in firmness.

Lots (6 kg) of whole carrots are blanched by immersion in a large excess of water at 60°C in a steam jacketed kettle fro 45 min; then blanched again for 6 min at 100°C in boiling water. The high temperature blanch was designed to inactivate enzymes that have the potential to generate off-flavours during storage in the dry conditions.

The carrots are then immediately peeled by immersion in 10% sodium hydroxide at 90°C for 1 min, passed through a rubber stud rolled peeler to remove loose skin, sprayed with cold water and trimmed by hand. They are diced into 9.5 mm cubes in an Urschle dicer and passed over a vibrating screen to remove small pieces.

The product may be spread on wire mash aluminum trays and conventionally air died in a cabinet dryer with cross-flow air for 1.5 hr at 82°C and then at 66°C for 3.5 hr to obtain a final moisture content of about 6-7%.

TECHNOLOGICAL FLOW-SHEET FOR DRIED/ DEHYDRATED MULBERRIES

Reception
↓
Control
↓
Sorting
↓
Washing
↓
Treatment
↓
Drying/dehydration
↓
Packing
↓
Labeling
↓
Storage

- Treatment before drying is as follows:

** Dipping fruits for 5 minutes in a solution containing

0.5% Potassium metabisulphite

and

0.2% Citric acid

- Technological steps and treatment are the same for white and for black mulberries.

9

Mango Products

INTRODUCTION

A large number of mango products are routinely prepared according to regional tastes in India. However, the Fruit Products Order (FPO) 1955 and the Prevention of Food Adulteration Act (PFA) 1954 have prescribed certain statutory regulations for better quality and consumer protection. Recently, greater emphasis has been laid on improvement in technology for preparation of mango products for domestic as well as export market. The methodologies for some of the products developed at this Institute are described below:

PUREE (PULP)

Mango puree is the base product preserved commercially for later use into ready to serve (RTS) beverages, juice, leather, powder, etc. Mango jam may preferably be prepared from only fresh fruits. It is important that mango puree is prepared hygienically, preserved in air-tight containers and stores in a cool dry place. Incidentally, it is a major export item in the list of mango products. The procedure for preparation of mango puree is as follows:

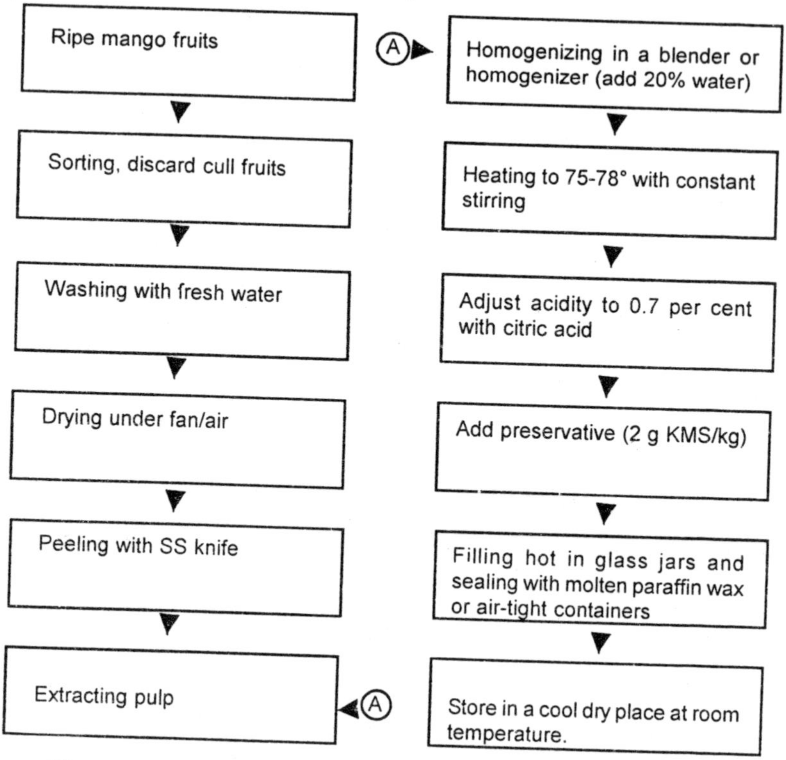

The puree stores well under ambient conditions for over a year. However, heat sterilized puree could be stored without any preservative under marginally freezing conditions (-5+-2°C) for one year.

The natural acidity of mango fruit may be in the vicinity of 0.2 per cent for sweet varieties which means citric acid at the rate of 5 g/kg of the pulp is to be added to make it 0.7 per cent in the final product. In sour mango varieties, there may not be a need to add citric acid. Moreover, heating of pulp may be accomplished as fast as possible. A quantified example for the preparation of mango puree is given below:

Materials

Mango fruits: 10 kg

Water: 1.5 l

Citric acid: 35-40 g

Potassium metabisulphite (KMS): 15 g

Procedure: Take fully ripe mangoes and extract the edible portion (pulp) manually with a stainless steel (SS) knife. Homogenize the pulp with 20 per cent water for about a minute. Heat the pulp to 75-78°C and then add citric acid dissolved in a little quantity of water. Take it off the flame and add KMS dissolved in distilled water. Fill it in pre-sterilized glass jars or air-tight containers. If the puree is filled in glass jars, the lids may be sealed with molten paraffin wax. Store the containers in a cool dry place.

BEVERAGES

Mango puree is used as base material for a variety of mango beverages. However, it is necessary that mango puree should be finely homogenized so that there is least sedimentation during storage and marketing of the beverage. There are commercial homogenizers available for fruit processing industries, but for home-scale or cottage-scale operations a simple method has been devises for fine homogenization of puree. The mango puree may be homogenized in a blender with approximately 50-60° Brix sucrose syrup for 30 seconds or so and then filtered through a sieve. The remaining amount of water may be added according to recipe later. In this way, we may get relatively uniform body of the mango beverage and lesser sedimentation. The general composition may be kept as given on the next page:

Description of	Puree	TSS	Acidity
Product	(%)	(°Brix)	(%)
Squash	40	50	1.1-1.2
Juice	40	15	0.3
Nectar (RTS)	20	15	0.3

Since mango puree already contains 20 per cent water so its concentration has been kept at higher range. Lesser quantity of puree could be used if the products are prepared from fresh fruits. As fresh fruits contain pectin of higher strength, squash with even 30 per cent puree could look like jam. However, there is no such problem with stored puree and it could be raised to even 40 per cent in the preparation of squash. The products so prepared would be of better quality and have more consumer acceptability although the constituent are slightly different than described by FPO. The general procedure for preparation of beverages may be as given below:

Homogenize puree and Sugar syrup

↓

Make up volume with water

↓

Heat the slurry to 95° (75-78°C for squash) with Intermittent stirring

↓

Add the required amount of acid (as citric acid dissolved in water)

↓

Remove from flame and fill hot into the pre-sterilized bottles.

↓

Crown cork the bottles

↓

Sterilize the filled bottles in Boiling water or under steam for 15 min (except for squash)

↓

Label and store the bottles in a Cool dry place.

The squash may be served after dilution of 4 times (1:3) or more with chilled water or as per taste, while juice and nectar could be served chilled without any dilution, the procedures for preparation of nectar, juice and squash are given below:

(i) Nectar

Materials

Mango pulp	1 kg
Water	5 l
Sugar	850 g
Citric acid	15-20 g

Procedure

One kilogram of pulp with good bright yellow colour may be taken and homogenized with sugar syrup and then the remaining water may be added in as stainless steel container. The mixture is heated to boil (> 95°C). Citric acid dissolved in little quantity of water is added prior to taking off the flame. It may be filtered through a nylon net cloth (sieve) before filling into pre-sterilized bottles and crown corked. The bottles are then sterilized for 15 minutes in boiling water. Label the bottles and store in a cool dry place. If the product is prepared from stored pulp then the amount of water already added may be adjusted in the calculations.

(ii) Juice

Materials

Mango pulp:	1 kg
Water:	2 l
Sugar:	350 g
Citric acid:	6-8 g

Procedure

The procedure for preparation of juice is exactly the same as described for mango nectar.

(iii) Squash

Materials

Mango pulp	1 kg (Fresh)	1.6 kg (Stored)
Water	1.2 l	0.7 l
Sugar	1.8 kg	1.7 kg
Citric acid	40 g	30-40 g
Potassium Metabisulphite (KMS)	3 g	-

Procedure

Dissolve sugar in water and filter. Homogenize mango pulp with sugar syrup. Heat the mixture up to 78°C, and citric acid dissolved in little quantity of water and take off the flame, finally add KMS dissolved in minimum quantity of water, fill the squash into pre-sterilized bottles, crown cork the bottles and store in a cool dry place.

BLENDS

Mango is a remarkable fruit which can be blended with a variety of other fruits for preparation of more palatable economical products with a difference. Dashehari mango has been successfully blended with papaya, pineapple and pear for beverage (RTS) preparation at this Institute. However, different varieties of mango may require different proportions of other fruits for better beverage preparations. The organoleptic score or sensory evaluation is an index of marketability of the product. The recommendations have been made after testing the preservability of the blends for six months or more. The preparation procedures of beverages from successfully blended fruits with Dashehari mango are given on the following pages:

(i) Mango-papaya blended beverage

Materials

Mango pulp	1 kg
Papaya pulp	500 g (100-500 g)
Water	7.5 l
Sugar	1.25 kg
Citric acid	5 g
Potassium Metabisulphite (KMS)	1.4 g

Procedure

Prepare around 50-60°C Brix sugar syrup and homogenize mango and papaya pulps with it. Mix the remaining water with pulp mixture and heat to 95°C. Add citric acid dissolved in small quantity of water prior to mixture attains 95°C temperature, add KMS also dissolved in water (if storage period is > 3 months). Fill the beverage into pre-sterilized bottles and crown cork them, the bottles are sterilized in boiling water for 15 minutes and then labeled and stores in a cool dry place.

(ii) Mango-pear blended beverage

Materials

Mango pulp	1 kg
Pear juice (pulp)	100g (up to 400 g)
Water	5.5 l
Sugar	850 g
Citric acid	18-19 g
Potassium Metabisulphite (KMS)	1 g

Procedure

The procedure is same as given for the preparation of mango-papaya blended beverage.

(iii) Mango-pineapple blended beverage

Materials

Mango pulp	1 kg
Pineapple juice	100 g (up to 400 g)
Water	5.5 l
Sugar	850g
Citric acid	18 g
Potassium Metabisulphite (KMS)	1 g

Procedure

The procedure is same as given for the preparation of mango-papaya blended beverage.

OTHER PRODUCTS FROM RIPE MANGOES

A variety of other products like leather, slices, toffees, powder, etc. could be prepared from ripe mango fruits, these products, not only have commercial value in domestic market, but they also have export potential, the preparation procedures of few such products are given below:

(i) Jam

Materials

Ripe mango fruits Or	10 kg
Mango pulp	6 kg
Water	1 l

Sugar	5 kg
Citric acid	50 g

Procedure

Extract the pulp from ripe mango fruits and homogenize it in a blender. Dissolve sugar in minimum quantity of water and filter through muslin cloth to remove dirt, suspended particles, etc. Mix mango pulp and sugar syrup and heat until the end point is attained which is indicated by either 'One thread mark' or the volume is reduced to approximately three fourth or temperature reaches 105°C. the citric acid is dissolved in a small quantity of water and added to the boiling slurry prior to the end point. If the TSS is 68° Brix or more, it is not necessary to add any preservative. The hot jam is poured into dry and pre-sterilized wide mouth jars and allowed to cool before sealing it with air-tight lid.

(ii) Slices

Materials

Ripe mango fruits Or	10 kg
Slice 1-2 cm thick	5 kg
Sugar	1.8 g
Water	3.0 l
Citric acid	14 g
Potassium Metabisulphite (KMS)	6 g

Procedure

Peel sound and firm ripe fruits and cut 1-2 cm thick slices with SS knife. Dissolve sugar in boiling water and filter. Add citric acid and KMS dissolved separately in little quantities of water to the sugar syrup. Put 500-550 g of mango slices in one kg wide mouth glass bottle and add 450-500 g hot sugar syrup (40° Brix) to it. Seal the glass bottles air-tight and store in a cool dry place.

(iii) Leather (Aam Papad)

Materials

Ripe mango fruits Or	10 kg
Mango pulp	6 kg
Citric acid	18 g
Potassium Metabisulphite (KMS) Or Sodium bisulphate	2-2.5 g

Procedure

Extract the pulp from ripe mangoes with SS knife and homogenize it in a blender. Add citric acid and KMS dissolved separately in small quantities of water to the pulp and mix thoroughly. Pour the pulp to 1 cm thickness in buttered SS Trays and dry in a solar dryer (the temperature is 20-30°C higher than the atmospheric temperature). After drying, another layer of 1 cm thickness of the pulp may be applied on it and dried. After drying to about 5-8 per cent moisture, the leather will have bright colour which may be cut into small pieces, packed in polythene pouches and stored in a cool dry place.

RAW MANGO PRODUCTS

Raw mango slices serve as a base product for pickles, chutney ad amchoor. It is normally prepared and preserved by the processing industries during the season for use at a later stage. It is also one of the major export items. The processes for the preparation of mango slices and amchoor are given below:

(i) Slices

Procedure

Raw mango fruits are washed in running water and infected fruits are discarded. After removing the stem, slices of desired thickness from peeled or unpeeled fruits are cut with a SS knife.

The slices are then dipped in 350 ppm SO2 (0.7 g KMS/l water) solution for 5 minutes, the solution may be drained and the slices are air dried and then mixed with the powdered salt. The treated slices may be filled into flexible pouches or any other container to avoid contact with air or water during storage. In this way, the slices could be stores for 3 months and during the period they could be utilized for preparation of desired product.

(ii) Amchoor

Procedure

Raw mango fruits, freshly harvested or dropped, are washed and peeled. Small slices are extracted and dipped in 0.2 per cent KMS solution for 10 minutes. The slices are drained and spread on wire net trays of aluminium or stainless steel in solar or electric dehydrators until the moisture is reduced to around 4 per cent. The dried slices may be powdered in a grinder or packed as such in suitable air-tight containers. If the slices are dried in the open air, there is a possibility of contamination with dust, insects, etc. Which must be avoided.

10

Method of Preparation and Keeping Quality of Reconstituted Skim Milk-based Mango Beverage

INTRODUCTION

Mango is the most popular tropical fruit of India, also known as "King of Asiatic fruits". India is the largest producer of mangoes, accounting for 52 percent of world production. In general, about 20-25 percent of the fruits are wasted due to lack of proper post-harvest facilities. There is a glut of mangoes during peak season. One of the major need of fruit industries is, therefore, to develop preserved mango products in order to reduce the post-harvest losses. India is also the largest producer of milk, its production being 78 million tones in 1998-99. But, still some areas (such as high mountain, defence service depot) are deficit in milk, where milk is distributed in the dried form. 'Mango shake' made from combination of milk and mango is extremely popular and a relishing beverage in northern parts of India. Blend of mango milk produces a nutritionally rich food as milk is an excellent source of protein, but deficit in vitamin C, Fe, Cu. While mango pulp is good source of carbohydrates, vitamin C, inorganic potassium, though lacks in protein. Little work has been cited on combination of reconstituted skim milk and mango. Therefore, the present investigation was carried to prepare and study the shelf life to the reconstituted skim milk based mango beverage.

MATERIALS AND METHODS

Preparation/preservation of the mango pulp

Mangoes of Chausa variety were procured from the local market. The fruit was sorted and washed thoroughly in water. Pulp was extracted using pulper. The pulp was then analysed for TSS, pH and total acidity. The sugar : acid ratio of the pulp was adjusted by the addition/deletion of sugar/water. Pulp was then adjusted by the addition/deletion of sugar/water. Pulp was then heated to 85°C, SO_2 @ 350 ppm was added, filled into sterilized glass bottles and then corked. The bottled pulp was stored at room temperature (9 to 17°C) and used after 5 months for the preparation of reconstituted skim milk based mango beverage.

Preparation of Reconstituted Skim Milk

Skim milk powder was procured from Verka Milk Plant, Ludhiana. Water was boiled, cooled to 28-30°C. then skim milk powder @ 10% was added to water slowly accompanied by stirring, followed by straining through muslin cloth to improve aesthetic quality of the reconstituted skim milk. RSM was analysed for various physico-chemical characteristics like TS (%), pH, acidity (%), lactic acid, specific gravity (g/cc), fat and SNF according to the standard procedure.

Preparation of reconstituted skim milk based mango beverage:

Preserved mango pulp was heated to temperature of 60°C for expelling out SO_2 gas and cooled to 5°C.RSM was prepared and cooled to 5°6C. RSM and mango pulp at 2,6 and 10% was mixed. T.S.S. of each mix was adjusted to 15°B by the addition/ deletion of sugar/H_2O. The method of preparation of reconstituted skim milk based mango beverage is given in the flow diagram (Fig. 10.1).

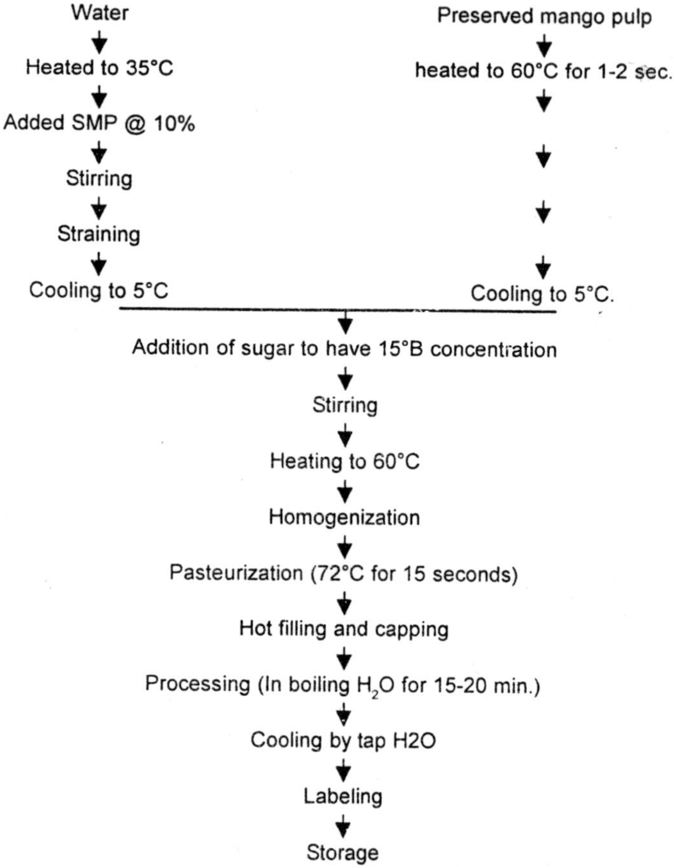

Fig. 1. Preparation of reconstituted skim milk based mango beverage

Storage studies

The prepared reconstituted skim milk based mango beverage was stored both at room (18-20°C) and refrigeration temperature (5-7°C). Microbiological and organoleptic changes were assessed at 7 days interval for the beverage stored at refrigeration temperature and at 3 days interval for the beverage stored at room temperature.

Microbiological Count

Microbiological status of the product was evaluated by measuring total plate count and yeast of mold count according to the standard procedures.

Organoleptic Evaluation

Sensory evaluation was done by panel of 7 semi-trained judges using 0.9 point hedonic scale (like extremely to dislike extremely) for different attributes like appearance, body texture, flavour and overall acceptability. The samples were tested at the same time by panelists and was asked to award marks for various sensory attributes, which could be best reflected by their perception of magnitude of that characteristics.

RESULTS AND DISCUSSION

Microbiological Count

Total plate count (Table 10.1) and yeast and mold count (Table 10.2) of the beverage stored at refrigeration temperature increased with the increase in storage. However, it was found within safer limit (<20,000 cfu/ml) even up to 32 days of storage.

Table 10.1. Effects of different levels of mango pulp and storage (Days) on Total Plate Count refrigeration (5-7°C) temperature

Pulp incorporation (%)	Storage days				
	0	8	16	24	32
2	0.12×10^2	0.18×10^2	0.23×10^2	0.23×10^2	0.27×10^2
6	0.12×10^2	0.14×10^2	0.18×10^2	0.24×10^2	0.30×10^2
10	0.12×10^2	0.15×10^2	0.16×10^2	0.26×10^2	0.31×10^2

Table 10.3 represents the TPC. Table 10.4 represents the yeast and mold count of the beverage stored at room temperature. The data reveals that total place count, yeast and mold of the beverage increased with the subsequent storages. The increase was more

at room temperature than at refrigeration temperature. The beverage became unacceptable after third day of storage due to increase in the microbial count leading to the production of off-flavour and odour.

Table 10.2. Effect of different levels of Mango Pulp and storage (days) on Yeast and Mold Count of RSM based Mango Beverage stored at refrigeration (5-7°C) temperature.

Pulp incor-poration (%)	Storage days				
	0	8	16	24	32
2	1	2	2	3	4
6	2	2	3	3	4
10	2	3	3	3	5

Table 10.3. Effect of different levels of Mango pulp and storage (days) on Total Plate Count of the RSM based Mango Beverage stored at room temperature (18-25°C).

Pulp incor-poration (%)	Storage days				
	0	8	16	24	32
2	2×10^2	10×10^2	176×10^2	287×10^2	225×10^2
6	5×10^2	14×10^2	198×10^2	291×10^2	291×10^2
10	6×10^2	19×10^2	212×10^2	315×10^2	315×10^2

Organoleptic evaluation

Various stages in organoleptic parameters of the beverage stored at refrigeration and room temperature is shown in Table 10.5 and Table 10.6 respectively. The various sensory attributes of beverage showed that there exists a perceivable variation among different formulations. Score for appearance, body, texture and overall acceptability was found to be highest for 10 percent pulp incorporation, followed by 6 per cent, further followed by 2 per cent pulp incorporation. Sensory panel judges also assigned the highest score for beverage with 10 per cent pulp incorporation, which is due to increase of mango flavour with increase in pulp content. The value of various sensory attributed like appearance, body and texture, flavour and overall acceptability decreased with the texture, flavour and overall acceptability decreased with the subsequent storage. This may be attributed to increase in acidity, total plate count, yeast and mold count with the advancement of storage.

Table 10.4. Effect of different levels of Mango pulp and storage (Days) on yeast and mold count of RSM based mango beverage stored at room (18-25°C) temperature.

Pulp incor-poration (%)	Storage days				
	0	8	16	24	32
2	2	4	7	14	15
6	2	5	11	16	18
10	3	5	13	15	21

CONCLUSION

Organoleptic and microbial changes were studied in reconstituted skim milk based mango stored at both room and refrigeration temperature. Changes were more at room temperature compared to refrigeration temperature. The beverage at room temperature storage had shelf life of only 3 days, while the beverage at refrigeration temperature storage had shelf life of 32 days. Therefore, refrigeration storage of beverage is preferred to room temperature.

Table 10.5. Effect of different levels of Mango Pulp and storage (days) on organoleptic characters of RSM based Mango Beverage at refrigeration (5-7°C) temperature.

	2%					6%					10%				
	0	8	16	24	32	0	8	16	24	32	0	8	16	24	32
Appearance	6.50	6.38	6.07	5.40	5.17	7.80	7.67	6.47	6.40	8.43	8.16	7.93	7.50	7.30	
Body & texture	6.60	6.60	6.17	5.80	5.40	7.57	7.50	7.00	6.90	6.80	8.10	8.05	7.87	7.30	6.77
Flavour	6.64	6.61	6.00	5.93	5.81	7.57	7.52	7.00	6.87	6.73	8.31	8.11	7.77	7.54	7.21
Overall acceptability	6.77	6.61	6.40	5.90	5.87	7.40	7.17	6.74	6.70	6.00	8.16	8.10	7.70	7.36	7.23

Table 10.6. Effect of different levels of mango pulp and storage (days) on organoleptic characters of RSM based mango beverage at room (18-25°C) temperature.

	2%					6%					10%				
	0	8	16	24	32	0	8	16	24	32	0	8	16	24	32
Appearance	6.30	6.42	4.41	1.38	1.00	7.68	7.27	5.18	2.07	1.03	8.40	8.37	6.20	3.77	1.00
Body & texture	6.30	5.56	3.89	2.21	1.00	7.23	7.07	4.13	1.77	1.00	8.36	7.30	4.97	2.65	1.00
Flavour	6.61	6.07	5.57	3.67	2.01	7.56	6.17	5.03	3.40	1.85	8.16	8.00	5.83	3.93	1.00
Overall acceptability	6.83	5.83	4.20	2.23	1.01	7.43	6.91	4.81	2.14	1.02	2.10	7.05	4.99	2.33	1.03

11

Processing Techniques of Mango Beverages

Mango (*Mangifera indica* L) belongs to the family Anacardiaceae. It is believed to be indigenous to South Asia, especially Indo-Burma region and is grown in Eastern India and Burma for over 4000 years. India contributes 50-60 per cent to the world's production of mango. It is grown in almost all the states. Andhra Pradesh tops in total production, whereas, Uttar Pradesh tops area-wise. Although, India is the home of about 1,000 varieties but only 20 varieties viz. *Dashehari*, *Langra*, *Chausa*, *Safeda*, *Totapuri*, *Fazli*, *Alphonso*. *Bombay Green*, *Banganapalli*, *Neelam*, etc., are grown commercially. Some mango hybrids like *Mallika*, *Amrapali*, *Ratna*, *Sindhu* and *Arka Puneet* have also been released by different research stations in the country.

Mango is rightly called "the king of fruits". Above all, it is the choicest of Indian table fruits having the premier place in the country. It is highly relished for its succulence, delicious sweet taste and excellent flavour throughout the world. Fruits are rich in Vitamin A and C besides being a good source of minerals like calcium, iron and phosphorus.

Constituents (per 100 g of edible pulp)

Moisture 86.1 g

Carbohydrate	11.8 g
Protein	0.6 g

Fat	0.1 g
Minerals	0.3 g
Calcium	12 mg
Iron	0.1 mg
Phosphorus	12.0 mg
Fibre	1.1 g
Vitamin A	4800 I.U.
Vitamin B	0.51 mg
Vitamin C	53 mg

Mango fruits are consumed both in raw as well as in ripe form. Besides consuming as table fruits, mango fruits show great potential for processing into many quality products which can have great demand in the national as well as in the international market. In order to avoid huge loss, stabilize the prices and utilize the surplus produce of mango fruits during glut in the main season, mango processing activities will also ultimately ensure greater availability of a wide variety of value added mango products which would help to improved the food intake and nutritional standards of the consumers during off season.

Among these products, mango beverages provide delicious cold drinks during hot summer in a tropical country like India. They are appetizing, thirst quenching, highly refreshing, easily digestible and nutritionally far superior to many synthetic and aerated drinks. If synthetic preparations are replaced by mango and other fruit beverages, it would be a boon to the consumers as well as to the fruit growers. Hence, scientific information about processing techniques of mango beverages should be disseminated on a countrywide scale to encourage its processing activities. Processing techniques of mango beverages i.e. juice, RTS, nectar, squash, juice concentrate and juice powder are described in the following paragraphs.

(A) EXTRACTION AND PRESERVATION OF PULP

Extraction of pulp from mango fruits is necessary for preparation of its various products. Varieties most suitable for this purpose are Safeda, Totapuri, Alphonso, Langra etc. select fully ripe fruits, wash them properly in running water. Peel off fruits, cut fruit slices and remove the stone. Add small quantity of water and pass through fruit pulper to obtain homogenized pulp. Screen homogenized pulp, heat up to 85°C, add 0.1 percent potassium metabisulphite (1g KMS per litre of water) and fill hot pulp in to clean, well sterilized cans (A2 ½). Exhaust filled cans, seal immediately and process sealed cans in boiling water for half an hour. Cool processed cans rapidly in cold water, label, pack in corrugated cardboard cartons and store in cool and dry place. The freshly extracted mango pulp as such or in preserve form can be used for preparation of various mango products including beverages.

B. PREPARATION OF BEVERAGES

1. Mango juice

Extract mango pulp as per technique given under extraction and preservation of pulp. Add half litre of water to one litre of extracted pulp and strain it though muslin cloth. Prepare sugar syrup by dissolving 200 g sugar and 2 g citric acid in 800 ml; water for each one litre pulp. Mix strained sugar syrup to the strained mango pulp, homogenize properly and heat at 85°C. Fill hot mango juice into clean, sterilized cans (A2 ½ size), seal immediately and process at 100°C for 20 minutes. Cool processed cans and store in a clean, cool and dry place. Prepared mango juice can also be bottled and crown corked before pasteurization.

2. Mango RTS Drink (ready-to-serve drink)

This is a fruit drink in which natural composition of fruit pulp is altered by addition of required amount of sugar, citric acid and water. According to Fruit Products Order, RTS beverage should contain minimum 10% fruit pulp/juice, 10% total soluble solids and 0.3% total acids. But mango RTS drink having 15% fruit pulp, 14 to 15% total soluble solids and 0.28% total acids is most acceptable.

Recipe

Mango	1 L
Sugar	828 g

Citric acid	13.5 g
Sugar syrup (sugar + citric acid + water)	5.7 L

Processing technique

Extract pulp from ripe mango fruits as per technique given under extraction and preservation of pulp. Weigh known quantities of sugar and citric acid as per recipe. Mix in one litre of water and boil for preparing sugar syrup. Remove scum from the syrup, cool slightly and strain through nmuslin cloth. The clear sugar syrup is then homogenized with the extracted fruit pulp. Add remaining quantity of water as per recipe and further homogenize the prepared product. Add recommended colour (lemon colour) and essence. Fill prepared mango RTS drink into clean, well sterilized RTS bottles (200 ml capacity), seal with crown corks and pasteurize on a false bottom in boiling water for half an hour. Cool in air and store in cool and dry place. Serve mango RTS beverage after proper chilling beverage filled RTS bottles in refrigerator.

3. Mango nectar

In mango nectar also, natural composition of fruit pulp is altered by adding of requisite amount of sugar, citric acid and water. According to FPO, this beverage should contain minimum 20% fruit pulp. 15% total soluble solids and 0.3% total acids. It may or may not require dilution before serving. For preparing RTS drink and nectar, the total soluble solids and acidity of extracted fruit pulp are first determined and then requisite amount of sugar and citric acid dissolved in required amount of water are added to the extracted fruit pulp for adjustment of TSS and acidity as per requirement in the finished product.

Recipe

Mango pulp	1 L
Sugar	600 g
Citric acid	10 g
Sugar syrup (sugar + citric acid+ water)	4 L

Processing Technique

Processing technique of mango nectar is similar to that of mango RTS drink. The differences are only in quantities of sugar, citric acid and water required for preparing the sugar syrup to be added to extracted pulp.

4. Mango squash

It is also a very delicious fruit beverage prepared from fully ripe fresh mango fruits. Mango squash should contain minimum 25% fruit portion and 40% total soluble solids as per FPO requirements, it also contains about 1.0% total acids and 600 ppm sodium benzoate or 350 ppm sulphur dioxide. It is diluted before serving.

Recipe

Mango pulp	1 L
Sugar	1.650 kg
Citric acid	28 g
Water	1 L
Sodium benzoate	3 gm

Processing Technique

Processing technique of mango squash is practically similar to that of mango RTS drink and nectar except that in mango squash, concentration of fruit pulp and sugar is increased and sodium benzoate is also added @ 1g per litre of prepared squash as a chemical preservative. Edible lemon yellow colour may also be added to the finished product after dissolving it in may also be added to the finished product after dissolving it in quantity of water. Mango squash is then filled into 700 ml capacity, clan, well sterilized squash bottles leaving 2.5 to 3.0 cm head space.

Properly seal, label and store mango squash bottles in cool and dry place. Serve it after diluting to four times with chilled water.

5. Mango Juice concentrate

Extracted mango juice from which water has been mostly removed by heating or freezing is known as mango juice concentrate. Juice is concentrated either by freezing and centrifuging or by evaporation under reduced pressure at low temperatures (5-12°C). The flavours volatilized and lost during evaporation are recovered and cut back into concentrate. Mango juice concentrate contain pure juice with at least 32% total soluble solids. Carbonated beverages are prepared from mango juice concentrate. Major method deployed for production of mango juice concentrate are i) low temperature, vacuum evaporation ii) high-speed, high-temperature evaporation iii) freezing and mechanical evaporation.

6. Mango Juice Powder

Extracted mango pulp/juice can also be converted into a free flowing, highly hygroscopic powder by drum frying, freeze drying, puff drying, spray drying or vacuum drying. Mango juice powder has a long shelf-life and is soluble in cold water. Much of the characteristic fresh flavour of mango juice is lost which is compensated by adding to juice powder natural fruit flavour in powder form. Reconstitution of mango powder mixture yields full strength mango juice drink.

12

Ready to Serve (RTS) Beverage based on Pomegranate and Mango

INTRODUCTION

During seasonal glut, the pomegranate fruit prices are fairly low and due to cracking problem, fruits need to be processed and preserved. Pomegranate can be processed into various products like juice, squash, syrup, jelly, wine, anar-rub and canned beverages (Adsule and Patil, 1995). However, the information on processing of pomegranate fruits for juice and ready-to-serve (RTS) beverage is scanty. Pomegranate flavour is delicate and it contains less amount of vitamin C. therefore, juice needs to be blended with some other juice having strong flavour and high nutritional quality for consumer acceptance. The present investigation was, therefore, undertaken to utilize mango pulp to blend pomegranate juice to make it suitable for preparation of ready-to-serve beverage having consumer appeal.

MATERIALS AND METHODS

Pomegranate fruits of Ganesh cultivar were obtained from Department of Horticulture of this University. The fruits of uniform size, colour and maturity were harvested. Mango pulp of Alphonso variety manufactured by Desai Bandhu at Pawas, Dist. Ratnagiri

(M.S.) under the trade name 'Vijay' was used for the research work.

The pomegranate juice was extracted by squeezing the arils gently by pressing through two layers of clean muslin cloth. Various steps in preparation of RTS beverage from the clarified pomegranate juice and blend of mango pulp are outlined in Fig. 12.1. The analysis of juice and RTS beverage for various chemical parameters was done according to standard A.O.A.C. (1975) procedures. The sensory evaluation of RTS beverage was carried out according to the method of Amerine by a panel of 7 judges on a 10 point score card.

Mixing of juice + pulp (10%)

↓

Adjustment of TSS to 15° Brix and acidity to 0.25 percent

↓

Filling into 500 ml bottles

↓

Keep the bottles in refrigerator (Temp. 4 +- 2 °C)

↓

RTS beverage

Fig. 12.1 Flow chart for preparation of ready-to-serve (RTS) beverage.

RESULTS AND DISCUSSION

Sensory evaluation of ready-to-serve (RTS) beverage

The pomegranate juice was the major constituent in making RTS beverage and mango pulp was used for blending to improve the colour, flavour and nutritional quality of the RTS beverage. The score for colour and appearance, flavour, taste, astringency and overall acceptability increased with the increased proportion of mango pulp in the blends upto 60:40 level (pomegranate: mango) and then decreased slightly for 50:50 level (Table 12.1). Begum et al., (1983) tried pineapple and mango pulp mixture and found 25:75, 50:50 and 75:25 blends more acceptable. Researchers indicated that 25-33 percent papaya pulp could be incorporated in mango pulp without affecting the quality and acceptability of the mango beverage.

Table 12.1. Sensory evaluation of ready-to-serve (RTS) beverage prepared from blends of pomegranate juice and mango pulp.

Proportion of juice (pomegranate: mango)	Characters*				
	Colour/ appearance	Flavour	Taste	Astringency	Overall acceptability
100:0	5.25	4.00	4.25	5.00	4.63
90:10	7.25	7.25	6.00	6.25	6.69
80:20	7.50	7.75	7.25	6.75	7.31
70:30	8.00	8.13	7.50	7.25	7.72
60:40	8.50	8.50	8.75	8.00	8.44
50:50	8.25	8.25	7.75	7.25	7.88
Mean	7.46	7.31	6.92	6.75	7.11
S.E. +-	0.21	0.18	0.17	0.16	0.15
C.D. at 5%	0.63	0.55	0.50	0.49	0.46

CHEMICAL COMPOSITION OF RTS BEVERAGE

There was no change in TSS, pH and acidity but the ascorbic acid content in RTS beverage changed with the levels of pomegranate juice. As the level of pomegranate juice decreased and mango pulp increased, the ascorbic acid content increased proportionately (Table 12.2).

Considering both the chemical composition and organoleptic properties of RTS beverage prepared by various combinations of pomegranate juice and mango pulp, it may be concluded that a blend of 60:40 (pomegranate: mango) is highly suitable for the preparation of good quality RTS beverage. These results are, however, based on the laboratory scale study. Therefore, pilot plant studies are required before the process of RTS beverage making from pomegranate and mango is commercialised.

Table 12.2. Chemical composition of ready-to-serve (RTS) beverage prepared from blends of pomegranate juices and mango pulp

Proportion of juice (° Brix)	Parameters						
	T.S.S.	pH	Acidity (%)	Reducing sugars (%)	Non-reduction sugars (%)	Total sugars (%)	Ascorbic acid
100:0	15.00	2.98	0.26	1.26	12.71	13.97	0.92
90:10	14.98	3.00	0.27	1.14	12.66	13.80	1.07
80:20	15.02	3.00	0.25	1.09	12.58	13.67	1.23
70:30	14.98	3.02	0.23	1.01	12.51	13.52	1.38
60:40	15.00	3.00	0.25	0.92	12.43	13.35	1.53
50:50	15.02	2.98	0.24	0.90	12.32	13.22	1.68

13

Mango (*Mangifera indica* L.) Varieties for Wine-making

INTRODUCTION

Mango is one of the most popular fruit crop in the tropical and sub-tropical regions of the world. It is termed as the "King of fruits" owing to its delicious taste, captivating flavour, attractive colour and excellent quality, besides begin good source of minerals and vitamins. Mango is commercially grown in more than 87 countries in the world. However, India ranks first with respect to both area of 10.63 Lakh ha with a production of 10 million tones. Mango in general, contains high amount of easily fermentable sugars, vitamins and minerals thus making it a suitable medium for the growth of wine yeasts. In India, nearly 100 varieties are under cultivation, but only twenty of these are grown on a commercial scale. Most of the commercially grown varieties are best suited for table purpose. There are no specific varieties specially meant for wine making in India at present. The fact that mango pulp can be used for making good quality, sweet and dry wines, not much work has been done on the suitability of mango varieties for wine making. The possibility of making wine from four varieties was investigated.

MATERIALS AND METHODS

Four varieties viz., *Alphonso*, *Mallika*, *Nekkare* and *Totapuri* fruits of optimum maturity were harvested from the mango orchard at G.K.V.K., Bangalore. Fifteen kilogram each of sound, healthy and ripe fruits were selected, peeled and pulp was separated from stones using stainless steel knife. The pulp was ameliorated to obtain 20° Brix by adding cane sugar and acidity was maintained at 0.5 per cent by adding citric acid. The pulp was diluted at 1:1 ratio with water after adding 50 ppm of SO^2 in the form of potassium metabisulphite. Preservative was added to prevent browning of juice by oxidation and to suppress wild yeasts present in the pulp. About 250 juice of each variety was collected and used for estimation of chemical parameters. The juice was kept in five litre conical flasks and plugged with cotton. After 6-8 hours of sulphiting the juice was inoculated with yeasts starter culture at the rate of two percent (v/v) for fermentation. The fermentation was carried out at ambient condition for 10-12 days. After the completion of fermentation, clear liquid was filtered through a clean muslin cloth and stored in sterile glass bottles for a month, when the suspended matter settled leaving clear wine on the top. The wine was further clarified and stored in bottles with 100 ppm SO_2 by adding potassium metabisulphite.

For preparing sweet wines, cane sugar at the rate of 5 g/l was added. The wines were filtered, clarified and stored under standard conditions.

RESULTS AND DISCUSSION

The composition of the juice varied with variety (Table 13.1). The TSS of the juices ranged from 13° to 23° Brix while titratable acidity as malic acid ranged from 0.25 to 0.57 per cent. The reducing sugars was from 0.64 to 2.94 per cent. Brix/acid ratio of the juices ranged from 28 to 91 and the tannin content of juices was from 58 to 86 mg/100 ml. the juice with low TSS were raised to 20° Brix by adding cane sugar. The fruit juices low in TSS are required to be ameliorated to obtain high alcohol content. Researchers stressed the need for sweetening of juices because of the low sugar content in majority of the fruits.

Effect on changes in the composition of the juice was influenced by various chemical constituents of different wines (Table 13.2). The titratable acidity in all the samples increased after fermentation. This might possibly be due to production of certain organic acid, reported that during the fermentation of apple juice, yeasts formed organic acids such as malic acid, lactic acid and succinic acid. The dry and sweet wines made from Alphonso had a high acidic taste as revealed by higher values of volatile acidity. The titratable acidity and volatile acidity were too high in the wine prepared from Alphonso, while alcohol content was only 4.4 per cent (Table 13.2). Low alcohol content and higher volatile acidity suggested the possibility of acidification of samples.

Table 13.1: Chemical composition of mango juices

Varieties	TSS (° Brix)	Titratable acidity (as % malic-acid)	Reducing sugars (%)	Brix/acid ratio	Tannins (mg/100 ml)
Alphonso	16.00	0.40	2.52	39.80	58.00
Mallika	22.80	0.25	1.87	91.20	80.00
Nekkare	13.00	0.30	0.64	43.19	62.00
Totapuri	16.00	0.57	2.94	28.12	86.00

Generally, sweet wines form all the varieties recorded higher amounts of reducing sugars than their respective dry wines. The maximum reducing sugar was found in Alphonso followed by Mallika and Totapuri wines. This might be due to the complete conversion of disaccharides to monosaccharides as well as improper utilization of sugars by the yeast cells for their growth and development during fermentation.

The tannin content in all the wine samples was significantly decreased after fermentation. The lowest tannin content was observed in wines of Alphonso. This could be due to the utilization of more tannins by the yeast cells during fermentation process. Wine made from variety totapuri contained 9.8 per cent alcohol while that of Mallika and Nekkare contained 6.9 and 5.3 per cent alcohol respectively, whereas the lowest alcohol was found in Alphonso (4.4%) wine. The variation in alcohol content of wines was due to several factors such as, initial sugar content, amount of by-products formed, quantity of sugars used by yeasts for their growth and the amount of cane sugar used for amelioration of juice.

Table 13.2: Chemical composition of mango wines

Parameters	Alphonso		Mallika		Nekkare		Totapuri	
	Dry	Sweet	Dry	Sweet	Dry	Sweet	Dry	Sweet
Titratable acidity (as % malic acid)	1.86	1.86	0.26	0.24	0.54	0.51	0.80	0.74
Reducing sugars (%)	0.82	1.52	0.76	1.35	0.21	0.56	0.73	1.31
Tannins (mg/100 ml)	13.00	15.50	44.00	49.42	30.00	32.00	32.00	34.10
Alcohol (% v/v)	4.36	4.72	6.89	7.24	5.29	6.45	9.80	9.84
Volatile acidity (as g acetic acid/100 ml)	0.30	0.08	0.07	0.02	0.04	0.06	0.01	0.01

Table 13.3: Organoleptic evaluation (mean averages) of Mango wines

Wine	Appearance (Out of 2)	Colour (Out of 2)	Flavour (Out of 2)	Aroma & Bouquet (Out of 4)	Overall (average) score (Out of 20)
Totapuri sweet	1.50	1.75	1.30	3.40	14.35
Dry	1.15	1.80	1.20	2.90	12.15
Mallika Sweet	1.75	1.80	1.20	2.70	12.90
Dry	1.35	1.80	0.90	2.00	10.65
Nekkare Sweet	2.00	1.70	1.45	3.40	13.20
Dry	1.80	1.80	0.90	2.20	11.20
Alphonso Sweet	0.40	1.10	0.45	2.20	10.65
Dry	0.35	1.10	0.25	1.30	6.05

Organoleptic evaluation of mango wines (Table 13.3) revealed that the sweet wines prepared from all the four varieties scored higher rankings than dry wines. This could be attributed to the characteristic fruity flavour of mango and by the addition of sugar. However, due to its complete dryness, dry wine was not as acceptable as sweet wine. The sweet wines prepared from Totapuri secured maximum (14.34 out of 20) overall score, followed by Nekakre (13.20 out of 20) and Mallika (12.90 out of 20) wines. However, the wine of Alphonso scored minimum points for quality, the highest acceptability of Totapuri, Nekkare and Mallika wines might be attributed to the excellent sugar to acid blend in the juice before fermentation, presence of pleasant light golden yellow colour and a distinct mild fruity flavcur. The results suggests that Brix/acid ratio of 28 and 43 is optimum for making good quality of dry wines from Totapuri and Nekkare varieties of mango under Bangalore conditions. Generally Alphonso and Mallika are good table varieties. Totapuri and Nekkare varieties are normally not very popular for table purpose. However, Nekkare stones are commonly used to raise root stocks after discarding the pulp.

Hence, the available fruits can be successfully utilized for wine making in the production centre.

14

Membrane Technology in Fruit and Vegetable Processing

Liquid foods like fruits and vegetable juices, milk, coffee, tea, extract etc., are very complex aqueous mixtures of organic and inorganic compounds. The solids content in most liquid foods is low, usually in the range of 8 to 16%. It is obvious that much of what the consumer eats and pays for in food is water. Partial removal of water, reducing the water content to a low level, can be the last step in food processing prior to packaging, the concentrate being the end product or can be a step prior to drying.

Objectives of producing concentrated end products are: reduction of packaging, transport and storage costs; reduction of water activity so as to enhance storage stability; improvement of convenience for the consumer and in few cases improvement of convenience for the consumer and in few cases improvement of sensory acceptability; reduction of overall dewatering costs including capital and energy costs prior to drying.

Concentration of liquid foods, particularly fruit juices, coffee and tea extracts, is a delicate affair. They are heat sensitive and their colour and flavour deteriorate rapidly as processing temperatures are increased. Even at moderate temperatures many of their components are unstable. Since it is the aroma volatiles that give a food product its wide variety of flavour sensations, even minor changes in aroma during concentration can greatly after the sensory qualities of the final product. Thijssen1 specified the conditions that must exist in order to obtain high quality concentrates. The conditions are, low process temperatures, short residence times in the process apparatus, nearly sterile operations, selective dewatering i.e. the major proportion of all the components expect water should be retained in the concentrate.

For the concentration of 'liquid foods three different main groups of processes can be used viz. evaporation with or without aroma recovery, reverse osmosis or ultrafiltration and freeze concentration.

At present evaporation is considered as the best developed, economically the most favourable, and the most widely used method for the concentration of liquid foods. However, loss of aroma compounds and higher energy requirements are the serious drawbacks of concentration by evaporation. Freeze concentration involves partial freezing of the product and removal of the water as pure ice crystals, thus bearing behind all of the nonaqueous constituents in the concentrated phase. The process, however, was seldom used because of the high investment cost and the considerable loss of concentrates in the withdrawn ice.

Ultrafiltration and reverse osmosis are the two pressure driven separation processes that clarify and concentrate fruit juice without change of phase using appropriate membranes. Whereas ultrafiltration at low pressure allows the low molecular weight components along with water to pass through the membrane retaining the high molecular weight components, reverse osmosis retains both low and high molecular weight components permitting only water to pass through thus concentrating the liquids. Since water is removed as permeate through a membrane without change of phase and heat is not applied for the separation of water, energy requirement is low, thermal damage to flavour, colour is minimized compared to thermal evaporation, mainly due to low energy requirements, membrane separation processes have attracted much attention in liquid food processing. Due to these advantages, the membrane separation techniques like reverse osmosis (RO) and ultrafiltration (UF) are assessed on a variety of fruits and vegetable juices like orange, apple, pears, tomato, kiwi, pineapple, passion fruit, cabbage, cucumber, etc. One of the prime considerations to evaluate the performance of RO is the choice of membrane type. Polyamide membranes are found to be more favourable in terms of retention so solutes and flavours than cellulose acetate membranes. One of the major problems associated with membrane processes is the membrane fouling, which is the deposition of dispersed particles and colloidal substances on membrane surfaces during the RO operation. One disadvantage mainly associated with this technique is the level of concentration attained which was a found in the range of 20-30° Brix compared to the industrial practices of concentrating juices upto 42° Brix. However, RO concentration process could be utilized to remove substantial amount of water spending less energy and thermal exposure. The partially concentrated juices/extracts can be utilized for making shelfstable consumer type products by aseptic packaging to reduce packaging and transportation cost. Alternatively, it can be further processed by thermal evaporation and other processing methods like spray drying and freeze drying to reduce energy consumption as well as to improve quality.

CONTRIBUTION OF DFRL

Processing

Studies were carried out at Defence Food Research Laboratory (DFRL) on the ultrafiltration (UF) of orange, mango, pineapple, guava, pomegranate juices using UF membranes (polysulphones) of different Molecular Weight Cut OFF (MWCO) and subsequent concentration by reverse osmosis (RO) using a UF-RO system of plate and frame configuration, watermelon, tomato and carrot were concentrated without ultrafiltration. Both cellulose acetate (CA) and thin film composite polyamide (HR) membranes were used for concentration. RO-UF system and the membranes were procured from DDS (De Danske Sukker Fabrikker), Denmark, Shelf stability of orange, pineapple and mango juice semi concentrates were evaluated. Physico chemical parameters as well as sensory characteristics for juices and extracts were evaluated at different stages of processing.

Figure 14.1 Illustrates the various steps involved in the preparation of mango juice and pulp semi-concentrates. Mango pulp after enzyme treatment and filtration was subjected to ultrafiltration and subsequent concentration by RO. Concentrated mango juice was then reconstituted with pasteurized with pasteurized retentate and reside (from filtration step) to obtain concentrated mango pulp.

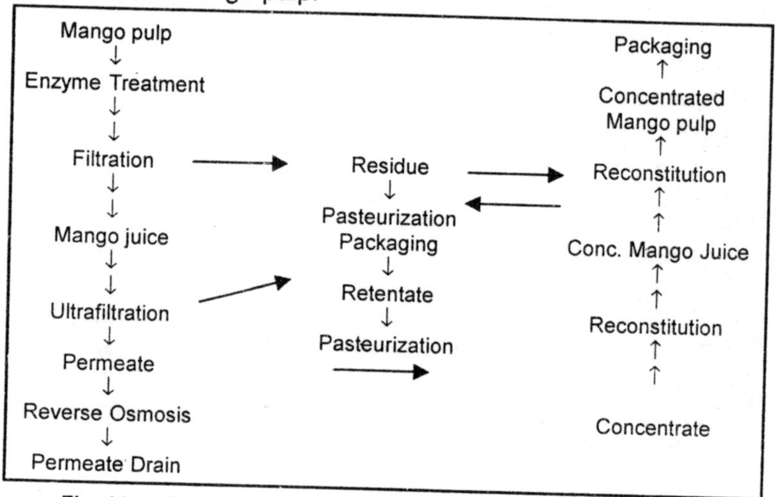

Fig. 14. 1. Flow Diagram of UF/RO System for Mango Juice/Pulp Concentrations

ULTRAFILTRATION

Performance of ultrafiltration membranes of three different MWCO's viz. 20,000, 50,000 and 1,00,000 on the composition of UF juices from guava as compared to feed juice 16 are shown in Table 14.1. Concentration of total solid, brix, sugar, acid, minerals and ascorbic acid in the UF juices were considerable less than that of feed juices. Performances membranes of 50,000 and 1,0,000 MWCO were almost same in most of the parameters studied including permeate flux. An UF membrane of 50,000 MWCO was found to be suitable for the clarification of fruits and vegetable juices.

Table 14.1. Performance of ultrafiltration membranes of different MWCO on the composition and flux of guava juice

Parameter	Feed Juice	Membrane		
		GR-6[1] (20000 MWCO)	GR-5[1] (50000 MWCO)	GR-40 (100000 MWCO)
° Brix	9.30	6.40	7.00	7.10
pH	3.48	3.50	3.50	3.50
Density (g/ml)	1.03	1.02	1.02	1.02
Total Solids (%)	11.30	6.50	8.10	8.20
Reducing Sugar (%)	4.50	3.50	4.30	4.40
Total Sugar (%) as dextrose	8.40	5.20	5.70	5.80
Acidity (%) (as citric acid)	0.44	0.40	0.39	0.39
Brix/Acid	21.14	16.25	17.95	18.21
Minerals	0.38	0.27	0.31	0.32
Ascorbic acid (mg/100 ml)	164.0	120.0	138.0	139.0
Av. Permeate flux (L/m2h)	-	18.7	26.6	28.7

PHYSICO-CHEMICAL EVALUATION

Physico chemical characteristics and acceptability of selected fruits and vegetable juices i.e. orange, pineapple, mango, guava, pomegranate, watermelon, carrot and tomato concentrated using HR (thin film composites) membranes are shown in Table 14.2. It was found that juices could be concentrated upto 21-27° brix at 50 bar pressure depending on the type of juices. There were no changes in pH and Brix/acid ratios and the overall acceptability was found to be comparable with feed juices.

EVALUATION OF RO MEMBRANES

The performance of a RO membrane could be judged by the rejection characteristics and permeation capacity which respectively shows the solutes retained in the concentrate and the rate of water removal. Percent rejection of total soluble solids and acids in case of mango, guava, orange and tomato were more in HR membranes compared to CA membrane. Rejection of ascorbic acid was also observed to be quite high in case of HR membranes whereas rejection of reducing sugar was higher in CA membranes in guava, orange and water-melon. Average permeate flux of CA membranes were much higher compared to HR membranes in case of all the juices studied (Table 14.3).

Table 14.3. Rejection characteristics and average processing capacity of different membranes during concentration of some fruit juices

Juice	Membrane type	Rejection (%)				Av. Flux (l/m²h)
		TSS	Acidity	Red. Sugar	Asc. Acid	
Mango	CA-992	95.5	82.2	93.5	-	18.9
	HR-95	97.5	96.3	97.3	-	16.2
Guava	CA-992	96.5	91.7	97.7	95.9	19.1
	HR-95	98.3	95.8	97.3	9.0	15.0
Orange	CA-992	-	87.2	94.7	90.8	19.5
	HR-95	-	93.6	94.2	99.5	16.8
Watermelon	CA-992	96.7	84.6	96.3	-	21.6
	HR-95	95.3	92.3	94.7	-	18.9
Tomato	CA-992	96.5	94.8	95.8	94.5	24.9
	HR-95	97.8	96.9	96.1	98.2	21.6

SENSORY EVALUATION

Sensory quality of the juices in terms of aroma and overall acceptability were much better in concentrated obtained using HR membranes (Table 14.4).

Loss of aroma was found to be more in case of CA membranes than that of HR membranes for all the juices. Consequently overall acceptability, which depends mostly in aroma in case of fruit juices, was also less in the juice concentrated by CA membranes.

Table 14.2. Physico-chemical characteristics of some fruit and vegetable juice semi-concentrates obtained by RO using HR-95 membrane at 50 bar pressure

Juice	Brix		pH		Acidity (%)		Brix/acid		OAA*	
	Feed	Cone.	Feed	Cone.	Feed	Cone.	Feed	Cone.	Feed	Cone.
Orange	10.0	26.0	3.60	3.63	0.37	0.92	27.0	28.3	7.2	6.5
Pineapple	15.0	25.0	3.48	3.48	0.50	0.78	30.0	32.0	7.5	7.1
Mango	14.0	27.0	4.05	4.05	0.22	0.42	63.6	64.4	7.8	7.4
Guava	9.0	24.0	3.50	3.45	0.52	1.27	17.3	18.9	7.3	6.9
Pomegranate	14.0	25.0	2.86	2.83	0.50	0.90	28.0	27.8	7.3	7.2
Watermelon	6.5	24.0	5.21	5.13	0.07	0.24	87.8	100.0	7.5	7.0
Carrot (acidified)	6.2	23.4	4.26	4.13	0.2	0.75	31.0	31.2	7.0	6.8
Tomato	4.0	21.0	4.06	4.10	0.49	2.40	8.16	8.75	7.2	6.9

Table 14.4. Sensory Quality of Fruit Juice Semi-concentrates as compared to Feed Juices

Juice	Aroma			Overall Acceptability		
	Feed	HR	CA	Feed	HR	CA
Orange	7.2	6.6	6.2	7.3	6.4	6.0
Pineapple	7.6	7.2	6.8	7.7	7.2	6.9
Mango	7.8	7.3	6.5	7.8	7.2	6.6
Guava	7.3	6.9	6.4	7.2	7.0	6.6
Watermelon	7.7	7.0	6.5	7.7	7.1	6.6

EVALUATION OF SHELF-LIFE

Storage studied of fruit juice semi-concentrated from orange, pineapple, mango, pretreated with sulphur dioxide, packed and pasteurized in polypropylene pouches, showed (Table 14.5) that those were acceptable up to 4 months at 37°C and 6 months at RT with initial SO_2 level of 550-660 ppm. Browning was considerable at the end of acceptable storage period and one of the main causes of unacceptability. Loss of SO_2 was also considerable and ascorbic acid was completely reduced after 6 months (in case of orange juice). Change in pH was negligible and loss of sulphur dioxide and cartenoids was found to be 48.5% and 28.5% respectively.

CONCLUSION

1. Studies showed that fruit juices could be concentrated to 23-27° Brix with an average permeate flux of 15-45 L/ m2h at 50 bar operating pressure depending on kind of juice, type of membrane and pretreatment given.
2. Rejection of solutes during RO concentration were found to be in the range of 90-99% depending on solutes, type of membrane and kind of juice.
3. Ultrafiltration with a membrane of 50,000 MWCO was found to be suitable for clarification with a view to improve

the permeate flux and reduce the fouling during RO concentration.

4. Fruit juice semiconcentrates from mango, pineapple and orange could be kept for 6 months and 4 months at RT and 37°C respectively.

Table 14.5. Storage stability of pineapple, orange and mango juice semi-concentrates

		Pineapple		Orange		Mango	
	Temp.	2	6	2	6	2	6
PH							
	LT	3.29	3.28	3.90	3.89	3.89	3.88
	RT	3.28	3.27	3.88	3.86	3.87	3.86
	37	3.28	3.27	3.86	3.84	3.87	3.86
SO_2 (ppm)							
	LT	528.00	336.00	576.00	340.00	502.00	368.00
	RT	352.00	208.00	356.00	256.00	307.00	283.00
	37	208.00	176.00	208.00	96.00	176.00	142.00
Browning (OD)							
	LT	0.13	0.13	0.29	0.33	0.55	0.55
	RT	0.20	0.24	0.32	0.62	0.58	0.60
	37	0.25	0.43	0.65	1.10	0.60	0.75
Asc. Acid (mg/100g)							
	LT	-	-	17.50	-	-	-
	RT	-	-	13.80	-	-	-
	37	-	-	6.30	-	-	-
Cartenoids (ug/g)							
	LT	-	-	-	-	52.50	42.90
	RT	-	-	-	-	48.30	40.00
	37	-	-	-	-	45.80	35.70
OAA							
	LT	7.20	6.80	6.50	6.00	7.440	6.60
	RT	7.10	6.50	6.30	5.20	7.10	6.00
	37	6.80	6.00	5.80	-	6.60	-

LT = 0-4°C, RT = 20-34°C; Initial SO_2 550 ppm; Initial SO_2 600 ppm; Initial SO_2 550 ppm.

15

Value Aaddition to Fruits and Vegetables by Mechanical Washing

INTRODUCTION

The unnecessary wastage of valuable commodities can be avoided if they are processed in value added products by adopting standard processing technologies with modern machineries.

Washing of fruits and vegetables is a vital step in any processing operation, which gives attractive and chemical free fruit. At present washing of fruits and vegetables is carried out manually which is a time consuming process. Very little work on mechanical washing for value addition of fruits and vegetables is reported in literature. Fruits and vegetables can be washed by adopting various methods. In view of this a mechanical fruit washer was designed, developed and performance was evaluated for mechanical washing of tomato, potato and mango.

MATERIALS AND METHODS

A prototype of mechanical fruit washer (Stirrer type) was designed and developed at Department of Agricultural Process Engineering, MPKV, Rahuri (Fig 15.1.). The fruit washer was tested for mechanical washing of tomato, potato and mango. The performance of the machine was tested for washing efficiency, capacity and performance index. The machine works on the principle of turbulent flow of water created by different rotors in the washing chamber. The fruits kept in the washing tray will come in contact with vortex created in the chamber and get washed.

The machine consists of Washing unit, Rotor assembly, Mainframe, Power transmission unit (drive unit) and body with lid. The overall dimension of machine was 1000 mm × 560 mm × 750 mm.

EXPERIMENTAL TECHNIQUE

The speed of the rotor (1466, 1476 and 1486) was kept variable while conducting the trials, the optimum depth of water, rotor speed and time was determined. The minimum depth of water in washing chamber was kept 20 cm (110 litre). The washing efficiency was calculated as per the method given below:

$$E_W = \frac{W_w}{W_1} \times 100$$

Where,

E_w = Washing efficiency (%)

W_W = Weight of washed fruits (kg)

W_1 = Weight of unwashed fruits (kg)

The performance index (PI) of the fruit washer was calculated as per the method given below:

$$Ew = \frac{\text{Efficiency (\%)} \times \text{Capacity (tonne/hr)}}{\text{Unit cost of operation (Rs/tonne)}}$$

PERFORMANCE EVALUATION

Potato, tomato and mangoes were used for testing the performance of machine, known quantity of foreign matter (FM) was added into original sample to study the effect of machine parameter on washing of fruits. Three replication of each fruit was taken and the results were analyzed. Three different blades (A, B and C) of different specification were used for each trial for creating desired vortex in the washing chamber of the machine.

RESULTS AND DISCUSSION

The results of the experiment in terms of capacity, washing efficiency and performance index at different rotor speeds are discussed.

Capacity of Water

Capacity of washer for three different rotor speeds for mango, potato and tomato was calculated and presented in Table 1. It was observed from the table that the capacity was found in between 258.25 kg/hr to 892.11 kg/hr. the higher capacity (892.11 kg/hr) was found in case of potato washing for rotor C at 1486 rpm. It may be due to the configurations of rotor C. It was observed during the trial that as speed increases capacity of the machine increases. It was also noted that there was no specific increase in capacity of machine beyond 1486 rpm.

Washing Efficiency

Washing efficiency was calculated for three speeds of 1466, 1476 and 1486 rpm for three rotors at 20 cm depth (110 litre) of water. The data obtained is given in table 2.

Washing Efficiency of Mango

It was observed from the table that higher (97.07%) washing efficiency was obtained for mango washing for rotor C. Followed by rotor B (96.56%) and rotor A (96.98%) at 1486 rpm. It was observed that there was less vortex created by rotor A and B; it may be due to its configurations. It was also noted that continuous stirring was required for rotor A and B. In case of rotor C stirring was not required and uniform Washington of fruits was observed.

Washing Efficiency of Potato

Washing efficiency of potato was recorded by keeping the machine variables constant as discussed above. The values obtained were presented in Table 15.2. It was observed from the table that higher (98.18%) efficiency was recorded for rotor C at 1486 rpm followed by (97.43% and 97.00% for rotor B and rotor A, respectively. It was observed that there was no significant increase in efficiency for different rotor speeds in case of potato washing.

Table 15.1: Capacity of machine for mango, potato and tomato washing.

Speed (rpm)	Rotor Type	Capacity (kg/hr)		
		Mango	Potato	Tomato
1466	A	258.25	340.87	538.66
1476		343.66	412.00	576.57
1486		391.20	512.00	620.15
1466	B	362.11	436.05	440.18
1476		378.88	4447.65	474.23
1486		396.69	520.03	575.57
1466	C	432.25	733.71	690.85
1476		629.14	790.00	779.80
1486		779.85	892.11	833.17

Rotor A - Height = 110 mm Effective width = 55 mm
Rotor B - Height = 110 mm Effective width = 65 mm
Rotor C - Height = 110 mm Effective width = 75 mm

Washing efficiency of tomato

It was observed from the Table 15.2 that higher (98.09%) efficiency was obtained for rotor C followed by rotor A (98.07%) and rotor B (97.92%) at 1486 rpm. It was observed during tomato washing that no stirring was required. It may be due to sufficient vortex created by different rotors. The tomatoes were found bouncing in the washing without tray due to higher velocity of water and get washed without any mechanical damage. Similar results were reported for washing of carrots in rotary vegetable washing machine.

Table 15.2. Washing efficiency (%) of mango, potato and tomato for Rotor

Sr. No.	Fruit used for Washing	Speed of Rotor Rpm	Rotor A				Rotor B				Rotor C			
			W1 gm	W2 gm	Time (min)	Efficiency	W1	W2	Time	Efficiency	W1	W2	Time	Efficiency
1	Mango	1466	5375	5165	1.20	96.09	5349	5130	0.85	95.90	5322	5115	0.71	96.11
2		1476	5347	5155	0.90	96.40	5302	5115	0.81	96.47	5320	5138	0.49	96.59
3		1486	5378	5216	0.80	96.98	5340	5157	0.78	96.59	5356	5199	0.40	97.07
1	Potato	1466	5356	5170	0.91	96.52	5346	5160	0.71	96.52	5320	5136	0.42	96.54
2		1476	53444	5150	0.75	96.36	5340	5148	0.69	96.40	5318	5135	0.39	96.54
3		1486	5340	5180	0.60	97.00	5340	5203	0.60	97.43	5300	5204	0.35	98.18
1	Tomaio	1466	4135	4040	0.45	97.70	4120	4035	0.55	97.93	4140	4030	0.35	97.34
2		1476	4125	4036	0.42	97.84	4135	4031	0.51	97.24	4126	4029	0.31	97.64
3		1486	4110	4031	0.39	98.07	4115	4029	0.42	97.92	4105	4027	0.29	98.09

Rotor A- Height = 110 mm Effective width = 55 mm
Rotor B- Height = 110 mm Effective width = 65 mm
Rotor C- Height = 110 mm Effective width = 75 mm

Performance index of washer

Performance index of washer for mango, potato and tomato for different rotors at three speeds was calculated and presented in Table 15.3. It was observed from the table that for tomato performance index was found higher (3.90) for rotor C at 1486 followed by 3.26 and 2.80 for same rotor at same speed for potato and mango washing respectively. It was observed that as speed increased performance index was found increased.

Table 15.3. Performance index of washer for different rotor sped and rotors (A, B and C) for mango, potato and tomato washing

Speed (rpm)	Rotor type	Capacity (kg/hr)		
		Mango	Potato	Tomato
1466	A	0.92	1.46	2.10
1476		0.22	1.77	2.25
1486		1.40	2.21	2.42
1466	B	1.28	1.87	1.72
1476		1.35	1.94	1.84
1486		1.42	2.26	2.25
1466	C	1.54	3.16	2.68
1476		2.25	3.40	3.04
1486		2.80	3.90	3.26

Rotor A- Height = 110 mm Effective width = 55 mm
Rotor B- Height = 110 mm Effective width = 65 mm
Rotor C- Height = 110 mm Effective width = 75 mm

CONCLUSIONS

From the experiment of mechanical washing of fruit and vegetables following conclusion could be drawn.

1. The capacity, efficiency and performance index of machine varied with respect to speed of rotor and type of rotor.

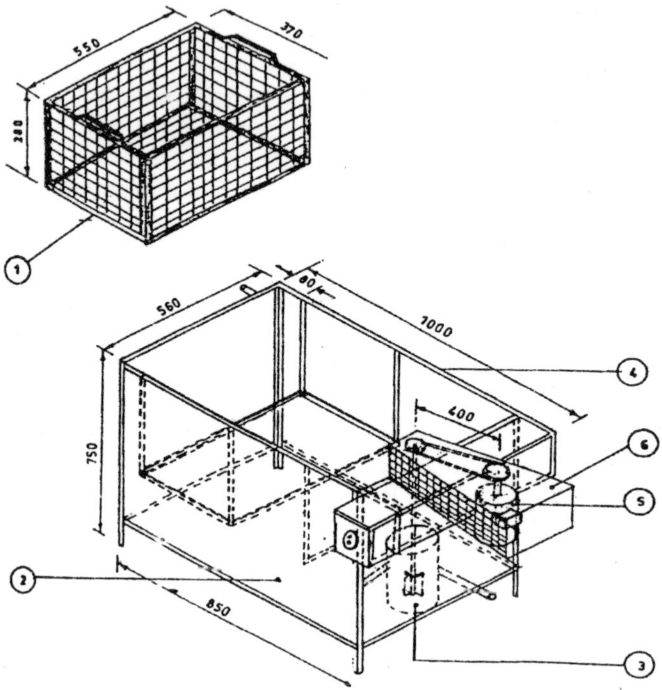

Fig. 15.1: Mechanical Fruit Washer

Sr. No.	Name of the Parts	MAT.	QTY.
1.	Cleaning unit	M.S.Angle	1
2.	Body and laid	G.I.Sheet	1
3.	Rotor Assembly		
	i) Rotor blade	M.S.	1
	ii) rotor shaft & Pully	STD	1
4.	Main Frames 25 mm T.	M.S.Angle	1
5.	Power Transmission Unit (Motor 1 HP Single Phase 1486 rpm)	STD.	1
6.	Motor Guard	M.S.	1

Dr. A.S. College of Agricultural Engg. M.P.K.V. Rahuri
Department of Agricultural Process Engineering

Title: Fig 15.1: Mechanical fruit washer

All dimensions are in mm.

2. The capacity of machine varied between 258.25 kg/hr to 833.17 kg/hr. The higher capacity (833.17 kg/hr) was seen in case of tomato washing.

3. The washing efficiency varied between 95.90% to 98.09% for mango, potato and tomato washing. Maximum efficiency of 98.09% was recorded in tomato washing for rotor C at 1486 rpm.

4. The performance index varied between 0.22 to 3.90. Higher performance index (3.90) was seen in case of rotor C at 1486 rpm at 98.09% washing efficiency.

5. The ratio of cost of manual to mechanical washing was 4.26: 1,5.89:1 and 7.58:1 for mango, potato and tomato washing, respectively.

6. The portable mechanical fruit washer was found suitable for washing of small batch of fruits.

16

Packaging of Fruit Juices

Fruits are an essential part of our diet. Most of them are available quite cheap during the glut season. Being highly perishable they have to be preserved and processed for later use. Canning, freezing and aseptic packaging as methods of preservation are very expensive and make the product of reach of the common man, the solution lies in the use of an appropriate technology for preserving them in the form of pulps and juice for their subsequent use for beverage industry. Fruit processing industry is an important agrobased industry. If properly harvested it has a great potential to improve nutritional status of our people as to improve horticultural economy to cater to the indigenous need and better returns to the growers. The major constraints caused by packaging and transport costs limit the scope and growth of fruit juice and beverage industry. In the absence of easy availability of surplus fresh fruits simulated flavours have enjoyed an open field. In many pockets of our country, juice from fresh fruits is accepted during certain seasons. However the cost of such products limits their consumption. If fruit juices are to be marketed on a national scale, there should be dependable availability of the raw material and proper economical packaging of fruit juices and pulps. The seasonal availability of fruits necessitates storage for round the year use. There is a crying need to increase the availability of fruits, to make them easily and economically accessible to the consumers and convert the surplus to their commercialized products. Packaging industry is still in its infancy in our country and processing industry faces a number of problems including multiple taxes and levels.

OBJECTIVES

Appropriate packaging is a pre-requisite for retaining the quality of the preserved product. At present juices and pulps are packed in glass container with chemical preservatives and tin container with a hermetic seal. These containers and to 20-50% of the wholesale price of the final product. Expensive nature of sanitary cans and their rising costs is one of the important factors which has affected the development of canned food industry in India. In foreign countries flexible pouches are also used as packaging material (Table 2). Hence experiments were carried out to find out the effectiveness of more economic alternatives like plastic containers and films for packing of pretreated fruit pulps and juices.

STUDIES ON THE STORAGE OF NON-COLOURED FRUIT PULPS AND JUICES

Feasibility of storage of fruit juices and pulps in different containers was studied both at room and low temperatures. Juices and pulps of sweet orange, kinnow orange, litchi, ber and mango were preserved with potassium metabisulphite or KMS (1000-2000 ppm) alone or in combination with 1.0% citric acid, sodium benzoate (500-1000 ppm) or a mixture of both KMS and sodium benzoate (500-1000 ppm KMS + 250-500 ppm sodium benzoate). Retention of colour and nutrients were better with KMS as compared to KMS plus sodium benzoate or sodium benzoate alone. However presence of citric acid along with KMS or sodium benzoate showed slightly more browning compared to KMS alone. with respect to organoleptic quality, retention of vitamin C and carrotenoids, glass bottles were found to be better as compared to high density polyethylene or PVC containers irrespective of storage temperature. These products could be stored for 6-12 months in glass, 4-8 months in high density and 2-4 months in PVC containers expect in mango where pulp could be stored for 7 months in PVC bottles when stored at room temperature (25-30°C). Low temperature (1-3°C) was found to be better for the retention of colour, flavour and nutrients and for reducing non-enzymatic browning in juices and pulps. Juices from three varieties of sweet oranges were preserved by heat processing and chemicals. As compared to Pineapple and common variety of the juice, the Red blood variety retained better colour and odour and did not turn bitter during storage for 6 months at room temperature. For the retention of vitamins in juices and pulps chemical preservation was better as compared to heat processing.

In case of mango pulp HMHD (200 g) films were also used. Heated pulp along with 0.5% citric acid was heat processed at 100°C for 20 minutes in these films. Pulp was found to be organoleptic acceptable upto 45 days in HMHD pouches whereas with chemical preservation it could be stored at room temperature for 7-8 months in plastic containers and 1 year in glass bottles. For banana pulp a combination of KMS (0.1%) alongwith ascorbic acid (0.1%) was best followed by KMS (0.1%) for the retention of colour and flavour in glass bottles upto storage of 6 months at room temperature.

SUITABILITY OF DIFFERENT CONTAINERS FOR STORING COLOURED JUICES/PULPS

1. Phalsa Juice

Loss of anthocyanins in the phalsa juice increased in temperature of processing from 50° to 90°C. Phalsa juice after heating to 85°C could be preserved both by addition of sodium benzoate (500 ppm) and by heat processing and storing in different containers. There was better retention of anthocyanins in the juice packed in glass bottles followed by HDPE & PVC containers. Light did not have much effect on the stability of pigments in the juice. At 3°C the phalsa juice could be stored well in HDPE and PVC bottles. At room temperature the juice could not be stored for more than 10 days in these bottles. Addition of cane sugar (20-65%) to the juice was found to have a beneficial influence on the stability of juice colour. It could be stored for 10 months at 3°C, 100 days at 20°C and 15 days at 37°C. formation of browning pigment (Hydroxal methyl furfural, HMF) decreased with increase in the sugar concentration in the juice during storage at 37°C.

2. Plum pulp

Studies carried out regarding preservation of plum pulp with potassium metabisulphite (1000 ppm) and sodium benzoate (600 ppm) in different containers revealed that no marked difference in colour and flavour was observed when pulp was stored at low temperature (1-3°C) in either plain or coloured bottles. Anthocyanin pigments of the pulp were affected by potassium metabisulphite which reappeared after heating the pulp. Pulp was found to be organoleptically acceptable for more than 5 months at low temperature (1-3°C) and upto 2 months at ambient temperature (25-30°C). Glass bottles were found to be better than PVC bottles regarding the retention of nutrients and preservatives.

Table 16.1. Packaging of food products in flexible packaging materials

Type of food products	Packaging materials used
Fruit and vegetable products and products requiring processing	Pouches made of polyester or polyamide/aluminium foil/HDPE or polyethylene polypropylene copolymer
Jams and pickles	Pouches of cellulose/polyethylene or nylon/polyethylene
Fruit juices and non-carbonated soft drinks	Pouches of polyester/aluminium foil/ polyethylene tetrapack/tetrabrick made of paper/aluminium foil/polyethylene.

Research has been done at CFTRI Mysore regarding the changes in orange juice packed in flexible and rigid containers. Storage studies were carried out under these conditions (i) 40°C and 35% RH (ii) 27°C and 65% RH and (iii) refrigerated condition to evaluate the protective qualities of polyester/aluminium foil/ polyethylene and metallized tinplate containers. Chemical, biological and organoleptic changes in the juice as influenced by the storage conditions and packaging materials were investigated. Based on the changes in the ascorbic acid, acidity, browning index and also microbiological and organoleptic analyses, it was found that foil laminate pouches afforded shelf life of 45, 65 and more than 90 days whereas metallized polyester/polyethylene pouches provided corresponding shelf life of 34, 65 and more than 90 days under the three conditions. There were minimal changes in the product packed in tin plate containers with only light feathering at high temperature storage.

RECOMMENDATIONS

To put the commercial fruit juice processing industry on a sound footing and to meet the challenges from a number of bottlenecks in the packaging industry some of the recommendations are:

1. There should be a processing unit which can claim to be actually utilizing the surplus or the overflow from fresh fruit markets.
2. Packaging line should be located near processing units.
3. Contract packaging of fruit juices/pulps should be encouraged. This would mean that processing firms should set up automatic packaging machinery.

17

Flexible Packages for Fruit and Vegetable Pulps

The increasing consumer demand for fruit and vegetables products has necessitated the search for suitable packaging materials which are economically proficient and safe. Canning is popular and well accepted all over the world. With the rising cost as compared with other packaging materials canning has become prohibitive. Besides high cost of cans, variable tinning quality and high rate of spoilage have compelled the food industries to look for replacement of cans.

Now aseptic packaging has been Standardised in advanced countries and some of these equipments are being used in India recently for packing export oriented foods. In this process, the product is sterilized at ultra high temperature for a very short time with the result there is a minimal loss of flavour or other nutrients. However, the success of aseptic packaging is to be seen in India as the fruit or vegetable products packed by this process need low temperature storage. In united Kingdom, orange juice is being marketed in polyester/aluminium foil/polyethylene type of pouches, while in Australia from developed polyester/aluminium foil/polyolefin pouches which can withstand temperatures above 100°C. Polypropylene films have been found suitable for sterilization and packaging ready-to-serve foods, but the preservative effect of these films may not be as good as that achieved in rigid containers.

MANGO

In India, some alternative materials have been tried for packaging of mango pulp. These include wooden barrels, high density polyethylene (HDPE) containers porcelain, HDPE and glass containers (Kalra, 1982) and flexible pouches. Alphonso and Totapuri mango pulp with 500 ppm SO2 stored at 25°C had a shelf life of more than 12 months in HDPE containers and 6 months in polyethylene and polypropylene pouches (Table 17.1). Ghosh et al., stored pasteurized mango pulp in 300 gauge polypropylene pouches at ambient temperature (22-28°C) for 4 months. They reported reduction of SO_2 from 700 to 146 ppm and loss of carotene and vitamin C upto 99 per cent.

In another study Kalra and Chadha evaluated polypropylene pouches (200 gauge) for packaging Lucknow Safeda mango pulp (Table 2) imposing the following three treatments.

T_1: Fresh pulp filled into pouches and heated in boiling water for 20 minutes.

T_2: Heated the pulp to 80°C for 10 minutes, cooled to 50°C, mixed with 350 ppm SO2 and filled.

T_3: Pulp sulphited to 100 ppm SO2, filled and sterilized the pouches for 20 minutes in boiling water.

The pouches were stored at ambient (32-35°C) and cold conditions (4-6°C). In all the treatments under ambient and T1 in cold conditions developed granulation/precipitation and mould growth in the stored pulp samples within 2-3 months. The remaining treatments were in good condition for 4 months of the study (Table 17.2). Composition changes in the pulp were low to moderate under cold conditions (Table 17.2). Juice prepared from pulp stored for 4 months had acceptable quality. High molecular weight high density (HMHD) film pouches pulp could be stored at ambient condition 24-28°C up to 2 months.

GUAVA

Cultivar Allahabad Safeda pulp pre-sterilized (76-78°C) and sulphited with 250, 500 and 750 ppm SO_2 stored under ambient

Table 17.1. Storage life and composition of Alphonso mango pulp packed in polyethylene (PL 400) and polypropylene pouches (pp 100 gauge) stored at 25°C

Treatment	Container	Storage Life (months)	° Brix	Acidity	Composition of pulp total carrotenoids mg/100 g	Free SO_2 ppm	Total SO_2 ppm
At packaging		-	16.8	0.56	16439	ND	ND
Hot pulp							
After Storage*							
Hot pulp							
+							
500 ppm SO_2	PE	6	17.0	0.82	14100	60	208
	PP	6	17.5	0.80	13900	78	180

*Composition of pulp refers to pulp stored for 4 months.
ND = not determined.

Table 17.2. Chemical characteristics of Lucknow Safeda mango pulp stored in polypropylene pouches at maximum storage period

Treatment	Storage Period (months)	Moisture %		Acidity % as citric acid		°Brix		Total SO_2 ppm		Vitamin C mg %	
		A	B	A	B	A	B	A	B	A	B
Mango Pulp	Initial	78.2	78.2	0.32	0.32	2.14	2.14	—	—	5.8	5.8
T_1	2	81.8	79.3	0.15	0.26	17.8	18.9	Not added	4.6	4.3	
T_2	2	70.8	78.8	0.26	0.21	19.4	20.5	70	160	3.5	6.8
	4	—	76.2	—	0.22	—	19.8	—	50	—	2.6
T_3	2	80.9	79.7	0.25	0.11	18.6	18.9	nil	64	3.3	5.0
	4	—	79.3	—	0.28	—	15.4			—	3.3

A = stored at ambient temperature 32-35°C; B = stored at 4-6°C.

temperature (15-30°C) was not spoiled up to 3 months. After that it developed pink discolouration. Ordinary and food grade polyethylene did not exhibit any significant difference in the chemical composition (Table 17.3).

Table 17.3. Changes in guava pulp compositions stored in food grade polyethylene pouches

Characters	Storage Period (months)	SO_2 level ppm		
		250	500	750
Moisture%	0	86.3	86.3	86.2
	3	85.9	85.9	85.7
TSS ° Brix	0	9.6	9.6	9.6
	3	12.5	12.3	11.6
pH	0	4.14	4.16	4.18
	3	3.97	3.93	3.88
Free SO_2 ppm	0	174	300	482
	3	60	60	66
Tannins mg%	0	320	322	342
	3	162	157	162
Reducing	0	4.08	4.05	4.19
sugars (%)	3	6.60	6.31	6.61

OTHERS

The flexible packaging of fruit products and vegetable products does not always present a successful story, solar dehydrated green peas when packed in transparent as well as black polyethylene pouched and butter paper bags and stored at room temperature (22-36°C), those packed in both types of polythene pouches were spoiled within two months, while butter paper bags retained the original quality of peas. Polythene pouches possibly restrict heat and moisture loss to the outside atmosphere which might create problems for such dehydrated materials. However, in case of materials such as tomato crush and tomato juice concentrate packed in polyethylene and polypropylene pouches could be stored at ambient temperature for about 2 months (Table 17.4). Similarly in high molecular weight high density film pouches. Maini et al., showed that tomato pulp could be stored upto 2 months at ambient temperature (24-28°C). In successful preservation of tomato crush in pouches, control of microflora responsible for spoilage is vital as a wide array of bacteria including heat resistant Bacillus, yeast and moulds, coagulam have been reported from spoiled tomato crush. Potassium, sorbate or propyliparaben individually or with ferric chloride as preservative prevent or check the spoilage micro-organisms effectively.

Table 17.4. Shelf life and composition of Pusa Ruby cultivar of tomato crush stored at 25°C polyethylene and polypropylene pouches

Container	Shelf life (weeks)	Composition		
		pH	Acidity	Vitamin C (mg/100 g)
At packing	-	4.02	1.77	19.44
After storage P.E. pouch	7	4.05	1.79	Traces
P.P. pouch	7	3.90	1.70	Traces

The flexible packaging material be it polyethylene, polypropylene or any other laminate could create some specific problems such as microbial storage under high temperature conditions. However, at low temperatures (below 20°C) some success has been achieved for the storage of mango pulp and guava pulp. Even aseptically packed pulps and juices would have to be stored under cold conditions. It is imperative that future researches pertaining to flexible packaging materials should invariably consider low temperatures (0-20°C), microbial spoilage and work out the most feasible and economic processes for storage of fruit products.

18

Developments in Packaging of Liquid Foods

Packaging to perfection can be seen in Nature. Let us look at it for the packaging of liquids, the smallest living forms, micro-organisms are liquid chemicals encapsulated in a membranous sac. Higher forms of life are aggregations of such cells. For example, a citrus fruit-cells filled with liquid (juice) are contained in multiple coverings to form the whole fruit. Similarly, coconut is a package which containers a nutritionally rich liquid; so is the case of egg, contained within a calcium carbonate shell. They all protect and preserve the contents as desired by nature to meet the specific needs. The contents are both highly perishable microbiologically and the packaging offers adequate protection.

Liquid food products have been packed, preserved and transported over the ages by a variety of methods. Preservation of food by choice of proper container goes back to the civilizations of the past. Wooden containers, earthern pots (glazed pottery or jars) and glass continue to be the major materials even in the present day. All these had the benefits of being non-reactive to the food material and also efficient to contain the material resisting deformation besides being leak-proof (if properly closed). We see details of such products as oils, wines, pickles and preserves served/packed in such containers from history of mankind either in their day to day life or in trade practices.

Over the years, with man's quest for newer technologies, packaging of liquid food products also gained greater importance.

The need for developing alternative materials and methods for liquid food packaging has arisen out of more than one reason. They include reduction in cost of packaging, improved shelf life, providing customers convenience in using the product, improvement in handling during transport or in retail outlets and also to promote consumer acceptance of the product. It was further necessitated due to changed distribution systems, competition, changing consumer needs and availability of new packaging materials and/or methods. A consumer pack may need redesigning also when the product enters the phase of its product life cycle where in a sales promotion activity in the form of a consumer benefit is needed.

When a packaging system for packaging liquid products is considered, we have to ascertain the quality of the product, the transport hazards to which it will be exposed, the type of marketing requirement (bulk or retail packs) and about the packaging materials and machinery *vis-à-vis* the cost. While looking at the nature of a product, the problems that we encounter are: the stability of the product; its viscosity properties; its shelf life requirements and possible interaction with the packaging material. The material can be corrosive, sticky, volatile, etc. the compatibility of the packaging material when liquid products are packed thus assumes primary importance.

Next we consider the transport hazards such as vibration, compression, deformation or cracking and piercing, puncturing, tearing, sagging, etc. also the possibilities of temperature variation, water vapour and chemical atmosphere, microbiological contamination, attack by rodents, mice and contamination by other goods (materials of adjacent packs) or leakage (in adjacent packs). Further, packaging has to take into account the shelf life requirements and the retail, wholesale packing needs also. In this connection, in a retail pack convenience of its opening or serving assumes importance. Since the pack also serves as a factor in selling, its design and looks are also of importance. Consumer convenience such as carrying, easy opening, serves of measured doses, easy grip and easy disposability would form attractive functions for sale of the commodity.

For transporting in bulk, liquid material can be carried in wooden drums or metal drums. Alternatively, containers can be packed in wooden crates or fibre mould cases, e.g. Glass carboys in crates, polythene or synthetic plastic carboys can be considered. A new development in this area is the bag-in-box type of packaging for liquids.

While we examine the shelf life requirements of the product, microbial spoilage in case of fresh food products such as milk and fruit juices, due to their high susceptibility such as milk and fruit juices, due to their high susceptibility to microbial contamination and hence requirement for sterilization/pasteurization procedures need be considered. Packaging material should withstand rigorous treatments during such packaging stages, systems are currently available for in situ sterilisation of packaging material while the pack is being formed, known as aseptic packaging systems.

With the present trend of Supermarket selling in the major cities, the pack has to sell the product and therefore the age-old definitions: Packaging contains, protects and preserves and informs" and "At its most sophisticated it provides two functions selling and convenience" are quite apt. In a world where quality of the product is high, the only difference between competitive brands lies in the packaging, and only the packaging influences the selling operations. Therefore a definition such as "Packaging is a techno-economic factor aimed at minimizing cost or delivery while maximizing sales (and hence profits)" becomes all the more meaningful.

As the industry grows and consumers demand more and more convenience, the need for quality packaging undoubtedly increases. Today, packaging is cost effective in the sense that the package is pivotal to the marketing philosophy of the urban markets offering a wide choice at a low cost. Thus the model food package has to hold down marketing cost and offer the consumer tangible price benefit. In the attempts to minimize cost of packaging, elimination of the labour content in the packaging operations and use of less costly packaging materials are of primary importance. The increased speeds on machine lines and use of flexible laminates in place of tin containers may be considered as a development.

Reduction in cost does not necessarily be a consumer

requirement for increased sales. For example, development of the aluminium end ring-pull can for beer and soft drinks was found more expensive than the flat topped cans it replaced. However, it added to customer convenience and thereby larger scales and greater profitability for the can manufactured and the beverages company, in practice, decisions often therefore have to be made on specific areas.

As outlined above, the selection of the packaging material and the packaging machines depends upon the food to be packed and the consumers needs. The materials, machines and the methods together can be called as a packaging system.

Such systems offered in majority of instances include the total package of operations such as making or forming sachets, erecting or closing cartons, feeding and seaming cans, presenting bottles to feeder heads and capping, over-wrapping cartons, etc. Secondary operations such as coding, labeling, check-weighing and palletization for despatch also involve the packaging system. Thus the product must be put in the package in the decided condition at the required speed and to the stated quantity with the utmost economic efficiency.

Today we find fruit juices, wines, water, oil, soup, concentrated vegetable purees, etc., packed in a variety of systems as Prepac, blockpak, Zupack, Purepak, Ceka, Tetrapak, thermo forming systems and bag-in-box systems. Facilities such as aseptic packaging, hot filling, nitrogen flushing, etc., for the product are also available.

There are the range of cartooning systems and form fill seal machines now available and are replacing the glass and tin containers for liquid food packaging. Among these aseptic packaging is yet another development. Developments considered in this paper is restricted to form fill seal machines including carton packs and sachets. Canning and bottling as packaging system have been deliberately omitted here.

In the list of liquid food products packed by the aseptic packaging systems, we can see a large number of products. Fermented milk yoghurt, non-dairy whitener, whipping cream substitute, fruit products such as papaya drink, water-melon drink, mango and guava, fruit nectars; juices such as sugar-cane, lemon, tomato; beverages such as coffee, tea and alcoholic beverages such as saki and wine; and soya based drink-soya milk can be listed among the aseptically packed products.

A cartoning system combines a special carton with machinery to erect it from a flat condition, fill it with a product and close it. The machinery varies from simple hand-fed machines to automatic stations coupled with means for packing the cartons directly into cases for despatch. In all these systems three main operations are involved; forming or erecting the container, loading or filling the container and closing, m or sealing, besides these, such systems may be required to carry out secondary operations such as handling, embossing codes, etc.

Full automatic machinery is used when forming, filling and closing has to be carried out on one machine in a single operation.

Requirements with respect to hygiene and impermeability are stringent with respect to liquid food products. Sealing must be tight.

The cartoning systems are of two types. One where the cartons are formed from a reel and filled in a continuous operation as in 'Tetra Pack' or the other which starts from a pre-manufactured blank as in 'Purepak'.

Machines for the packaging of liquids are frequently availed on rent because of the special working conditions and importance of perfect servicing.

Form fill seal machines use a reel of flexible material (paper, film or laminate of paper/film/foil). They form the laminates to tubular shapes and seal and fill it at regular intervals. They may also fold lengthwise and seal it at right angles to the fold to form a serried of pockets (sachets) which are filled and closed.

Machines of the first type form pouches with a seal at each end and down the center of one face, while the second type of operation produces sachets with three or all four edges sealed.

There are basically three types of machines. Vertical form fill seal machine, horizontal form fill seal machines and sachet forming machines.

All the types can be used for liquid food product packing.

They can have such secondary facilities as gas flushing, vacuumizing, etc., introduced.

Standipacks and gusseted sachet packs are quite accepted for liquid food products for their consumer convenience.

All these automated packaging systems thus enable (a) faster speeds for production, (b) introduction of flexible packaging materials as an alternative to tin and glass containers, (c) reduction in labour requirement and (d) convenience to consumers such as price advantage and easy disposability.

19

Drying of Fruits and Vegetables

Preservation of foods by drying them is perhaps the oldest method known. Large quantities of fruits are dried in the sun in different parts of the world such as Asia Minor, Greece, Spain, and other Mediterranean countries, Arabia, Afghanistan, Australia, etc. The modern method of dehydration, i.e. drying fruits and vegetables under controlled conditions of temperature and humidity is, however, assuming importance as a major industry. The dehydration industry got an impetus during the World War II. On account of their concentrated form, low cost, convenience and easy transportability, dried fruit and vegetable products and also other dehydrated foods became highly popular among the armed forces.

Dehydrated vegetables, however, lost some of their popularity owing to some undesirable changes in colour, taste and flavour during storage and distribution. Dehydration techniques have since been greatly improved to get over most of these defects so that the modern dehydrated food is really a first class product in every way. It is sometimes said that the dehydration industry will one day be the most important one among the food preservation industries employing various other well-known methods of preservation such as canning, freezing, addition of chemical preservatives, etc. There is scope for advanced scientific as well as development work in the field of food dehydration, especially of fruits and vegetables.

MANUFACTURING PROCESS

1. Fruits and vegetables are sorted and graded.
2. Then these are washed with clean water by automatic washing machine to remove soil and attached pesticides.
3. The washed fruits and vegetables are peeled to remove outer skin.
4. These are then sliced or diced into thickness of 2mm - 4mm.
5. The diced fruits & Vegetables are steam blanched for 5 minutes.
6. The vegetables are dipped in potassium Metabisulfite solution for 3-5 minutes and fruits are dissolves in water containing L-Ascorbic Acid (Vitamin C).
7. These fruits & vegetable treated products are now freeze dryed by automatic freeze-drying by automatic freeze-drying.
8. These dryed products are now packed in pouches by automatic vacuum packaging form-fill-seal machine. These pouches are now packed in cartons or cardboards, stored and market.

PLANT ECONOMICS FRUITS AND VEGETABLES DRYING BY (FREEZE DRYING METHOD)

Rated Plant capacity = 500.00 kgs./day

LAND & BUILDING

1. Land 2 Acres Rs. 27,50,000.00

PLANT AND MACHINERY

1. Automatic Washing machine for fruits & vegetables
2. Automatic peeling machine
3. Blanching machine

4. Diceing or cubing machine (Automatic)
5. S.S. Tank
6. S.S. Strainer
7. Freeze Drying machine
8. Boiler
9. Automatic Vacuum pouch packaging machine
10. Laboratory testing equipment.
11. Weighing balance water pump valves motors and other accessories.

RAW MATERIALS

1. Fruits 32 MT.
2. Vegetables 32 MT.
3. Chemicals as potassium metabisulfite, vitamin C

TOTAL WORKING CAPITAL/MONTH

1.	RAW MATERIAL	Rs.	2,89,000.00
2.	SALARY & WAGES	Rs.	42,120.00
3.	UTILITIES & OVERHEADS	Rs.	2,43,500.00
	TOTAL	Rs.	5,74,620.00

TOTAL CAPITAL INVESTMENT

TOTAL FIXED CAPITAL	Rs.	1,63,57,000.00
TOTAL WORKING CAPITAL FOR 1 MONTH	Rs.	5,74,620.00
TOTAL	Rs.	1,69,31,620.00

TURN OVER/ANNUM

1. By sale of 75000 kgs of Dehydrated Fruits
2. By sale of 75000 kgs.

TOTAL Rs. 1,57,50,000.00

PROFIT SALES RATIO = Profit / Sales x 100 = 23.53 %

RATE OF RETURN = Operating profit / T.C.I x 100 = 21.89 %

BREAK EVEN POINT (B.E.P) = 63.76 %

20

Dehydration Fruits and Vegetables by Vacuum Drying Method

MANUFACTURING PROCESS

Manufacturing process of Dehydration of Fruit & Vegetable by Vacuum Drying Method.

CANNING

Apples, Bananas, Grapes, Guavas, Litchi, Mangoes, Oranges Papaya, pears & Pineapples among fruits and Cabbage, carrot cauliflower, Mushroom, Lady's Jigoes, peas, potato & tomato are choosen for the canning process. The details of the process are given below.

The whole process can be divided into following steps.

1. Sorting and Grading

After preliminary sorting, the fruits and vegetables are graded. This is necessary to obtain a pack of uniform quality as regards size, colour, etc. and is done by hand or with the help of grading machines.

2. Washing

The graded fruits and vegetables are washed with water indifferent ways, such as soaking or agitating in water, washingwith cold or hot water sprays, etc.

3 Peeling, Coring and Pitting

The washed fruits and vegetables are prepared for canning by peeling, coring pitting by machines. Some cases it is done by hand, by heat treatment and by lye solution.

4. Can Filling

The cans are washed with water to remove any adhering dust or foreign matter. In large canneries, the cans are washed with jets of compressed air water.

PLANT ECONOMICS OF DEHYDRATION OF FRUIT AND VEGETABLES BY VACUUM DRYING METHOD

Rated Plant capacity = 500.00 kgs./day

LAND AND BUILDING

Land Area 5,000 sq.mt Rs. 1,81,20,000.00

PLANT AND MACHINERY

1. Automatic Washing machine
2. Automatic peeling machine
3. Blanching machine
4. Diceing or cubing machine(Automatic
5. S.S. Tank
6. S.S. Strainer
7. Freeze Drying machine
8. Boiler

9. Automatic Vacuum pouch packaging machine
10. Laboratory testing equipment.
11. Weighing balance water pump valves motors

RAW MATERIALS

1. Fruits
2. Vegetables
3. Chemicals as potassium metabi-sulfite, vitamin C

TOTAL CAPITAL INVESTMENT

TOTAL FIXED CAPITAL	Rs. 3,17,27,000.00
TOTAL WORKING CAPITAL FOR 3 MONTHS	Rs. 19,73,055.00
TOTAL	Rs. 3,37,00,055.00

TURN OVER/ANNUM

1. By sale of 75000 kgs of Dehydrated Fruits
2. By sale of 75000 kgs.

TOTAL Rs. 2,17,50,000.00

PROFIT SALES RATIO = Profit / Sales x 100 = 28.30 %

RATE OF RETURN = Operating profit / T.C.I x 100 = 18.26 %

BREAK EVEN POINT (B.E.P) = 60.62 %

21

Fruit Drink Rasna Type Mango and Pineapple Pulp and Concentrates

MANUFACTURING PROCESS (FRUIT PULP MANUFACTURING (MANGO AND PINEAPPLE)

The fruits of semi solid texture are taken and sorted byeither manually or by automatic sorting machine. Then the fruitsare washed either by detergent solution or clean water thoroughlyto remove dirt, soils and other impurities sticking on thesurfaces of fruits. This washing or cleaning operation isfollowed by automatic washing machine or manually washed. Thefruits are now ready for steaming operation. By steamingoperation the fruits become soft. These are now passed through apulper machine which is power driven and comprises of aperforated cylinderical sieve and revolving wooden or metallicpaddles. The pulp passing through the sieve is collected inwooden barrels. The pulp is then heated in open pan evaporatorat temperature 84-88oC. Then suitable preservative such aspotassium metabisulfite (sulphur dioxide) or sodium benzoate atamout 350 PPM is added and mixed homoginiously. Then it isfilled in sterilized cans, and sealed by double seaming machine.The sealed cans are pastevrized in boiling water for 15-35minutes. After pastevrization process is complete the cans aretaken out and cooled and stored in cool dry place.

MANGO JUICE

The operation describes in this report are, where possible,performed by mechanical equipment, however, substitution of hand operations is not precluded if the same principles are followed :

WASHING

Washing fresh Mangoes accomplished one or more of the following purposes :-

a) Remove soil or earthy substances.

b) Remove mild, yeast, bacteria and/or spores of these micro organism.

c) Remove insects, insect eggs, larve of fragments,

d) Remove downy or spinery portions of skin.

e) Remove toxic and flavour or odour bearing residues of

• sprays and dusts.

Soak tank into which raw Mangoes are discharges. Tank may contain cold or warm water (to 120°F) with or without addition of a harmless detergent. The time in soak tank is 2 -3 minutes.

Mangoes are elevated to brush washer with transverse revolving fibre or nylon brushes which fumable the product under sprays or water or high pressure. Washed fruit is now ready for final inspection and/or trimming.

PLANT ECONOMICS OF FRUIT PULP AND JUICE CONCENTRATES

Rated Plant capacity = 1166.67 DOZ/day

LAND AND BUILDING

1. Total land area required 1300 Sq.mt Rs. 15,30,000.00

PLANT AND MACHINERY

1. Automatic Fruit washing machine
2. Pulper with 5Hp motor
3. Steam Heating tank
4. Mixer (S.S) lined equipped
5. Fruit Washing Machine
6. Sorting Table or Belt
7. Baby Boiler, Steam generating
8. Automatic can Filling Machine
9. Double Seaming Machine
10. Can Labelling Machine
11. Chilling Plant 10 MT/Hr
12. Storage and mixing tanks made of s.s complete
13. Material Handling Equipments
14. Evaporator
15. Lab Testing Equipments
16. Misc. equipments pipes,valves, fittings, motors, pumps, small tanks and other essential equipments

RAW MATERIALS

1. Mango of suitable variety 70 MT
2. Pine Apple 50 MT
3. Preservatives like citric acid, sod. Benzoate, sugar, salt, Barley, flavours, essence
4. Packaging Materials, labels

TOTAL CAPITAL INVESTMENT

TOTAL FIXED CAPITAL	Rs. 38,65,000.00
TOTAL WORKING CAPITAL FOR 3 MONTHS	Rs. 11,88,437.00
TOTAL	Rs. 50,53,437.00

TURN OVER/ANNUM

1. By sale of Mango pulp 300 MT
2. By sale of Pine Apple Pulp 300 MT
3. By sale of Mango Juice Concentrate 300 MT.
4. By sale of Pine Apple Juice Concentrate 300 MT

TOTAL Rs. 2,28,00,000.00

PROFIT SALES RATIO = Profit / Sales x 100 = 74.18 %

RATE OF RETURN = Operating profit / T.C.I x 100 = 334.68 %

BREAK EVEN POINT (B.E.P) = 13.27 %

22

Jam, Jelly, Chutney, Pickles and Squashes

Among preserved fruits, Jams, Jellies, Marmalades, Pickles, squahes forms an important class of products. during World War II, fairly large quantities of these were imported to into India from the U.S.A. the U.K. and Australia. Now a days, such products are being manufactured extensively in several factories in this country, as by products or joint products in fruits.

They are also made in many of the homes all over the country. Their production and demand can be increased manifold by making better use of fruit that is being wasted at present. A Jam differs from a preserve in that it does not contain pieces of the whole fruit as in the case with a preserve. In preparing the jam, the fruit is crushed or otherwise finely cut, so that when cooked, the mass is fairly uniform throughout. Itis rich in flavour, because the ripe fruit, which have developed full flavour, are used in its preparation.

MANUFACTURING PROCESS FOR SQUASHES

1. Orange Squash

First of all oranges are peeled and rags sticking to the the segments is removed. Now the juice from segments is extract byusing screw type s juice extractor and juice is collected andsieved to remove coarse seeds etc. and if necessary heated andpacked in bottles.The formulation is given below:-

Orange juice 10° Brix	45 Kgs.
0.8% acidity	45 Kgs.
Sugar	74 Kgs.
Citric Acid	2.33 Kgs.
Essence of orange	1.125 Kgs.
Water	57 Litres.
Orange colour qs	
Potassium metabisulphite	110 gms.

From the above formula, the squash obtained will have the following specification :

Juice	25%
Brix	45°
Acidity	1.5%

2. Formulation for Other Squashes

In all types of squashes the method is same that is extraction of juice and addition of ingredients. Therefore, it is needless to repeat the process but to be familiar with formulations is essential.

PLANT ECONOMICS

Rated Plant capacity = 800.00 Kgs/day

LAND AND BUILDING

Total are 450 sq.mts. Rs. 28,22,500.00

PLANT AND MACHINERY

1. Screw type juice extractor
2. Filter Press (S.S.)plate and frame type
3. Pasteuriser

4. Mixer
5. Bottle Washer
6. Bottle sealer hand operated (Manual operation)
7. Pulper (S.S.)
8. Cooking Pan (S.S)
9. Bottle filling m/c
10. Fruits and Vegetables Washing Tank (P V C)
11. Stainless Steel Tank
12. Aluminium table size 5 ft. x 10 ft.
13. Laboratory testing equipments
14. Pipes, fitings, motors, valves, pumps,
15. Baby boiler
16. Deaerator Vacuum type

RAW MATERIALS

1. Fruits of different varieties
2. Vegetables
3. Sugar
4. Spices, Salts
5. Bottles and Labels

TOTAL CAPITAL INVESTMENT

TOTAL FIXED CAPITAL	Rs. 41,06,500.00
TOTAL WORKING CAPITAL FOR 1 MONTH	Rs. 11,79,420.00
TOTAL	Rs. 52,85,920.00

TURN OVER/ANNUM

1. By sale of 60000 kgs. of Jam
2. By sale of Squash 60000 kgs.
3. Chutney 600000 kgs.
4. Pickles 60000 kgs.

TOTAL	Rs. 1,71,00,000.00

PROFIT SALES RATIO = Profit / Sales x 100 = 10.80 %

RATE OF RETURN = Operating profit / T.C.I x 100 = 34.94 %

BREAK EVEN POINT (B.E.P) = 64.67 %

23

Mango Pappad (*Aam Pappad*)

MANUFACTURING PROCESS

The manufacturing process of Mango pappad is the process of making ordinary pappad of different pulses, rice etc. in addition to mango processing and complete and thorough mixing of mango juice and other ingredients of mango pappad.

Let us start, firstly, with the mango processing. The operation is performed by mechanical equipment, however, substitution of hand operations is not precluded if the same principles are followed.

WASHING

Washing fresh mangoes accompanied one or more of the following purposes.

a) To remove soil or early substances.

b) To remove mold, yeast, bacteria and/or spores of these micro-organisms.

c) To remove insects, insect eggs, larva of fragments.

d) To remove downy or spinery portions of stzin.

e) To remove toxic and flavour or odour bearing residues of sprays and dusts.

Soak tank, into which raw mangoes are discharges, may contain cold or warm water (to 120oF) with or without addition of a harmless detergent. The time in soak tank is 2-3 minutes.

Mangoes are elevated to brush washer with transverse revolving fibre or nylon brushes which fumble the product under sprays or water on high pressure. Washed fruit is now ready for final inspection and/or trimming.

SORTING AND TRIMMING

The sorting and trimming operations remove whole units by sorting, or portions of units by trimming with knives for any one or more of the following reasons:-

a) Insect damage or insect removal.

b) Pathological damage (decay)

c) Inbedded roots or early substances.

d) Roots or other tough, inedible portion of the fruit.

e) A typical colour.

f) Mechanical injury.

PLANT ECONOMICS

Rated Plant capacity = 160.00 kgs/day

LAND AND BUILDING

1. Total Land required, 350 sq. mts.

TOTAL Rs. 16,37,500.00

PLANT AND MACHINERY

1. M.S. Kettle for washing of mangoes
2. Juice Extractor
3. Stainless Steel Juice collecting pot
4. Mixer S.S. Lining equipped
5. Miscellaneous

RAW MATERIALS

1. Ripe Mango,
2. Black Pepper,
3. Edible Soda (Sodium Bicarbonate)
4. Zeera,
5. Heeng Water,
6. Saef
7. Red Chillies
8. Miscellaneous (Packing materials)

TOTAL CAPITAL INVESTMENT

TOTAL FIXED CAPITAL	Rs. 23,72,500.00
TOTAL WORKING CAPITAL FOR 1 MONTH	Rs. 3,44,335.00
TOTAL	Rs. 27,16,835.00

TURN OVER/ANNUM

Receipt by sale of 48,000 kgs of Mango Pappad
Rs. 60,00,000.00

PROFIT SALES RATIO = Profit / Sales x 100 = 21.30 %

RATE OF RETURN = Operating profit / T.C.I x 100 = 47.05 %

BREAK EVEN POINT (B.E.P) = 54.93 %

24

Mango Pulp Processing and Canning

India is the home of mangoes. A large number of varieties are found in almost all parts of the country. According to statistics collected by the Fruit Development Adviser, Government of India, out of the total fruit acreage of 12,79,000 ha mangoes alone covered 8,19,000 ha in 1948-49 i.e. nearly 70 per cent of total area under fruits. Uttar Pradesh, Tamil Nadu, Karnataka, Bihar and West Bengal lead in mango growing.

Among the numerous varieties, 'Safaida' and 'Duschri' of U.P. 'Alphonso' of Ratnagiri, 'Badami' of Mysore, 'Benishan' of East Coast, and 'Raspuri' 'Neelam' and 'Mulgoa' of Tamil nadu and Karnataka are the most important varieties for canning. The 'Bangalora' or `Totapari' mango which is an assured and heavy annual beater, and also yields an excellent pulp or juice, is sometimes canned to give a fairly good canned product. Juicy and fibrous varieties are not quite suitable for canning. They are mostly used for making juice, squash, nectar, chutney and pickles.

MANUFACTURING PROCESS

The fruits of semi solid texture is taken and sorted by either manually or by automatic sorting machine. Then the fruits are clean water thoroughly to remove dirt, soils and other impurities sticking on the surfaces of fruits. This washing or cleaning operation is followed by automatic washing machine or manually washed. The fruits are now ready for steaming operation. By steaming operation the fruits become soft. These are now passed through a pulper machine which is power driven and comprising of a perforated cylindrical sieve and revolving wooden or metallic paddles. The pulp passing through the sieve is collected in wooden barrels. The pulp is then heated in open pan evaporator at temperature 84-88°C. Then suitable preservative such as potassium metabisulfite (sulphur dioxide) or sodiumbenzoate at about 350 PPM is added and mixed homogeneously. Then it is filled in sterilized cans, and sealed by double seaming machine. The sealed cans are pasteurized in boiling water for 15-35 minutes. After pasteurization process is complete the cans are taken out and cooled and stored in cool dry place. Mango pulp is prepared out of fully ripe mangoes. Fully ripe mangoes are peel and passed through a pulper to get fine pulp. The pulp as such are sweetened is heated to 80-85%, fulled hot in sterilized cans sealed and processed for 30 minutes in boiling mater. The cans are then cooled to 37%, dried labelled and stored. Firm Ripe mangoes that are Just developing colour are picked and ripened in straw. As they ripen, They are washed in water and peeled. The pulp obtained are placed in a 2 % common salt solution to prevent their enzymic browning . It is necessary to add 0.3 to 0.5 percent Citric Acid to the syrup for safe processing of the cans in open cookers. Now a days ,The practice is to sterilised the cans first in open corks, and then sterilize them in closed retort, at 1 to 2 pound steam pressure (psi) i e 0. 07 to 0.14 kgs per sq cm as an additional safety measure.

PLANT ECONOMICS

Rated Plant capacity = 6.67 MT/day

LAND AND BUILDING

1. Total land required 5000 sq.mts. Rs. 1,00,00,000.00

PLANT AND MACHINERY

1. BSB Reforming unit: consisting of rotary flat body reformer and hand flanger.

2. BSB Double seaming machine
3. Equipped with 1 HP,3 phase, 440 V motor and starter.
4. DK 65 Double seaming machine : can remain still semiautomatic, heavy duty, capacity about 200 cans, per hour. Equipped with 1.5 HP motor & starter, but without seaming rollers & seaming chucks.
5. Seaming chucks/rollers will be supplied at extra cost
6. BSB treadle bid embossing machine designed to emboss can lids without damaging the tin coating, without alphabets and numerals & with 2 row 6 digits die
7. Cost of alphabets and numerals
8. BSB seam checking gauge (stainless steel)
9. BSB Round can body beading machine for no. 1 Tall or A 2 1/2 cans with 1 HP 3 phase motor with 1,
10. set size of beading tools
11. BSB Rotary Fruit & Vegetable washing machine, length of drum is 8' overall length is 9.3',
12. Width = 3.3' & height = 6' 1 HP motor, capacity 2/3 tonnes per hour

RAW MATERIALS

1. Ripe mangoes
2. Preservatives like sodium benzoate
3. Cans (printed)
4. Other like sugar, salt, flavours etc.
5. Cartons

TOTAL CAPITAL INVESTMENT

TOTAL FIXED CAPITAL	Rs. 1,51,51,456.00
TOTAL WORKING CAPITAL FOR 3 MONTHS	Rs. 1,47,14,250.00
TOTAL	Rs. 2,98,65,706.00

TURN OVER/ANNUM

By sale of 40,00,000 nos Cans of Mango Pulp
Rs. 8,00,00,000.00

PROFIT SALES RATIO = Profit / Sales x 100 = 20.35 %

RATE OF RETURN = Operating profit / T.C.I x 100 = 54.51 %

BREAK EVEN POINT (B.E.P) = 33.10 %

25

Mango Powder

MANUFACTURING PROCESS

Raw material for ripe mango powder is mango which abundantly available in India every where. Manufacturing process for it is simple subdivided in following manner.

1. Washing process
2. Peeling, shorting and trimming.
3. Extraction of juice.
4. Deareation.
5. Straining, fltration and classification.
6. Preservation of juice.
   a) Pasteurisation
   b) Chemicals
   c) Sugar.
7. Drying process.

PLANT ECONOMICS OF MANGO POWDER

Rated Plant capacity = 3.00 TON/day

LAND AND BUILDING

1. Land Area 800 sq.mt. Rs. 34,00,000.00

PLANT AND MACHINERY

1. Washing Tank of Concrete
2. Storage Tank
3. Shortening and Trimming Equipments
4. Juice Extractor
5. Deareation Tank
6. Sedimentation Tank
7. Filtration Screen
8. Steam Jacketed Vessel
9. Chemical Treatment Inking Tank
10. Spray Dryers
11. Boiler
12. Packing Machine

RAW MATERIALS

1. Ripe Mango
2. Sodium Benzoate
3. Sugar

TOTAL CAPITAL INVESTMENT

TOTAL FIXED CAPITAL	Rs. 58,91,000.00
TOTAL WORKING CAPITAL FOR 1 MONTH	Rs. 29,12,531.00
TOTAL	Rs. 88,03,531.00

TURN OVER/ANNUM

By sale of 500000 kg. Ripe Mango Powder Per year Rs. 4,40,00,000.00

PROFIT SALES RATIO = Profit / Sales x 100 = 16.50 %

RATE OF RETURN = Operating profit / T.C.I x 100 =82.47 %

BREAK EVEN POINT (B.E.P) = 28.01 %

26

Mango Kernel Seed Powder (Starch)

All fruits' seed contain same valuable materials and products which are very useful in various composition like food powder, oil, some acids like malic, citric and tartaric acids in various proportion. Mango seed is one of them which contain valuable things when we analyse it. The artificial flavours that follow are used flavouring bakery goods, condiments, soft drinks and various other food products from mango seed. Flavours should be used sparingly, since they are very aromatic, odorous substance. The amount to be used per unit of food or liquid must be decided upon after experimentation. Oil soluble food colours may be added to flavours, if desired.

MANUFACTURING PROCESS

For the manufacture of kernel seed powder (starch), mango kernel seeds are taken and washed in a Rotary washer equipped with Jet spray arrangement. Washing is necessary to free the mango kernel seeds from any adhering contaminants.

After washing the mango kernel seeds are passed into Rotary Dryer to remove the water. Then temperature of drying is about 60-65°C to dispel off the moisture. Now, the dried mango seed kernels are subjected to Decortication process, for which they are passed through a Decorticator to remove the outer pericarp.

After decortication the inner mango seeds are subjected to

washing process again. Here they are washed in a Rotary Washer equipped with Jet spray arrangement. After washing operation, they are subjected to drying process in a Rotary Dryer at 60-65°C to remove the water. After drying operation, the grading of seeds is done to prepare feed for pulverizing. Grading section is the section where more kernels are separated by grading decorticated seeds. The kernels as obtained from the decorticator have about 5% of undecorticated seeds. This process of grading is carried out mechanically. Grading will thus increase the efficiency of the pulverizing step. To maintain the overall efficiency and performance of the process of manufacture of decorticated seeds from grading section are again fed to the decortication Unit.

PLANT ECONOMICS

Rated Plant capacity = 16.00 MT/day

LAND AND BUILDING

Total Land Area required Rs. 43,20,000.00

PLANT AND MACHINERY

1. Rotary washer (S.S.)
2. Decorticator
3. Crusher/Impact Grinder
4. Air Blower
5. Rotary Drier
6. Micro-pulverizer
7. Rotary Screen
8. Packing machine (Automatic)
9. Lab Testing equipments
10. Instrumentation & Process control equipments
11. Miscellaneous equipments viz. pipe fittings, pumps, motors, tools, jigs & fixtures.

RAW MATERIALS

1. Mango seeds
2. Packing material (H.D.P.E.) Woven sacks
3. Miscellaneous

TOTAL CAPITAL INVESTMENT

TOTAL FIXED CAPITAL	Rs. 81,75,000.00
TOTAL WORKING CAPITAL FOR 2 MONTHS	Rs. 86,08,710.00
TOTAL	Rs. 1,67,83,710.00

TURN OVER/ANNUM

By sale of Mango kernel seed powder (Starch)
Rs. 6,72,00,000.00

PROFIT SALES RATIO = Profit / Sales x 100 = 18.13 %

RATE OF RETURN = Operating profit / T.C.I x 100 = 72.58 %

BREAK EVEN POINT (B.E.P) = 26.30 %

117. MANUFACTURE OF TIN CONTAINERS
118. MANUFACTURE OF STORAGE TANKS, PRESSURE VESSELS, HEAT EXCHANGERS
119. MARK II HAND PUMPS
120. MARUTI WORKSHOP CUM - SERVICE STATION
121. MECHANICAL JACKS
122. METAL CUTTING DIE DESIGN
123. METAL CUTTING OF AND GRINDING WHEELS (ABBRASIVE CUTTING WHEELS)
124. METAL HOOKS & CLIPS
125. METAL SEPARATION (COPPER, TIN, LEAD) FROM SPENT WASH ACID
126. METALLIC RING JOINTS
127. METALLIC GASKET (SPIRAL WOUND)
128. MICROVEE & ABSOLUTE FILTER
129. MICROWAVE OVEN
130. MILD STEEL INGOTS
131. MINI STEEL PLANT
132. MODERN VEHICLE WORKSHOP
133. MOPED
134. M.S.HINGES
135. M.S.INGOT AND HR. STEEL STRUCTURALS
136 M.S.INGOT BY INDUCTION FURNACES
137. M.S.PIPES
138. M.S. WELDING ELECTRODE
139. MUFFLERS & SILENCERS FOR THREE WHEELERS
140. NAIL CUTTER WITH FILER & MANICURE
141. NICHROME WIRE
142. NICKEL LINED SCREENS
143. NON-FERROUS ALLOY ROLLING
144. NON-FERROUS FORGING
145. NON-FERROUS FOUNDRY
146. NON PRESSURE
147. INCANDESCENT LAMP
148. NUMBER COMBINATION LOCKS FOR LUGGAGES
149. NUTS & BOLTS
150. PAPER COATED ALUMINIUM AND COPPER WIRE
151. PETROMAX CONTAINER
152. PHOTO ETCHING OF STAINLESS STEEL PLATES
153. PIPE GALVANIZING PLANT
154. PISTON RING-AUTOMOBILE
155. PLANT PROTECTION EQUIPMENTS
156. PLATINUM LABORATORY APPARATUS
157. PRESSURE COOKER & ALUMINIUM UTENSILS
158. PRESSURE COOKER (ALUMINIUM)
159. PRESSURE DIE CASTING
160. PRINTED ALUMINIUM COLLAPSIBLE TUBES
161. PRINTED TIN CONTAINERS
162. PRINTING PRESS (CYLINDER MACHINE)
163. PUMPS FOR CHEMICAL INDUSTRY (SPECIAL)
164. RAILWAY SLEEPERS (M.S.)
165. RAZOR TWIN BLADE
166. R.C.C SPUN PIPES
167. RECONDITIONING OF M.S. DRUMS/BARRELS
168. RE-ROLLING COPPER AND BRASS SHEET AND RODS
169. RE-ROLLING MILLS
170. RESIN COATED SAND
171. RESIN CORED SOFT SOLDER WIRES
172. ROLLING MILL (BY INDUCTION FURNACE) & MANUFACTURE OF BARS, ANGLES, SQUARES, TUBES AND OTHERS
173. ROLLER BEARING & FORGING
174. ROLLING OF STAINLESS STEEL PATTA
175. RUBBER INSULATED PLIERS (HAND TOOLS)
176. RUBBING COMPOUND FOR AUTOMOBILES
177. SCIENTIFIC LABORATORY EQUIPMENTS
178. SCOOTER ASSEMBLING
179. SECONDARY LEAD EXTRAC -TION BY SCRAP BATTERY PLATES,PIPES & SHEET
180. SEAMLESS M.S. TUBES & PIPES
181. SELF TAPPING STEEL SCREW
182. SEWING NEEDLES
183. S.G. IRON & ALLOY STEEL
184. SHEET METAL PRODUCTS, (FERROUS/NON-FERROUS)
185. SHIP/MARINE CONTAINER
186. SHOCK ABSORBERS
187. SHOE EYELETS
188. SHOT AND GRITS BY AUTOMIZATION PROCESS
189. SHOVELS
190. SILICO MANGANESE ALLOYS
191. SILENCERS (MUFFLERS) EXHAUST & TAIL PIPE FOR ALL TYPES OF VEHICLES
192. SINTERED BEARING
193. SINTERED BUSHES
194. SINTERED METAL PRODUCTS
195. SOFT AND HARD FERRITES
196. SPANNERS
197. SPARK PLUGS
198. STEEL PLANT (ELECTRIC ARC FURNACE BASED- EAF)
199. SPHERIODAL GRAPHITE CAST IRON
200. SPRAY DRYER
201. STAINLESS STEEL HINGES
202. STAINLESS STEEL SHEET ROLLING TO PRODUCE STAINLESS STEEL UTENSILS
203. STAINLESS STEEL UTENSILS
204. STAPLE PINS,PAPER PIN, GEM CLIPS ETC.
205. STEEL CASTINGS
206. STEEL CHAIN
207. STEEL FOUNDRY
208. STEEL FURNITURES AND ELECTRICAL APPLIANCES
209. STEEL PLANT (MINI)
210. STEEL RODS AND COILS FROM SCRAPS
211. STEEL ROLLING MILL
212. STEEL STRIPS (COLD ROLLED) SILICON WITH GRAIN RIENTED FOR ELECTRIC USE
213. STEEL TRANSMISSION LINE TOWERS & ROLLING MILL TO PRODUCE STEEL SECTION
214. STEEL FURNITURES AND ELECTRICAL APPLIANCES
215. STEEL WIRE DRAWING AND GALVANIZING
216. STEEL WOOL
217. SUBMERGED ARC WELDED PIPES
218. SUBMERSIBLE PUMP MANUFACTURING
219. SUPER ENAMELLED COPPER WIRE
220. THREE WHEELERS
221. TIE-ROD ENDS
222. TIN CONTAINERS
223. TOOLROOM AND SHEET METAL PRODUCTS
224. TRACTOR TRAILERS
225. TRANSMISSION POWER FITTING
226. TUBULAR POLES
227. SUPER ENAMELLED COPPER WIRES
228. TUBULAR POLES FOR ELECTRICAL TRANSMISSION (BY FABRICATION PROCESS)
229. TUBULAR POLES OF M.S. & HIGH TENSILE STEEL
230. VACUUM CLEANERS
231. VACUUM FLASK (STAINLESS STEEL)
232. VALVES FOR REFRIGERA TION AND AIR-CONDITION
233. VEHICLE WELDING & PAINTING
234. VENETION BLIND
235. WASHING MACHINES (AUTOMATIC & COMPUTERISED)
236. WATER CONTROLLER (AUTOMATIC)
237. WATCH STRAPS/CHAINS/ BRACELETS/BELT BRASS & STAINLESS STEEL
238. WATER COOLERS
239. WELDED WIRE MESH
240. WELDING ELECTRODES
241. WICK STOVES
242. WIND MILL WINDOW FRAME (FERROUS & NON-FERROUS)
243. WRIST WATCH

359. DI ETHYL OXALATE
360. DI METHYL ORTHOPHTHALATE
361. DI-METHYL PHTHALATE
362. DICLOFENAC GEL
363. DIOCTYL PHTHALATE (DOP)
364. DI PHENYL GLYCERINE
365. DI PHENYL OXIDE
366. DINITRO-CHLORO BENZENE
367. DISTILLED WATER
368. DODECYL BENZENE SULPHONATE
369. DUSTLESS CHALK
370. EDTA & ITS SALTS
371. ELECTROLESS NICKEL PLATING ON PLASTICS
372. ENDOSULFAN
373. EPOXY RESIN BASED COMPOUND
374. ETHYL ACETATE
375. EHTYL ETHER
376. ETHYL ALCOHOL (POTABLE LIQUOR)
377. ETHYL HEXANOL
378. EXTRACTION OF ESSENTIAL OILS BY SUGAR CRITICAL FLUID (CARBON DIOXIDE) METHOD FROM FLOWERS, HERBAL & SPICES
379. FERRIC ALUM
380. FERRO CHROME LIGNO SULPHONATE
381. FERRO MANGANESE
382. FERRO SILICONE
383. FERRO VANADIUM FROM VANADIUM SLUDGE
384. FERROUS SILICATE
385. FERROUS SULPHATE
386. FERTILIZER FROM ANIMAL BLOOD & LEATHER WASTE
387. FLUORESCENT TUBE LIGHT POWDER
388. FOAMED PVC COMPOUNDING & ITS PRODUCTS
389. FORMALDEHYDE
390. FRACTIONAL DISTILLATION OF D.M.O (DEMENTHOLIZED OIL)
391. FRACTIONAL DISTILLATION OF ESSENTIAL OIL & MEDICINAL PLANT EXTRACT
392. FRICTION DUST (LIQUID & POWDER) FROM CNSL
393. FRUIT FLAVOURS
394. FURFURAL FROM RICE HUSK
395. GARLIC ACID
396. GASKET SHELLAC COMPOUND
397. GEAR OIL
398. GIBBERELLIC ACID
399. GLASS PUTTY
400. GLYCERINE
401. GOSSYPOL (POLY PHENOL) FROM COTTON SEED OIL
402. GUAR GUM POWDER
403. HAIR FIXER (HAIR GEL TYPE)
404. H - ACID
405. HENNA PASTE MAKING
406. HEPTAL DEHYDE
407. HIGH CARBON FERRO CHROME
408. HYDRATED CALCIUM SILICATE BRICK
409. HYDRATED LIME FROM SEA SHELL
410. HYDROCHLORIC ACID
411. HYDRO FLUORIC ACID
412. HYDROGEN PEROXIDE (BY AUTO-OXIDATION PROCESS)
413. ICE PACKS (SOLUTIONS TYPE, WHITE GEL TYPE, VIOLET SEMI SOLID POLYMER TYPE)
414. IMPROVING DROP POINT PARAFFIN WAX FROM 45-50^{0}C TO 75-80^{0}C
415. INDUSTRIAL ALCOHOL
416. INTEGERATED COMPLEX OF EASTER & ALLIED PRODUCTS (D.O.P, D.B.P, ETHYL ACETATE WIRE ENAMEL & CABLE JELLY)
417. IMFL (WHISKY) & COUNTRY LIQUOR
418. IRON OXIDE FOR MAKING FERITTE
419. IRON SULPHIDE
420. JUTE BATCHING OIL
421. KESH KALA TEL (HAIR DYE LOTION) (VASMOL 33, BLACK NITE TYPE)
422. L-LYSINE MONOHYDROCHLORIDE
423. LACTIC ACID FROM WHITE SUGAR BY FERMENTATION PROCESS
424. LDPE GRANULES FROM VIRGIN (LDPE RESIN)
425. LEAD EXTRACTION FROM BATTERY SCRAP
426. LEAD OXIDE (A) LEAD MONOXIDE (B) LEAD TETRA OXIDE (C) GREYLEAD OXIDE
427. LIQUID GLUCOSE & ITS BY PRODUCTS
428. LIQUID OXYGEN BOTTLING PLANT
429. LIQUID SHOE POLISH
430. LIQUID FLOOR POLISH
431. LUBE OIL VISCOSITY IMPROVED FOR P.P.G/P.E.G
432. LUBRICANTS ASHLESS 100% COMBUSTION
433. MAGNESIUM CARBONATE AND MAGNESIUM BICARMONATE
434. MAGNESIUM HYDROXIDE POWDER
435. MAGNESIUM SILICATE
436. MAGNESIUM SULPHATE
437. MALACHITE GREEN
438. MALEIC ANHYDRIDE
439. MANGANESE SULPHATE
440. MANUFACTURING OF CARBON MONO-OXIDE WATER GAS
441. MENTHOL BOLD CRYSTALS FROM FLAKES
442. MENTHOL CRYSTAL & MENTHA OIL
443. MERCURIC OXIDE
444. METAL PRE-TREATMENT CHEMICALS
445. METHANE GAS BY SODIUM ACETATE & SODA LIME
446. METHYL ACETYL RICINOLATE
447. METOL
448. METOL FROM HYDROQUINONE & METHYLAMINE
449. MICANITE
450. MICRO NUTRIENT MIXTURE
451. MINERAL WATER
452. MINERAL WATER AND PET BOTTILNG PLANT
453. MINERAL WATER IN BOTTLES, GLASS AND POUCHES
454. MINI CEMENT PLANT (BY ROTARY KILN PROCESS)
455. MIXED FERTILIZER
456. MOSQUITO & FLIES REPELLENT AGARBATTI (INCENSE STICKS)
457. MONO CHLORO ACETIC ACID
458. MONOCROTOPHOS (TECHNICAL)
459. MOSQUITO COIL
460. MOSQUITO COIL & MAT
461. MOSQUITO MAT
462. MOTHER TINCTURE & BIO CHEMIC MEDICINES
463. NAPHTHALENE & PHENYL (INTEGRATED UNIT)
464. NATURAL MINERAL WATER BY REVERSE OSMOSIS PROCESS
465. NICKEL PLATING BRIGHTNER (PRIMARY OR CARRIER BRIGHTNER & SECONDARY BRIGHTNER)
466. NICKEL SULPHATE
467. NICOTINE FROM TOBACCO WASTE
468. NICOTINE SULPHATE FROM TOBACCO WASTE
469. NITRO BENZENE
470. NITRO CELLULOSE SANDING SEALER/LACQUER
471. NITRO MUSK
472. NITROGEN & OXYGEN GAS PLANT
473. NON-IONIC SURFACTANT (WETTING AGENT)
474. NO-CARB PASTE
475. OCTANOL
476. ORTHO NITRO PHENOL
477. OXALIC ACID FROM MOLASSES
478. OXALIC ACID FROMRICE HUSK
479. OXALIC ACID FROM TREE BARK
470. OXALIC ACID FROM WASTE VEGETABLES
471. OXYGEN GAS PLANT
472. OXYGEN GAS PLANT (AIR SEPERATION METHOD)
473. PARA-AMINO BENZOIC ACID
474. PARA-AMINO PHENOL
475. PARA TOLUENE SULPHONIC ACID
476. PECTIN FROM RAW PAPAYA
477. PERFUME (LEMON & OTHERS)

Pay Rs. 8,000/- Only

for Tailor made Report We (EIRI) are fully capable to prepare any report as per your requirements

478. PESTICIDE PREPARATION USING NEEM FRUIT & SEEDS (MARGOSA)
479. PET BOTTLES FROM PRE-FORM
480. PET PREFORM FROM RESIN FOR PET BOTTLES
481. PETROLEUM JELLY
482. PHENOL
483. PHENYL
484. PHENYL (BLACK) IN LIQUID FORM
485. PHTHALIC ANHYDRIDE
486. PHOSPHORIC ACID FROM ROCK PHOSPHATE
487. PHOSPHORUS BY CHEMICAL PROCESS
488. PHOTO EMULSION FOR ROTARY SCREEN PRINTING
489. PHTHALOCYANINE BLUE
480. PIGMENT EMULSION FOR TEXTILE
481. PIGMENT GUM
482. PLANT GROWTH REAGEN BASED CHLOROTHYL TRIMETHYL AMMONIUM CHLORIDE
483. PLANT HARMONES BASED ON 2,4-DICHLORPHENOXY ACENTIC ACID & NAPHTHALENE
484. PLASTICINE (MODELLING CLAY)
485. PLASTIC WASTE REPROCESSING
486. PLASTER OF PARIS BANDAGES
487. POLYESTER RESIN (G.P. GRADE LAMINATE GRADE, ELECTRICAL GRADE)
488. POLY VINYL ACETATE
489. POLYVINYL ACETATE EMULSION
490. POLYURETHENE FOAM
491. POTASSIUM DICHROMATE/ BICHROMATE
492. POTASSIUM IODATE
493. POTASSIUM NITRATE
494. POTASSIUM PERMAGNATE
495. POTASSIUM PER SULPHATE
496. POTASSIUM SULPHATE (FERTILIZER GRADE)
497. POTASSIUM PER OXY DI-SULPHIDE
498. POTASSIUM SILICATE
499. POTASSIUM STEARATE
500. POWER ALCOHOL
501. PVC RESIN FROM ETHYL ALCOHOL
502. PYRIDINE & ITS DERIVATIVES
503. RAPID FAST DYES (ONLY PROCESS)
504. REACTOR (CHEMICAL)
505. RECLAMATION OF USED ENGINE OIL (BY CLAY & VACUUM DISTILLATION PROCESS)
506. RECLAMATION OF SPENT BLEACHING EARTH
507. RECLAMATION OF NICKEL SPENT CATALYST FROM VANASPATI INDUSTRY
508. RECTIFIED SPIRIT FROM MOLASSES & MAHUA FLOWERS
509. RECTIFIED SPIRIT FROM RICE STRAW
510. RED OXIDE PAINT/PRIMER (ANTI CORROSIVE) BASED ORGANIC RED PIGMENTS
511. REMOVAL OF ANTIMONY FROM LEAD SCRAP
512. RESORCINOL
513. ROSIN SIZING AGENT
514. RESORCINOL
515. SALINE AND INJECTION WATER
516. SALICYLIC ACID
517. SANTONIN
518. SENNOSIDES FROM SENNO LEAF
519. SHOE POLISH
520. SILICA GEL (BLUE SELF INDICATING PROCESS)
521. SILICONE EMULSION
522. SILICONE FROM RICE HUSK
523. SILICON FROM SILICA (SEMI CONDUCTOR GRADE)
524. SILICONE RESINS
525. SILICONE SPRAYSILVER BRAZING FOIL
526. SILVER EXTRACTION FROM WASTE HYPO SOLUTION
527. SILVER NITRATE
528. SILVER PARTS FOR CERAMIC CAPACITOR SINGLE SUPER PHOSPHATE & MIXED FERTILIZER (NPK)
529. SINGLE SUPER PHOSPHATE (S.S.P) & SULPHURIC ACID
530. SODA ASH
531. SODA ASH FROM NATRON
532. SODA WATER BOTTLING PLANT (CARBONATED BEVERAGE)
533. SODIUM ALUMINATE
534. SODIUM BI-CARBONATE (BAKING SODA) FROM SODA ASH
535. SODIUM CHLORITE
536. SODIUM CHROMATE SODIUM CYCLAMATE
537. SODIUM DI-CHROMATE
538. SODIUM DI-CHROMATE & SODIUM SULPHATE AS BYE PRODUCTS
539. SODIUM HEXA META PHOSPHATE
540. SODIUM HYDROSULFITE
541. SODIUM HYPO CHLORIDE (BLEACH LIQUOR)
542. SODIUM ISO-PROPYL XANTHATE
543. SODIUM LAURYL SULPHATE
544. SODIUM LAURYL SULPHATE & SODIUM LAURYL ETHER SULPHATE
545. SODIUM NITRATE
546. SODIUM PETROLEUM SULPHONATE (EMULSIFIER)
547. SODIUM SILICATE FROM SILICA & SODA ASH
548. SODIUM SILICATE FROM (1) PADDY SILK HUSK 2) & SILICA
549. SODIUM CARBONATE & SILICA
550. SODIUM SULPHATE
551. SODIUM SULPHIDE BY BARIUM SULPHATE PROCESS
552. SODIUM SULPHIDE FROM AMMONIA & SODIUM CHLORIDE
553. SODIUM SULPHITE
554. SODIUM TRI-POLY PHOSPHATE
555. SOFTENER (CATIONIC ANIONIC & NON-IONIC)
556. SPIRIT FROM PINE APPLE
557. STANNOUS CHLORIDE
558. STEARIC ACID
559. STEARATES MANUFACTURE (CALCIUM, ZINC, ALUMINIUM, MAGNESIUM STEARATES)
560. SULPHUR FROM PYRITES & SLAG
561. SULPHUR CRYSTALS/LUMPS
562. SULPHURIC ACID
563. SULPHURIC ACID FROM DCDA PROCESS
564. SUPER PHOSPHATE (S.S.P)
565. SYNTHETIC IRON OXIDE (YELLOW)
566. SYNTHETIC RED & WELLOW IRON OXIDE FROM IRON FILLING & PICKLE LIQUOR
567. TARTARIC ACID
568. TOILET CLEANER
569. TOLUENE AND SBP FROM

"Detailed Project Report" Payable in advance through Draft/Cash/M.O. in favour of *"ENGINEERS INDIA RESEARCH INSTITUTE"*. 4449, Nai Sarak (D), Main Road Delhi - 110 006 (INDIA) ● Ph : 23918117, 2391 6431, 2384 0361 ● Mob : 098114 37895 ●Fax : 91-11- 2391 6431 ●E-Mail : eirisidi@bol.net.in ● WebSite : www.eiriindia.org

CRUDE NAPHTHA
570. TRIMETHYL AMMONIUM CHLORIDE
571. TRIPHENYL PHOSPHITE (T.P.P)
572. ULTRAMARINE BLUE (LIQUID)
573. UREA FORMALDEHYDE & MELAMINE FORMALDEHYDE POWDER
574. UNDECYLINIC ACID
575. VINYL ACETATE MONOMER
576. VITAMIN C
577. VITAMIN E
578. WASTE WATER TREATMENT PLANT FOR INDUSTRIAL SECTOR IN INDIA (ONLY MARKER SURVEY)
579. WIRE DRAWING LUBRICANT
580. WIRE ENAMEL
581. XANTHATES
582. YELLOW DEXTRIN
583. ZINC CHLORIDE
584. ZINC OXIDE
585. ZINC PHOSPHATING BY COLD PROCESS
586. ZINC SILICATE
587. ZINC STEARATE
588. ZINC SULPHATE
589. ZINC SULPHATE MONOHYDRATE
590. ACID BLACK
591. AURAMINE'O'
592. AZO DYES STUFF
593. DYE & DYE INTERMEDIATE
594. DYE INTERMEDIATES
595. MALACHITE GREEN
596. METHYLENE BLUE
597. PHTHALOCYANINE BLUE
598. PHTHALOCYANINE BLUE & GREEN
599. REACTIVE DYES
600. SULPHUR BLACK DYE
601. VAT DYES
602. WATER CHILLING PLANT
603. WADDING OIL (100%) FOR WADDING OF COTTON HOSIERY CLOTH IN THE DYEING PROCESS
604. WHITE OIL
605. WAX FLOOR POLISH

ELECTRICAL, ELECTONICS, COMPUTERS AND INFOTECH/IT PROJECTS

606. AIR CONDITIONING
607. ALUMINIUM ALLOY CONDUCTOR
608. ALUMINIUM CABLE
609. ALUMINIUM ELECTROYTIC CAPACITORS
610. AUDIO CASSETTE ASSEMBLING & RECORDING
611. AUDIO CASSETTES DUPLICATING RECORDING
612. AUDIO CASSETTES & AUDIO STUDIO
613. AUDIO CASSETTES PLANE & RECORDED
614. AUDIO MAGNETIC HEADS
615. AUDIO MAGNETIC TAPE
616. AUDIO/VIDEO CASSETTES
617. AUTO BULB/LAMPS
618. AUTOMATIC VOLTAGE STABILIZER
619. BATTERY PLATES
620. BACK OFFICE (Rs. 5000/-)
621. B/W TV & COMPUTER MONITOR PICTURE TUBE
622. BREAD BOARDS
623. CALL CENTRE
624. CAMERA (35 MM)
625. CAPACITORS
626. CARBON ELECTRODE USED FOR BATTERY CELL
627. CARBON POTETIOMETERS
628. CEILING FAN
629. CERAMIC INSULATOR
630. CHILDREN INFOTECH TRAINING INSTITUTE (Rs. 5000/-)
631. CHOKE AND PATTI
632. CHOKE AND STARTER
633. CHOKE USED FOR FLUORESCENT LAMPS
634. COLOUR TELEVISION
635. COLOUR AND BLACK & WHITE TELEVISION
636. COMPACT DISC
637. COMPACT DISC PLAYER (AUDIO/VIDEO)
638. COMPUTER EDUCATION INSTITUTE
639. COMPUTER ASSEMBLY
640. COMPUTER HARDWARE
641. COMPUTER KEYBOARD
642. COMPUTER PERIPHERALS
643. COMPUTER PRINTERS
644. COMPUTER RIBBON
645. COMPUTER RIBBON REINKING OR REFILLING
646. COMPUTER STATIONERY
647. COMPUTER STATIONERY &

IMPORTED HARDWARE PARTS
648. COMPUTER TERMINALS
649. COMPUTERISED WASHING MACHINE (AUTOMATIC)
650. COMPUTER SOFTWARE
651. CONDENSER FOR MOTOR USING MPP FILM
652. CONTENT DEVELOPMENT CENTRE (EOU) (Rs. 5000/-)
653. CONTROL PANEL BOARD
654. COOLING COIL FOR AIR CONDITIONERS
655. COPPER STRIP COIL FROM SCRAP
656. CORDLESS TELEPHONES
657. CYBER CAFE
658. CYBERKIOSK (Rs. 5000/-)
659. DATA PROCESSING CENTRE (Rs. 5000/-)
660. D.C. MICRO MOTORS
661. D.G.SETS
662. DISH ANTENNA AND CABLE T.V. NETWORK EQUIPMENT
663. DISTRIBUTION TRANSFORMERS & REPAIRS
664. DOMESTIC ELECTRICAL APPLIANCES- ROOM COOLER, WASHING MACHINE, WATER HEATER, ELECTRIC ROOM HEATER
665. E-SCHOOL
666. E-COMMERCE/BUSINESS
667. ELECTRIC ENERGY METER
668. ELECTRIC FANS
669. ELECTRIC HORN FOR AUTOMOBILE
670. ELECTRIC LAMP/GLS (INCANDESCENT LAMP)
671. ELECTRIC MIXER
672. ELECTRIC MOTORS UP TO 10 HP. REWINDING OF ALL TYPES OF MOTORS WATER PUMPS
673. ELECTRIC MOTOR WINDING (FOR FAN, MIXIES, ETC.)
674. ELECTRIC STEAM IRON
675. ELECTRICAL APPLIANCES
676. ELECTRICAL FIXTURES
677. ELECTRICAL STAMPING
678. ELECTROLYTIC CAPACITORS
679. ELECTROMAGNETIC RELAY
680. ELECTRONIC BALAST/CHOK
681. ELECTRICAL CHOKE
682. ELECTRONIC DIGITAL WATCHES
683. ELECTRONIC DIGITAL WEIGHING MACHINE
684. ELECTRONIC FIRE ALARM
685. ELECTRONIC GAS STOVE LIGHTERS
686. ELECTRONIC PRESSURE INDICATORS, ELECTRICALS, ELECTRONIC LIQUID LEVEL INDICATORS, ELECTRONIC TEMPERATURE INDICATOR, DIGITAL TACHOMETER
687. ELECTRONIC TELEPHONE INSTRUMENTS
688. ELECTRONIC TOYS
689. ELECTRONIC WATCHES & CLOCKS
690. FAX MACHINES
691. F.H.P MOTORS
692. FLOPPY DISKETTES
693. FLUORESCENT LAMP STARTER
694. FLUORESCENT TUBULAR

LAMPS WITH INTRODUCTION TO MERCURY VAPOUR LAMP
695. FRANCHISEE COMPUTER EDUCATION CENTRE (Rs. 5000)
696. GAS DETECTOR (L.P.G)
697. GENERATOR SET & PUMP SETS
698. GENERATOR (BATTERY OPERATED)
699. GIS SERVICE CENTRE (GEOGRAPHICAL INFORMATION SYSTEMS)
700. HARDWARE FITTING FOR TRANSMISSION LINE OVERHEAD LINE MATERIAL
701. HEADERS FOR TRANSISTOR ICS SEMI CONDUCTOR
702. H.T & L.T INSULATORS
703. H.T & M.V INDUSTRIAL CUBICAL SWITCH BOARD
704. INFORMATION MOVING DISPLAY (L.E.D TYPE)
705. INSURANCE CLAIM PROCESSING CENTRE (EOU) (Rs. 5000/-)
706. INTEGRATED CIRCUITS
707. INTERNET BASED STOCK TRADING (Rs. 5000/-)
708. INTERNET SERVICE PROVIDER (I.S.P.)
709. JELLY FILLED TELEPHONE CABLES
710 LAP TOP COMPUTERS
711. LEAD ACID BATTERIES
712. LEAD ACID BATTERY PLATES AND ASSEMBLING OF BATTERY
713. LEGAL TRANSCRIPTION & SECRETARIAL SERVICES CENTER (EOU)(Rs. 5000/-)
714. LIGHT EMITTING DIODES (L.E.D)
715. LINEAR ICS TRAINER KIT
716. LOUD SPEAKER
717. L.T TRANSFORMER REPAIRING
718. MEDICAL TRANSCRIPTION CENTRE
719. METAL FILM RESISTORS
720. METALLISED POLYPROPYLENE, POLYESTER FILM CAPACITOR
721. MICA BASE ELECTRONIC COMPONENTS
722. MICA PAPER WASTE PAPER FROM MICA WASTE
723. MICRO PROCESSORS TRAINER KITS BASED ON MICRO PROCESSORS
724. MINI COMPUTER (PERSONAL COMPUTER)
725. MINIATURE CIRCUIT BREAKER (M.C.B)
726. MINIATURE WATCH BATTERIES (BUTTON CELL)
727. MIXER/GRINDER (MIXI)
728. MONO CHROME COMPUTER MONITOR
729. MOTOR START ELECTROLYTIC CAPACITOR
730. MULTI LAYER P.C.B
731. MULTIPLE RELAY FOR LOW VOLTAGE
732. NEON INDICATOR
733. NEON SIGN MANUFACTURE
734. OPTICAL FIBRE CABLES
735. ON LINE SHOPPING MALL (Rs. 5000/-)
736. OPTO MECHANICAL & ELECTRICAL EQUIPMENTS
737. PHOTO COLOUR LAB
738. PICTURE TUBE (B/W)
739. PLAIN PAPER COPIER
740. PLASTIC FILM CAPACITORS
741. POLYESTER CAPACITORS
742. PORTABLE GENERATOR SET
743. PORTAL
744. PORTABLE TELEVISION(TV)
745. POWER CAPACITORS
746. POWER INVERTERS
747. POWER PLANT
748. POWER TRANSFORMERS UP TO 600 KVA
749. PRINTED CIRCUIT BOARD
750. PVC WIRES & CABLES
751. RE-CONDITIONING OF PICTURE TUBE
752. RESIN CAST CT & PT (1 KV)
753. SEMI CONDUCTOR DEVICE
754. SEMI CONDUCTORS FOR TRANSISTORS & DIODES
755. SETTING UP OF A VIDEO STUDIO
756. SMOKE DETECTORS
757. SOLAR CELLS
758. SOLAR MODULES
759. SOLAR PHOTO VOLTAIC SYSTEM
760. SOLDER FLUXES
761. SOLAR WATER HEATING PANELS
762. STEEL FURNITURE & ELECTRICAL APPLIANCES
763. STEREO AMPLIFIERS
764. STEREO CASSETTE RECORDERS/PLAYERS
765. STREET LIGHT FITTINGS SURGE SUPPRESSOR
766. TANTALUM CAPACITORS
767. TEFLON COATED ELECTRIC CABLE
768. TELEMEDICINE (DISTANCE HEALTH CARE) (Rs. 5000/-)
769. TELEPHONE CORD/CABLE
770. TELEPHONE (PUSH BUTTON TYPE)
771. TELEPHONE (PUSH BUTTON & CORDLESS)
772. TELEVISION (CTV & B/W)
773. TELEVISION (3-D)
774. TELEVISION DEFLECTION COMPONENTS
775. TELEVISION SIGNAL BOOSTERS
776. TELEVISION TUNERS
777. TRACTION BATTERIES
778. TRAINING INSTITUTE OF MEDICAL TRANSCRIPTION
779. TRANSFORMER FOR B/W TV
780. TRANSFORMER FOR VOLTAGE STABILIZER & E.H.T
781. TRANSMISSION POWER LINE FITTING
782. TRANSMISSION TOWER FITTING
783. TV AUDIO EQUIPMENT CABINETS & THEIR ASSEMBLING UNIT
784. UN-INTERRUPTED POWER SUPPLY (U.P.S)
785. VARIABLE FREQUENCY
786. VARIABLE VOLTAGE A.C. DRIVE
787. VIDEO CASSETTES (COMPLETE MANUFACTURING & ASSEMBLING)
788. VIDEO CASSETTES RECORDER (V.C.R)
789. VIDEO FILM STUDIO
790. VOLTAGE REGULATOR FOR AUTOMOBILES
791. VOLTAGE STABILIZERS
792. VOLTAGE STABLIZER & T.V. GAIN BOOSTER
793. WAX AND CHEMICAL COATED, BRAIDED TINSEL WIRE
794. WEBSITE DESIGN & E-MAIL REGISTERING
795. WELDING ELECTRODES
796. WIND ENERGY POWER PROJECT (10 MW) WIRE WOUND POTENTIOMETERS

FOOD, AGRO FOOD, PROCESSED FOOD, AGRO PLANTATION, CULTIVATION, FARMING, DAIRY/MILK, TOBACCO/PAN MASALA, BREWERY & DISTILLERY, EDIBLE OILS, EOU FOOD PRODUCTS AND ALLIED PRODUCTS

797. ALCOHOLIC BEVERAGES & VENEGAR FROM COCONUT WATER
798. ALCOHOL DRINKS FROM ETHYL ALCOHOL BY MIXING OF VARIOUS FLAVOURS
799. ANTI SCALE COMPOUND FOR ADDING INTO SUGAR JUICE BOILING
800. APPLE JUICE CONCENTRATED & DEHYDRATED FRUIT & VEGETABLES
801. ARTIFICIAL FISH MEAL FOR POULTRY FEED
802. AUTOMATIC BISCUIT PLANT
803. BABY CEREAL FOOD AND MILK POWDER
804. BACTERIA FOR CANE JUICE
805. BAKER'S YEAST
806. BAKERY INDUSTRY
807. BANANA PUREE
808. BEER & WINE
809. BEER PLANT (BREWERY)
810. BIDI
811. BIDI & CIGARETTE
812. BISCUIT PLANT

813. BREAD (AUTOMATIC PLANT)
814. BLACK PEPPER (SPICES)
815. BREAD AND BISCUITS
816. BREEDING FARM
817. BROILER CHICKEN
819. BUTTON MUSHROOM CULTIVATION & PROCESSING
820. CANNING OF RASAGULLAS IN METAL CANS
821. CAFFEIN FROM TEA WASTE
822. CANNING OF FRUITS & VEGETABLES
823. CASEIN AND BY-PRODUCTS
824. CASHEW FRUIT JUICE FROM CASHEW FRUIT APPLE
825. CASHEWNUT KERNEL EXTRACTION FROM CASHEWNUT FRUIT
826. CASHEWNUT SHELL LIQUID & KERNEL PROCESSING
827. CASHEW FENI
828. CATECHEU (BY CHEMICAL PROCESS)
829. CATTLE FEED FROM TAPIOCA
830. CHEWING & BUBBLE GUM
831. CHICKEN/SHEEP MEAT PROCESSING
832. CHOCOLATE (MILK)
833. CIGARETTE AND BEEDIES
834. COCOA BUTTER FROM COCOA MASS
835. COCONUT PRODUCTS & BY PRODUCTS PROCESS COMPLEX
836. COLD/SOFT DRINKS
837. COLLECTION OF MILK AND MILK MAKING POWDER
838. COLLECTION OF MILK AND PACKING IN POLYTHENE POUCH (1/2 KG. 1 KG. & 2 KG.)
839. CONDENSED MILK (SWEETNED)
840. CONFECTIONERY INDUSTRY (TOFFEE & CANDY, SEMI-AUTOMATIC PLANT)
841. COUNTRY LIQUOR FROM MOLASSES
842. CIGARETTE
843. DAIRY FARM AND DAIRY (MILK) PRODUCTS (PASTEURISED MILK, BUTTER, GHEE, PANEER)
844. DAIRY FARM TO PRODUCE MILK & PACKING IN POUCHES (50%) & CAN(50%)
845. DAIRY FOR MILK PROCESSING
846. DAIRY FARM (BUFALO)
847. DAL (PULSE) MILL UNIT
848. DEHYDRATION OF CARROT & GARLIC
849. DEHYDRATION & CANNING OF FRUITS & VEGETABLES
850. DEHYDRATION OF FIGS
851. DEHYDRATION OF FRUITS AND VEGETABLES
852. DEHYDRATED ONIONS AND ONION POWDER
853. DRY ICE BY BREAKING OF AIR
854. DRYING OF RED CHILLIES, HALDI, DHANIA, AND GREEN PEAS
855. EGG POWDER (40,000 EGGS PROCESSING PER DAY)
856. EXPORT OF PROCESSED FOODS AND MARINE PRODUCTS
857. FISH CANNING & POUCHING
859. FISH FARMING (PRAWN & OTHER MARINE PRODUCTS)
860. FISH MEAL
861. FLOUR MILL AND MUSTARD OIL
862. FOOD COLOUR & ORASTED GROUNDNUT GRAM PEAS, ETC IN POUCHES
863. FROG LEGS PROCESSING
864. FROZEN MEATS PROCESSING
865. FOOD FLAVOURS (WHISKY) VODKA, GRAPE, BUTTER SCOTCH)
866. FOOD PRODUCTS COMPLEX (DEHYDRATED ONIONS, GARLIC POWDER & FLAKES, CATTLE FEED, TOMATO POWDER, TOMATO PRODUCTS, CANNED FRUITS & VEGETABLES, TOMATO PURE, GROUN NUT OIL, REFIND OIL, DEHYDRATED GRAPES, BANANA POWDER & WAFFERS)
867. FRUIT JUICE, JAM, JELLIES & ALLIED PRODUCTS
868. FRUIT JUICE, PICKLES PROCESSING AND CANNING
869. FRUIT JUICE MAKING & PACKING IN PLASTIC CONTAINER/POUCHES
870. FRUIT PROCESSING (JAM & JELLIES)
871. FRUIT PULP & JUICE CONCENTRATES
872. FRUIT & VEGETABLE DRYING (FREEZE DRYING METHOD)
873. GOAT & SHEEP FARMING
874. GRAM DALL/PULSE MILL
875. GRAPE DEHYDRATION
876. HARD BOILED CANDY (TOFFEE & CANDY)
877. HERBAL CIGARETTES
878. HONEY PROCESSING & PACKAGING
879. ICE CREAM OF DIFFERENT FLAVOURS
880. ICE CREAM STABILIZER
881. ICE MAKING PLANT
882. INDIAN MADE FOREIGN LIQUOR (I.M.F.L)
883. INSTANT FOOD (IDLI MIX, DOSA MIX, GULAB JAMUN MIX)
884. INSTANT FOOD (INSTANT FOOD & FAST FOOD PARLOUR)
885. INSTANT NOODLES
886. INSTANT TEA
887. INSTANT TEA FROM BLACK TEA
888. INTEGERATED STARCH BAKING POWDER/YEAST INDUSTRY
889. IODIZED SALT
890. IODIZED SALT (ORDINARY MOISTURE-LESS/FREE FLOWING IN PLASTIC BAGS AND CONTAINERS)
891. JAM, JELLIES, FRUIT JUICE & ALLIED PRODUCTS
892. KATHA AND CUTCH
893. KHANDSARI SUGAR
894. KHANDSARI SUGAR & IMFL
895. LACTIC ACID FROM WHITE SUGAR BY FERMENTATION PROCESS
896. LACTOSE & BY PRODUCTS PROCESSING FROM MILK
897. LIQUID GLUCOSE AND ITS BYE PRODUCTS
898. MACRONI AND VERMICILLI
899. MALT EXTRACTION FROM BARLEY
900. MANGO PROCESSING (MANGO PULP, JUICE & SLICES)
901. MAYUR BRAND TYPE CHEWING TOBACCO
902. MINERAL WATER
903. MILK PRESERVATION & MARKETING TO WHOLE SELLERS (INPOUCH PACKING BY UHT TECHNOLOGY)
904. MILK PROCESSING AND PACKAGING OF MILK PRODUCTS
905. MILK PRODUCTS (CASEIN, LACTOSE, GHEE & WHEY POWDER)
906. MILK TOFFEE
907. MINI FLOUR MILL
908. MINI SUGAR PLANT
909. MISRI (PEARL SUGAR CANDIES)
910. MODERN RICE MILL
911. MURABBA
912. MUSTARD OIL EXTRACTION & REFINING
913. MUTTON TALLOW
914. NAMKEEN INDUSTRY (BHUJIA, CHANA CHUR ETC.)
915. NAMKEEN & SWEETS
916. NON-BASMATI RICE FROM PADDY
917. OLEORESIN, ESSENTIAL OIL, DYES & POWDER OF SPICES
918. OLEORESIN EXTRACTION FROM DIPTERO-CARPUT TURMINATUS AND PINUS KHASYANA
919. OLEORESIN EXTRACTION FROM CHILLI
920. PAN MASALA AND POUCH

1059. BUFFALO HORN TIP, HOOF
1060. BANQUET HALL
1061. BUTTON
1062. CALCINED PETROLEUM (C.P) COKE
1063. CANVAS SHOES
1064. CANVAS SHOES, JUNGLE BOOTS
1065. CARBON BRUSH, BRUSH HOLDER & SLIP RING
1066. CEMENT SHEETS WITH COIR FIBRE & OTHER SEGMENTS
1067. CERAMIC TILES (GLAZED) BY DOUBLE FIRING/HEATING
1068. CHILDREN RECREATION CENTRE
1069. COAL BRIQUETTES
1070. COLD STORAGE & ICE
1071. COLD STORAGE FOR FRUITS AND VEGETABLES
1072. COMPRESSOR (HERMETIC) FOR AIR CONDITIONER
1073. COSTUME JEWELLERY/ IMITATION JEWELLERY
1074. DECORATIVE LAMINATED SHEET (SUNMICA)
1075. DIAMOND CUTTING & EXPORTS
1076. DRINKING STRAW FROM PROPYLENE
1077. ENGINEERING COLLEGE
1078. ENTERTAINMENT CLUB
1079. FASHION TECHNOLOGY INSTITUTE
1080. FAST FOOD PARLOUR
1081. FAST FOOD (INSTANT FOOD & FAST FOOD PARLOUR)
1082. FIRE EXTINGUISHERS (SODA ACID TYPE)
1083. FISH NET
1084. FLORICULTURE (CUT FLOWER ROSE) WITH GREEN HOUSE
1085. FLOOR COVERING SHEET
1086. FILM STUDIO (VIDEO)
1087. FLUSH DOOR, CHIP BOARD, WOOD WOOL & OTHER INSULATING BOARDS
1088. GAS DETECTORS OF L.P.G
1089. GEMS MANUFACTURING
1090. GLASS BOTTLE BY SCRAP
1092. GOAT & SHEEP FARMING
1093. GOLD ELECTROPLATING
1094. GOLD JEWELLERY (E.O.U)
1095. GOLD PLATED SILVER JEWELLERY & CUTLERY
1096. GRANITE SLAB AND TILES
1097. GREEN HOUSE
1098. HARD CHROMIUM PLATING
1099. HEALTH CLUB AND BEAUTY PARLOUR CUM HAIR SALOON WITH SONA BATH
1100. HEALTH CLUB CUM BEAUTY PARLOUR TRAININGINSTITUTE
1101. HORN TIP,HOOVE BUTTON
1102. HOSPITAL
1103. HOSPITAL (100 BEDS)
1104. HOSPITAL (200 BEDS)
1105. ICE MAKING PLANT
1106. IMITATION AND COSTUME
1107. JEWELLERY (NECKLACE, EARRINGS EAR TOP ETC.)
1108. INITMATE SCENT CHEMICALS FROM ALL TYPES OF FLAVOUR
1109. INVESTMENT CASTING
1110. JUTE, COIR, GLASS ROPE/ SUTLI
1111. JUTE TWINE
1112. L.P.G BOTTLING PLANT
1113. L.P.G REGULATOR (DOMESTIC PURPOSE)
1114. LAMINATED PARTICLE BOARD & HARD BOARD
1115. LAMINATED SAFETY AND TOUGHENED GLASS
1116. LEASING & HIRE PURCHASE
1117. LICHEN (CHARILA)
1118. MANILA ROPES
1119. MEDICAL COLLEGE
1120. MATCH UNIT FROM WAXED PAPER
1121. MEDIUM DENSITY FIBRE BOARD
1122. MELAMINE CROCKERY
1123. MINERAL WATER
1124. MINI CEMENT PLANT
1125. MIRROR SILVER, GOLDEN, PINK, BLACK & SMOKES
1126. MODERN ADVERTISING AGENCY WITH DTP & FILM STUDIO
1127. MOTEL/SMALL HOTEL
1128. MULTI COLOUR PRINTING
1129. MULTI STOREY COMMERCIAL COMPLEX ALONGWITH RESIDENTIAL AND DELUX FLATS FOR FOREIGN TOURISTS & REVOLVING RESTAURANT AT THE TOP
1130. MULTIPLE LAMINATION INDUSTRY
1131. MUSHROOM GROWING AND PROCESSING (BY DEEP FREEZING METHOD)
1132. NEWS PAPER PRINTING
1133. NICKEL LINED INDUSTRIAL SCREEN
1134. OFFSET COLOUR PRINTING PRESS (SIX COLOUR)
1135. OFFSET PRINTING PRESS
1136. P.C.C ELECTRIC POLES
1137. PHOTOGRAPHIC DEVELOPER & FIXER
1138. PVC EXTRUSION PROFILE (DOOR & WINDOWS)
1139. POP-CORN
1140. PHOTO ETCHING OF S.S.
1141. PRE STRESSED CEMENT CONCRETE PIPES
1142. PILFER PROOF CAPS
1143. PILFER PROOF CAPS AND CROWN CAP
1144. POUCH MAKING & GRAVURE PRINTING (ROTO PRINTING)
1145. POULTRY & FISH FARMING (INTEGERATED UNIT)
1146. PRINTING OF TIN SHEETS
1147. READYMADE GARMENTS
1148. RESTAURANT
1149. ROSE PLANTATION AND ROSE OIL EXTRACTION
1150. ROTOGRAVURE PRINTING
1151. SAFETY BELTS
1152. SAFETY MATCHES
1153. SHOE LACES
1154. SILK COCOON CULTIVATION (GROWING OF SILK COCOON WARM)
1155. SILK SCREEN PRINTING FORMULATIONS FOR PLASTIC, PAPER & CLOTH
1156. SPIKENARD (JATAMANSI)
1157. STENCIL COATING SOLUTION
1158. SUGAR CANDY (MISRI)
1159. SUGAR CANE PLANTATION
1160. SUGAR CANE JUICE PRESERVATION
1161. SURAT ZARI
1162. SYNTHETIC SHOES & SOLES
1163. TEA PACKAGING INDUSTRY
1164. TENNIS BALLS
1165. THREE STAR HOTEL
1166. TRAVELLING AGENCY
1167. TRAYS, TROLLEYS FOR HOSPITAL WITH SCRATCHLESS COATING
1168. WAX EXTRACTS (TANNING POWDER)
1169. WIRE ROPE SLINGS
1170. WOOD WOOL SLAB
1171. WOODEN CANE FURNITURE WITH EXPORT POTENTIAL
1172. WOODEN FURNITURE
1173. WOODEN PANEL INCLUDING KILN SEASONING
1174. WOODEN FURNITURE
1175. WATCH CASE BUFFING
1176. WATCH DIAL
1177. WRIST WATCHES
1178. WATCHES (ELECTRONIC)
1179. ZEDOARY (KACHUR)

EDIBLE OILS, ESSENTIAL OILS LURICATIING OILS, GREASES, VEGETABLE OILS, WAXES, CAMPHOR, PERFUMES & PERFUMERY COMPOUNDS AND REFINED OILS ETC.

1180. AROMATIC PERFUMERY COMPOUND
1181. AEROSOL
1182. AGARBATTI PERFUMERY COMPOUND
1183. BEES WAX MANUFACTURE
1184. CAMPHOR
1185. CARDANOL FROM CASHEW NUT SHELL LIQUID
1186. CASTOR OIL
1187. CASTOR OIL DERIVATIVE OLEORESINS
1188. CHILLI OIL
1189. CITRONELLA OILS
1190. CLOVE OIL
1191. CONCENTRATE OF ROSE JASMINE & LILY ETC.
1192. COLOURED FLAME CANDLE

1193. CANDLES (SEMI-AUTOMATIC)
1194. CORN OIL (MAIZE OIL)
1195. DEHYDRATED CASTOR OIL
1196. EUGENOL FROM CINNAMON LEAF OIL
1197. EXTRACTION OF ESSENTIAL OIL (CARDAMON, JEERA, AJOWAN, GINGER OILS ETC. & PACKAGING OF GROUND SPICES)
1198. EXTRACTION OF JASMINE ESSENCE
1199. EXTRACTION OF ESSENTIAL OILS BY SUPER CRITICAL FLUID METHOD FROM FLOWERS, HERBS & SPICES
1200. EUCALYPTUS OIL
1201. EXTRACTION OF OIL FROM OIL SEED EXPANDEREXTRUSION TECHNOLOGY)
1202. FAT LIQUOR SULPHATED OIL
1203. FLAVOURS FOR FOOD
1204. GARLIC OIL & POWDER
1205. GINGER OIL, SANDALWOOD OIL AND NAGARMOTHA OIL
1206. GINGER OIL
1207. GINGER OIL & GINGER DUST
1208. INTEGERATED WAX COMPLEX
1209. IONONE FROM LEMON GRASS OIL
1210. JASMINE & LILLY FLOWER OIL
1211. LEMON GRASS OIL
1212. LIQUID PARAFFIN
1213. LUBE OIL & GREASE
1214. LUBRICATING OIL
1215. MENTHOL CRYSTALS
1216. MENTHOL OIL & CRYSTAL
1217. MICRO CRYSTALLINE WAX
1218. MUSTARD OIL (EDIBLE OIL)
1219. OIL FROM ARTEMISIA HERBS
1220. PALM OIL CRUSHING UNIT
1221. PAN MASALA
1222. PARAFFIN WAX
1223. PARAFFIN WAX FROM SLACK WAX
1224. REFINED OIL-SUN FLOWER OIL, GROUNDNUT OIL, STAFF FLOWER OIL & COTTON SEED OIL
1225. REFINED VEGETABLE OIL
1226. RECLAMATION OF USED ENGINE OIL
1227. RICE BRAN OIL (R.B.O)
1228. ROSE OIL EXTRACTION
1229. SMOKE LESS CANDLE
1230. SPICE OIL & OLEORESINS
1231. SOLVENT EXTRACTION PLANT (OIL CAKE BASED)
1232. SYNTHETIC ALMOND OIL
1233. SYNTHETIC TALLOW
1234. SYNTHETIC GHEE
1235. VEGETABLE OIL EXTRACTION & REFINING
1236. WADDING OIL (100%) FOR WADDING OF COTTON HOSIERY CLOTH IN DYEING PROCESS
1237. WAX EMULSION FOR TEXTILE
1238. WAX FLOOR POLISH

PAINT, ENAMEL, SOLVENTS, THINNERS, INKS & VARNISH

1239. ACRYLIC EMULSION PAINTS
1240. ALUMINIUM PAINT
1241. AUTOMOBILE PAINTS
1242. BALL POINT PEN REFILL INK
1243. BITUMINIOUS ROAD EMULSION
1244. BITUMEN
1245. BITUMINIOUS FELTS FOR WATER & DAMP PROOFING
1246. BITUMINIOUS ROAD EMULSION RAPID MEDIUM & SLOW SETTING
1247. BUFFING & POLISHING
1248. CEMENT PAINT FOR WHITE & GREY CEMENT

1249. DISPERSANT
1250. DRY DISTEMPER
1251. DRY DISTEMPER & CEMENT PAINT
1252. DUPLICATING INK BLACK FOR GESTNER DUPLICATOR
1255. EMULSION PAINTS (WATER BASED)
1256. HAMMERTONE PAINT
1257. INSULATING VARNISH & WIRE ENAMEL
1258. IRON OXIDE PIGMENTS
1259. INSULATING VARNISH (POLY VINYL BUTYRAL BASED, FFC GRADE)
1260. LIME COLOUR (CEMENT COLOUR)
1261. SYNTHETIC RED OXIDE FOR FLOORINGS
1262. SOLVENT & THINNERS
1263. MARKING INKS (WATER PROOF)
1264. METAL NAPHTHANATE (AS DRIER FOR PAINTS)
1265. N.C.PUTTY
1266. OFFSET PRINTING INK
1267. OIL BOUND DISTEMPER PAINT
1268. PAINT BRUSHES
1269. PAINT REMOVERS
1270. PAINT INDUSTRY
1271. PAINT & VARNISH
1272. PICTURE VARNISH
1273. POWDER COATING PAINT
1274. PRINTING INKS (OFFSET, FLEXO & ROTO GRAVURE)
1275. PRIMER PAINT & ENAMEL PAINT
1276. PUTTY & WATER PROOFING PAINT
1277. PRINTING INKS (FLEXO-GRAPHIC INK)
1278. PUTTY (METAL CASEMENT)
1279. RED OXIDE PRIMER (ANTI CORROSIVE)
1280. REFRACTORY PAINT (GRAPHITE BASED)
1281. SCREEN PRINTING INKS
1282. SILK SCREEN PRINTING INK FORMULATION FOR PLASTIC, PAPER, CLOTH
1283. STAMP & PAD INK
1284. STOVING PAINT
1285. SPIRIT SOLUBLE MALEIC RESIN
1286. TEXTURE PAINT
1287. THINNERS AND ITS ALLIED PRODUCTS
1288. TONER INK
1289. VARNISH THINNER (SOLVENT)
1290. VACUUM METALLIZING LACQUERS
1291. WOOD PRIMER

PHARMACEUTICAL, DRUGS, AYURVEDIC/HERBAL COSMETICS & MEDICINES, HOMOEOPATHIC MEDICINES, DISPOSABLE SYRINGE, DENTAL COLLEGE & FINE CHEMICALS ETC.

1292. AROMATIC PILLS
1293. ASPIRIN
1294. AYURVEDIC PAIN BALM OINTMENTS
1295. AYURVEDIC CHURAN AND TABLETS
1296. AYURVEDIC TABLETS (HAJMOLA TYPE)
1297. AYURVEDIC/HERBAL PHARMACY
1298. AYURVEDIC SHERBATS
1299. AYURVEDIC PRODUCTS
1300. BULK DRUGS (E.O.U)
1301. BLOOD BAGS
1302. CALCIUM GLUCONATE
1303. CAPSULE, TABLET & INJECTION WITH MODERN INSTRUMENTS
1304. CASHEW FENI
1305. CHLOROQUINONE PHOSPHATE (BULK DRUGS)
1306. CLINICAL THERMOMETER
1307. DENTAL CLINIC

1308. DENTAL COLLEGE
1309. DENTAL GRADE EUGENOL
1310. DEXTROSE MONOHYDRATE, LIQUID GLUCOSE
1311. DEHYDRATED ONION & ONION POWDER
1312. DEXTROSE POWDER (ANHYDROUS FROM STARCH)
1314. DEXTROSE SALINE SOLUTION
1315. DISTILLERY (I.M.F.L)
1316. DISPOSABLE NEEDLES FOR SYRINGES
1317. DISPRIN
1318. DISTILLED WATER
1319. EMPTY HARD GELATINE CAPSULES
1320. FILLING & PACKING OF CAPSULES
1321. GLUCOSE - D - POWDER
1322. GLYCERINE
1323. HERBAL COSMETICS
1324. HERBAL SHAMPOO
1325. HERBAL HAIR OILS (AYURVEDIC)
1326. HOMOE & BIO-MEDICINES WITH MOTHER TINCTURE
1327. HOMOEPATHIC MEDICINES
1328. HYPODERMIC NEEDLES
1329. I.V. FLUIDS
1330. IBUPROFEN
1331. INFUSION & TRANSFUSION SETS (I.V. SET)
1332. INJECTABLE FOR PHARMACEUTICALS
1333. INJECTION AMPOULES PACKAGING BOX
1334. INTEGERATED SURGICAL COTTON
1335. ICE MAKING PLANT
1336. ICE & COLD STORAGE
1337. LACTOSE & BY PRODUCTS PROCESSING FROM MILK
1338. LICHEN (JATAMANSI CHARILA)
1339. LIQUID GLUCOSE AND ITS BY-PRODUCTS
1340. L-LYSINE MONOHYDRO CHLORIDE
1341. LIQUID GLUCOSE FROM POTATOES
1342. MEDICAL COLLEGE
1343. NICOTINE FROM TOBACCO WASTE
1344. OINTMENT-AYURVEDIC (YELLOW & WHITE)
1345. PHARMACEUTICAL AND FOOD GRADE GELATINE
1346. PHARMACEUTICAL INDUSTRY (TABLETS, CAPSULES, LIQUID, GEL, OINTMENT POWDER INJECTABLE)
1347. PHARMACEUTICAL UNIT (EOU) WITH FORMULA TIONS, INJECTABLES, ETC. PYRIDINE & DERIVATIVES
1348. SALT (IODIZED SALT)
1349. SALINE & INJECTION WATER
1350. SALINE WATER & DEXTROSE SOLUTION (I.V.FLUID IN PLASTIC BOTTLES)
1351. SORBITOL
1352. STARCH (MAIZE)
1353. SURGICAL ADHESIVE PLASTER
1354. SURGICAL BANDAGES
1355. SURGICAL GLOVES
1357. SURGICAL COTTON
1358. SURGICAL COTTON AND BANDAGE
1359. SYNTHETIC CAMPHOR POWDER
1360. TABLETS & CAPSULES
1361. TISSUE CULTURE
1362. TINCTURE FROM RECTIFIED SPIRIT
1363. TRIMETHOPIME
1364. VETERENARY MEDICINES (ONLY FORMULATIONS)
1365. VITAMIN 'C', SORBITOL' ANHYDROUS DEXTROSE, STARCH

PULP, PAPER, STRAW/GREY BOARD, KRAFT PAPER, PACKAGING, PAPER CARRY BAGE, PAPER FROM AGRO WASTE & STATIONERY ETC.

1366. AMMONIA PAPER
1367. AUTOMATIC BOOK BINDING
1368. ADHESIVE (FEVICOL TYPE)
1369. ALL PIN & GEM CLIPS
1370. CARBON PAPER
1371. CARD BOARD
1372. CARBON LESS PAPER
1373. CELLPHANE PAPER
1374. COMPUTER FORMS & SECURITY PRINTING PRESS
1375. CORRUGATED BOARD & BOX (PRINTED & LAMINATED)
1376. CORRUGATED BOARD AND BOXES FROM FROM CARD BOARDS
1377. CORRUGATED CARTONS FROM PLAIN PAPERS
1378. CORRUGATRED PACKING & MATERIAL (BULB & TUBES PACKING)
1379. DESK TOP PUBLISHING
1380. DEFOAMING AGENT FOR PAPER PLANT
1381. DRINKING STRAW PAPER
1382. D.T.P CUM OFFSET PRESS
1383. EGG TRAYS
1384. EXERCISE NOTE BOOK, REGISTER AND PAD
1385. FLEXOGRAPHIC INK
1386. GREETING CARD BY OFFSET PRESS
1387. HAND MADE PAPER FILTER PAPER
1388. HARD BOARD
1389. INJECTION AMPOULES PACKAGING BOXES
1390. INSULATIING PAPER
1391. KRAFT PAPER
1392. KRAFT PAPER FROM BAGASSE
1393. LAMINATED PACKAGING PAPER WITH PRINTING
1394. LAMINATION & COATING ON PAPER
1395. M.G. PAPER FROM WASTE PAPER
1396. MILL PAPER FROM WASTE PAPER
1397. MILL BOARD FROM RICE & WHEAT STRAWS
1398. MILL BOARD FROM WASTE PAPER
1399. MINI PAPER PLANT FROM SISAL
1400. MINI PAPER PLANT
1401. MULTI WALL PAPER SACKS
1402. NEWS PAPER FOR CHILDREN
1403. NEWS PRINT PAPER FROM RICE STRAW BAGASSE
1404. NEWS PAPER CHILDRENS
1405. NEWS PRINT PAPER
1406. OFFSET AND TREADLE TYPE PRINTING PRESS
1407. MILL BOARD BASED ON RICE STRAW
1408. PAPER AND BOARD FROM STRAW
1409. PAPER & PAPER PRODUCTS
1410. PAPER ENVELOPES
1411. PAPER CARRY BAGS
1412. PAPER BOARD CARTON
1413. PAPER CONES FOR LOUD SPEAKERS
1414. PAPER FROM AKRA
1415. PAPER FROM BAGASSE WITH CORRUGATED BOARD & BOXES
1416. PAPER FROM BAMBOO
1417. PAPER GLASSES FOR BEVERAGES
1418. PAPER FROM RICE HUSK & WHEAT HUSK
1419. PAPER FROM TREE BARK, EUCALYPRUS WOOD
1420. PAPER PRODUCTS
1421. PAPER PLANT (WHITE WRITING & NEWS PAPER FOR PULP & WASTE PAPER)
1422. PAPER PLATES, PAPER GLASS
1423. PAPER CONES & TUBES
1425. PAPER PLANT WITH DTP & PRINTING & PUBLISHING UNIT
1426. PAPER BASED PHENOLIC SHEET
1427. PAPER CUP FOR ICE CREAM
1428. PAPER TUBES SPIRAL WINDING COMPOSIT CONTAINER
1429. PAPER LABLE FOR BEER BOTTLES
1430. PARTICLE BOARD & BLACK BOARD WITH SANDING & LAMINATION OF PARTICLE BOARD
1431. PARTICLE BOARD FROM RICE HUSK
1432. POUCH FILLING & MAKING FOR TOMATO SAUCE
1433. POUCH MAKING &

GRAVURE PRINTING
1434. PROCESSING OF PAPER FOR FEEDING IN COMPUTER
1435. PULP FROM BAMBOO & WOOD
1436. PAPER FILES
1437. PLAYING CARDS
1438. ROSIN SIZING AGENT (FOR PAPER PLANT)
1439. SAND PAPER
1440. SANITRY NAPKINS
1441. SILICON COATED PAPER
1442. STENCIL PAPER
1443. STRAW BOARD AND GREY BOARD
1444. STRAW BOARD & MILL BOARD
1445. STRAW BOARD AND PAPER BOARD
1446. TISSUE PAPER FACIAL
1447. TISSUE MOIST TOILETERY CLEANSING TISSUE AND RELATED PRODUCTS
1448. TISSUE PAPER ROLLS
1449. TETRA PACK FOR MILK PACKAGING, GHEE & OTHER LIQUIDS
1450. TOILET PAPER ROLLS
1451. TOILET PAPER & NAPKINS
1452. WAX COATED PRINTED PAPER
1453. WET FACE FRESHNER TISSUE
1454. WHITE WRITING & PRINTING PAPER
1455. WRITING & PRINTING PAPER (PAPER MILLS)

PLASTIC, B.O.P.P, ACRYLIC, DISPOSABLE PLASTIC PRODUCTS, PET PRODUCTS, P.V.C, H.D.P.E, P.P, L.D.P.E., P.U, A.B.S, THERMOFOARMING, MASTER BATCHES, & POLYMER AND RUBBER PRODUCTS, TYRE, TUBE, ADHESIVE, SHEET, COIR & MANY OTHERS

1456. ABS GRANULES FROM ABS SCRAPS FROM OLD T.V. CABINETS, WHITE GOODS ETC.
1457. ACRYLIC BEADS
1458. ACRYLIC COPOLYMER EMULSION
1459. ACRYLIC LATEX
1460. ACRYLIC SHEET
1461. ACRYLIC SHEET & MOULDED PRODUCTS
1462. ACRYLIC TEETH
1463. AUTO TUBES
1464. AUTO FLAPS FOR TRUCKS & BUSES
1465. AUTO TYRES & TUBES
1466. BABY BOTTLES (PLASTIC) WITH WHITESILICON RUBBER NIPPLES
1467. B.O.P.P. FILM
1468. B.O.P.P. PRESSURE SENSITIVE SELF ADHESIVE TAPE
1469. BABY NIPPLE (SILICON)
1470. BABY NIPPLE (BIG SIZE)
1471. BALLOON PLASTIC ADVERTISING
1472. BLISTER FILM PVC
1473. BLISTER PACKAGING & POUCH PAKAGING
1474. BLOW MOULDING PLASTIC CONTAINER
1475. COATING ON METALIZED POLYESTER FILM/METALISED PAPER/ ALIMINIUM FOIL
1476. COATING ON PLASTIC (ELECTROLYSIS) & GLASS
1477. COIR FOAM (RUBBERISED)
1478. COLOUR COATING ON PLASTICS
1479. COLOUR MASTER BATCHES FOR VARIOUS PLASTICS
1480. CYCLE TYRES AND TUBES
1481. DISPOSABLE PLASTIC CUPS GLASSES, ETC.
1482. DISPOSABLE PLASTIC SYRINGES & NEEDLES
1483. DISPOSABLE PLASTIC SYRINGES
1484. DOUGH MOULDING COMPOUND (D.M.C)
1485. EPOXY RESIN
1486. EXPANDED POLYESTRENE MOULDING (THERMOCOLE)
1487. F.R.P AUTO, SCOOTER ROOFS & CEILINGS
1488. F.R.P PRODUCTS (HELMET, WASHBASIN SHEETS, ROOFING SHEETS)
1489. FIBRE REINFORCED PLASTIC (HIGH PRESSURE MOULDING WITH SMC BMC AND DMC)
1490. FIELD RUBBER CONVERTED TO THE 60% LATEX RUBBER
1491. FLEXIBLE P.U. FOAM
1492. FORMALDEHYDE CROCKERY & OTHER ITEMS
1493. FORMALDEHYDE RESIN (UREA, PHENOL,MELEMINE)
1494. GASKET SHEET
1495. GUM BOTTLE (PVC)
1496. GLASS BEADS
1497. HDPE COATED PAPER SACK
1498. H.D.P.E. BAGS
1499. H.D.P.E. CONTAINERS (BLOW MOULDING)
1500. H.D.P.E. CONTAINER, POLY JARS BY INJECTION MOULDING (FOOD GRADE)
1501. H.D.P.E. JERRY CANS
1502. HDPE MANUFACTURING FROM ETHYLALCOHOL
1503. H.D.P.E PIPE AND FITTINGS
1504. H.D.P.E. PIPES
1505. H.D.P.E PRINTED BAGS
1506. H.D.P.E TWINES AND ROPES
1507. H.D.P.E. & L.D.P.E PIPES AND FITTINGS
1508. H.D.P.E/PP BOX STRAPPING
1509. H.D.P.E/PP WOVEN SACKS USING PLAIN LOOMS
1510. HOLOGRAM STICKERS-3D
1511. H.M BAG PLANT WITH PRINTING UNIT
1512. HAWAI CHAPPALS (RUBBER)
1513. I.V PLASTIC BOTTLE
1514. ICE CREAM CUP (PLASTIC)
1515. INJECTION MOULDED AUTO COMPONENTS
1516. INJECTION & BLOW MOULDED PLASTIC PRODUCTS
1517. INJECTION MOULDED PLASTIC PRODUCTS
1518. INTEGERATED COMPLEX ESTER'S & ALLIED PRODUCTS (D.O.P.D.B.P, & ETHYL ACETATE, BUYTL ACETATE, WIRE ENAMELS, JELLY CABLE COMPOUND)
1519. L.D.P.E. (LOW DENSITY POLY ETHYLENE) GRANULES FROM VIRGIN (L.D.P.E. RESIN)
1520. INTEGERATED SURGICAL RUBBER GOODS INDUSTRY
1521. INJECTION MOULDED PLASTIC BALLS
1522. L.D.P.E FROM ETHYL ALCOHOL
1523. LDPE MOULDED PRODUCTS
1524. LAMINATION OF COEXTRUSION MULTILAYER FILM IN ROLL FORM
1525. LATEX RUBBER
1526. LATEX RUBBER CONDOM
1527. MASTER BATCHES (COLOURED, P.V.C, L.D.P.E, H.D.P.E, ETC.)
1528. MELAMINE FORMALHYDE RESIN
1529. MOULDED LUGGAGE
1530. MULTI-LAYER (3 LAYER BAGS)
1531. MULTI-LAYER (3 LAYER) FILM WITH LAMINATION & PRINTING
1532. OIL SEAL
1533. PET BOTTLE/CONTAINERS
1534. PET BOTTLES FROM PRE FORM
1535. PET BOTTLE & MINERAL WATER
1536. PET PRE-FORM FROM PET RESIN
1537. PET PRE-FORM CUM PET BOTTLES
1538. PET PRE-FORM PET BOTTLES CUM MINERAL WATERS
1539. POLY CARBONATE RESIN
1540. PTFE COMPONENTS
1541. PU/PVC SOLE FOR SPORT SHOE BY IMPORTED M/C.
1542. PVC BATTERY SEPARATOR
1543. P.V.C COMPOUNDS (FRESH)
1544. P.V.C COMPOUNDS (SCRAP)
1545. P.V.C ELECTRICAL INSULATING TAPE
1546. P.V.C. EXTRUSION PROFILES
1547. P.V.C FITTINGS
1548. P.V.C FLEXIBLE FUSIBLE POWDER HEAT FUSIBLE POWDER
1549. P.V.C GRANULES (FOR

INSULATION & SHEETS GRADES)
1550. P.V.C GRANULES FROM PVC SCRAPS (WITH POLLUTION CONTROL)
1551. P.V.C HOSES
1552. P.V.C LEATHER CLOTH
1553. P.V.C FLEXIBLE PIPES
1554. P.V.C PIPES AND FITTINGS
1555. POLYTHENE BAGS (PRINTED)
1556. PVC PLASTICS FILM SHEET SOFT/RIGID
1557. PVC RESIN AND COMPOUND
1558. PVC RULAR
1559. PVC STABLIZERS (SINGLE PACK SYSTEM)
1560. PVC WIRE AND CABLES
1561. PAPER BASED PHENOLIC SHEET FOR ELECTRICAL
1562. PHENOL FORMALDEHYDE RESIN
1563. PHENOLIC RESIN
1564. PLASTIC BEADS FROM PLASTIC SCRAPS
1565. PLASTIC BUTTONS
1566. PLASTIC CANS
1567. PLASTIC COLLAPSIBLE TUBE
1568. PLASTIC CORRUGATED SHEET & BOXES
1569. PLASTIC FILM AND SHEETS WITH PRINTING FLEXO & ROTO/LDPE/HDPE/PP/HM/PVC
1570. PLASTIC FILTER MASTER BATCH & OTHER MASTER BATCHES FOR VARIOUS PLASTICS
1571. PLASTIC JERRY CANS
1572. PLASTIC GRANULES OR POWDER FROM PLASTIC SCRAP
1573. PLASTIC INJECTION MOULDED T.V. CABINETS
1574. PLASTIC ITEMS MANUFAC TURE FROM POWDER MELAMINE
1575. PLASTIC GOODS
1576. PLASTIC PIPES & TARPAULINES
1577. PLASTIC SHEET FROM SCRAP
1578. PLASTIC PLANT (BLOW MOULDING & INJECTION MOULDING)
1579. PLASTIC PRODUCTS (GOLD, SILVER, NICKEL)
1580. PLASTIC TOYS
1581. POLYESTER BEADING
1582. POLYESTER FILM
1583. POLYTHENE BAGS & AUTOMATIC PRINTING
1584. POLYTHENE PRINTED BAGS
1585. POLYURETHANE FOAM AND ITS PRODUCTS
1586. PROPYLENE FILM (PRINTED) & BAG MANUFACTURING
1587. PLASTIC MATS
1588. RAINBOW COLOUR ON PVC FILM & SHEET
1589. RED MUD PVC PIPES AND FITTINGS
1590. RE-RUBBERISED OF SOLID TYPE
1591. RESIN COATED SAND REXINE
1592. REXINE CLOTH & ALLIED PRODUCTS
1593. RUBBER ADHESIVE
1594. RUBBER AUTO PARTS
1595. RUBBER BELTING
1596. RUBBER MOULDING UNIT INCLUDING LINING RUBBER SHEETING
1597. RUBBER RECLAIMING
1598. RUBBER ROLLERS FOR TEXTILE MILLS & PAPER INDUSTRIES
1599. RUBBER & PLASTIC SHEETS, MATS & FLAPS
1600. RUBBER SHEET AND ALLIED HOSPITAL RUBBER GOODS
1601. RUBBERIZED PVC GASKET
1602. RUBBERISED COIR
1603. RUBBER COMPOUND FOR AUTOMOBILES
1604. SAFETY BELTS
1605. SILVER AND GOLD PLATING ON PVC AND NYLON-6
1606. SILICONE RUBBER NIPPLES/ TEATS
1607. SPECTACLE FRAMES (PLASTIC)
1608. SPUNGE RUBBER
1609. SURGICAL EXAMINATION GLOVES
1610. SYNTHETIC PEARL COATING ON POLYSTYRENE BEADS
1611. SYNTHETIC RUBBER ADHESIVE
1612. TEFLON MANUFACTURING
1613. TEFLON TAPE
1614. TEFLON TAPES & CABLES
1615. THERMOCOLE SHEET AND MOULDED PRODUCTS EXPANDED POLYESTERENE EXTRUSION PROFILES
1616. THERMOFORMED PACKAGING (BLISTER PACKAGING & POUCH PACKAGING)
1617. THERMOPLASTIC POLYURETHANE
1618. THERMOFORMED CUPS, PLATES & GLASS WITH HIPS SHEET
1619. THERMOCOLE
1620. THERMOCOLE BASED DISPOSABLE GLASS, CUPS & PLATES
1621. TOOTH BRUSHES
1622. TOY BALLOON, DECORA TIVE & INDUSTRIAL BALLOONS
1623. TREAD RUBBER
1624. TYRE RETREADING (HOT)
1625. TYRE RETREADING BY COLD PROCESS
1626. TYRE TUBES & FLAPS
1627. TYRE & TUBES
1628. UNSATURATED POLYESTER FOR REXINE
1629. V-BELT AND FAN BELT
1630. VINYL ASBESTOS AND PVC WALL PAPER
1631. VITON (FLUORO ELASTOMER)

SOAP, COSMETICS & PERFUMES

1632. ACID SLURRY, SYNTHETIC DETERGENT POWDER
1632. ACID SLURRY
1633. AGARBATTI SYNTHETIC, PERFUMERY COMPOUND
1634. AFTER SHAVE LOTION
1635. ANTISEPTIC CREAM
1636. BETA IONONE
1637. BLEACHING POWDER
1638. BLUE DETERGENT POWDER
1639. CLEANING POWDER (VIMTYPE)
1640. COLD CREAM
1641. COLOURED FLAME & PERFUMED CANDLES (RED, BLUE, GREEN FLAME)
1642. COSMETIC INDUSTRY (MODERN)
1643. COSMETIC INDUSTRY (SHAMPOO, SPRAY PERFUME, TALCUM POWDER
1644. DETERGENT POWDER (ARIEL TYPE)
1645. DETERGENT POWDER (NIRMA TYPE) FULLY AUTOMATIC PLANT
1646. DETERGENT WASHING POWDER
1647. FISH OIL SOAP
1648. GLYCERINE TRANSPARENT SOAP
1649. HAIR REMOVING CREAM
1650. HERBAL COSMETICS
1651. HERBAL SHAMPO & CREAM
1652. HERBAL/AYURVEDIC COSMETICS
1653. INCENSE POWDER, INCENSE STICKS & INCENSE CAKE
1654. OPTICAL WHITENERS
1655. ROSE OIL EXTRACTION
1656. SHAMPOOS (COCONUT OIL BASED COLD PROCESS)
1657. SHAVING CREAM
1658. SINDUR (KUMKUM)
1659. SOAP COATED PAPER
1660. SPRAY DRIED DETERGENT POWDER
1661. STAIN REMOVER
1662. TALCUM POWDER (FACE & TOILET POWDER)
1663. TOILET AND HERBAL SOAP
1664. TOOTH PASTE & POWDER
1665. WASHING DETERGENT POWDER AND WASHING SOAP
1666. WASHING POWDER LIQUID DETERGENTS, LOTION & SHAMPOO

TEXTILE INDUSTRIES, READYMADE GARMENTS, COTTON, DYEING, BLEACHING, CLOTH, HOSIERY, POWER LOOM, HAND LOOM, WOOLLEN, SILK, SOCKS, SURGICAL COTTON & MANY OTHERS

1667. ANGORA RABBIT WOOL
1668. BUCKRAM
1669. CANVAS SHOES, JUNGLE BOOT, BOOT RUBBER KNEES & BOOT COMBAT
1670. CARPET FROM COTTON WASTE
1671. CERAMIC THREAD GUIDE
1672. COTTON BUDS/SWABS
1673. COTTON FROM WASTE YARN
1674. COTTON ROLLS
1675. COTTON SPIDERS FOR LOUD SPEAKERS
1676. DENIM CLOTH
1677. DENIM CLOTH (INTEGERATED UNIT WITH BLEACHING, DYEING AND PRINTING)
1678. DISPERSENT FOR TEXTILE
1679. DYEING & BLEACHING
1680. DYEING OF HANK YARN
1681. EMULSIFIER FOR WOOL BATCHING OIL
1682. EMBROIDERY ON FABRICS
1683. GARMENT DYEING, WASHING & STITCHING (JEANS, JACKETS, SKIRTS & SHIRTS)
1684. GOVES KNITTING
1685. GUNNY BAGS
1687. HDPE WOVEN SACKS
1688. HDPE TARPAULINS USING PLAIN LOOM WITH LAMINATION
1689. HDPE/PP WOVEN SACKS USING CIRCULAR LOOMS
1690. HOSIERY CLOTH (COTTON) PROCESSING (BLEACHING, DYEING, FINISHING OF CLOTH)
1691. HOSIERY INDUSTRY
1692. HOSIERY MERCERISING
1693. HOSIERY PRODUCTS LIKE VEST, BRIEF, T-SHIRTS & SOCKS
1694. JACQUARD FABRICS
1695. JUTE COIR, GRASS ROPE/ SUTLI MAKING
1696. JUTE FELT
1697. JUTE TWINES
1698. KNITTED FABRICS
1699. LAMINATED JUTE BAGS
1700. LAMINATION OF HDPE WOVEN CLOTH (JUTE,COTTON, PAPER)
1701. NYLON YARN CRIMPING, DOUBLING AND BLEACHING
1702. PIGMENT BINDER FOR TEXTILE PRINTING
1704. POLYESTER RESIN FOR WIRE ENAMEL
1705. POLYESTER RESIN
1706. POLYESTER YARN FROM WASTE POLYESTER ZIP FASTENERS
1707. POWER LOOM
1708. READYMADE GARMENTS & HOSIERY
1709. READYMADE GARMENTS MERCHANDISE
1710. READYMADE GARMENTS & COVERS
1711. READYMADE GARMENTS & EMBROIDERY OF GOWNS, SHIRTS, BLOUSES, T-SHIRTS ETC. (ONLY LADIES)
1712. READYMADE SALWAR SUIT
1713. RECOVERY OF NYLON FROM NYLON WASTE
1714. ROTARY PRINTING AND DYEING ON COTTON, SYNTHETIC TEXTILE
1715. SANITARY NAPKINS
1716. SCREEN PRINTING ON COTTON CLOTH
1717. SEWING THREAD REELS & BALLS MAKING INDUSTRIES
1718. SCREEN PRINTING ON COTTON, POLYESTER & ACRYLIC
1719. SHAWLS (WOOLLEN)
1720. SHOE LACES
1721. SILK FABRICS ON HANDLOOM
1722. SOCKS KNITTING
1723. SPINNING, DOUBLING DYEING MERCERISING & BLEACHING OF COTTON YARN
1724. SPINNING & CARDING OF WOOL INTO YARNS
1725. STARCH BOOK BINDING CLOTH
1726. SURAT JARI
1727. SURGICAL COTTON & BANDAGE
1728. SYNTHETIC TEXTILE INDUSTRY(SUITING, SHIRTING, SAREES) TERRY CLOTH
1729. T-SHIRTS
1730. TOWELS, BED SHEET COVERS
1731. TERRY TOWEL
1732. TERRY FABRICS WEAVING UNIT
1733. TEXTILE AUXILLIARIES & CHEMICALS
1734. TEXTILE BLEACHING, DYEING & FINISHING & PRINTING OF COTTON FABRICS
1735. TEXTILE (HOSIERY)
1736. TEXTILE MILL
1737. TEXTILE DYEING & PRINTING
1738. TEXTILE PRINTING (JOB WORK)
1739. TEXTILE PIGMENT PRINTING BINDER
1740. TOWEL (TERRY)
1741. VELVET CLOTH BY FLOCKING PROCESS
1742. VISCOSE STAPLE FIBRE
1743. WADDING OIL (100%) FOR WADDING OF COTTON HOSIERY CLOTH IN THE DYEING PROCESS
1744. WEAVING OF DASUTI CLOTH WITH PRINTING, DYEING, EMBROIDERY & FINISHING
1745. WASHING OF JEANS & OTHER GARMENTS
1746. WORSTED WOOLLEN YARN CLOTH
1747. ZARI GLITTER SALMA SITARA OF PLASTIC FILM

INFOTECH/IT, HOSPITALITY, HOSPITAL, COLLEGE, SCHOOL, MEDICAL, ENTERTAINMENT CLUB, WARE HOUSING & REAL ESTATE, PROJECTS

1748. AMUSEMENT PARK
1749. AMUSEMENT PARK CUM WATER PARK
1750. BANQUET HALL
1751. CALL CENTER (DOMESTIC)
1752. CALL CENTER (INTERNATIONAL)
1753. CHILDREN RECREATION CENTRE
1754. COLD STORAGE
1755. COMMUNITY HALL
1756. COMPUTER EDUCATION INSTITUTE
1757. COMPUTER SOFTWARE
1758. COLLEGE
1759. CYBER CAFE
1760. DENTAL CLINIC
1761. DENTAL COLLEGE
1762. DIAGONOSTIC CENTRE
1763. E-COMMERCE/BUSINESS
1764. E-SCHOOL (Rs. 5000/-)
1765. ENGINEERING COLLEGE
1766. ENTERTAINMENT CLUB
1767. ENTERTAINMENT CLUB, HOLIDAY RESORT, 4 STAR HOTEL, AMUSEMENT PARK CUM WATER PARK, MUSHROOM & ITS PRODUCTS, FISH FARMING, LAKE FOR BOATING, DEER PARK
1768. FASHION TECHNOLOGY INSTITUTE
1769. FAST FOOD PARLOUR
1770. FIVE STAR HOTEL
1771. FOOD PARLOUR
1772. FRANCHISE TRAINING PROGRAMME FOR IIT & ENGINEERING ENTRANCE EXAMS.
1773. GOLF COURSE
1774. HEALTH CLUB, BEAUTY PARLOUR
1775. HEALTH CLUB AND FITNESS CENTER
1776. HEALTH RESORTS
1777. HOLIDAY RESORTS
1778. HOLIDAY RESORT CUM

ENTERTAINMENT CLUB WITH 4 STAR HOTEL
1779. HOSPITALS
1780. ICE CREAM PARLOUR
1781. INTERNET SERVICE PROVIDER (I.S.P.)
1782. MEDICAL COLLEGE
1783. MEDICAL COLLEGE, HOSPITAL & RESEARCH INSTITUTE
1784. MEDICAL TRANSCRIPTION CENTRE
1785. MENTAL RETARDATION HOSPITAL & CEREBRAL PALSY
1786. MOTEL/SMALL HOTEL
1787. MULTISTOREY COMMERCIAL COMPLEX
1788. MULTISTOREY RESIDENTIAL COMPLEX
1789. NURSERY SCHOOL
1790. NATURE CARE CENTRE
1791. NURSING HOME
1792. ONLINE SHOPPING MALL (RS. 5000/- REPORT)
1793. PORTAL
1794. REHABILITATION CENTRE FOR AGED & NEEDY PERSONS
1795. RESIDENTIAL CUM COMMERCIAL COMPLEX
1796. RESTAURANT
1797. RESTAURANT WITH PUB
1798. SCHOOL (PRIMARY)
1799. SCHOOL (HIGHER SECONDARY)
1800. THREE STAR HOTEL
1801. TOURIST CLUB
1802. TRAINING INSTITUTE FOR MEDICAL TRANSCRIPTION
1803. VIDEO FILM STUDIO
1804. WARE HOUSE
1805. WEBSITE DESIGN & E-MAIL REGISTERING

AGRO BASED INDUSTRIES

1806. COAL BRIQUETTES FROM AGROWASTE
1807. FURFURALFROM RICEHULL
1808. MUSHROOM CULTIVATION & PROCESSING (BUTTON)
1809. MUSHROOM GROWING & PROCESSING WITH AIR CONDITIONING
1810. MUSHROOM CULTIVATION & PROCESSING UNIT DEHYDRATION & PACKAGING OF OYSTER & PADDY STRAW MUSHROOMS
1811. ORGANIC MANURE
1812. PAPAYA CULTIVATION
1813. PAPAYA & TOMATO CULTIVATION
1814. PROCESSING & UTILISATION OF COCONUT
1815. PROCESSING OF SHEEP HAIR TO PRODUCE WOOL

BAKERY, CONFECTIONERY & FOOD PRODUCTS

1816. AGROLACTOR SOYA MILK
1817. APPLE FRUIT JUICE WITH CANNING BOTTLING
1818. AYURVEDIC SHARBAT
1819. BAKERY UNIT (PASTRIES, BREAD, BUNS, CAKE, TOFFEE ETC.)
1820. BAKING POWDER
1821. BANANA & ITS BY PRODUCTS
1822. BANANA POWDER
1823. BANANA WAFERS
1824. BANANA CULTIVATION
1825. BEER INDUSTRY
1826. DEHULLING OF JAUN FOR BEER
1827. BEER & WINE
1828. BEER, ALCOHOL, IMFL
1829. BESEN PLANT
1830. BISCUIT PLANT
1831. BREAD & BISCUIT PLANT
1832. BOTTLING PLANT COUNTRY LIQUOR FROM RECTIFIED SPIRIT
1833. BRANDY
1834. BREAD RUSKS
1835. CANNED FRUITS & VEGETABLES
1836. CANNING & PRESERVATION OF MEAT
1837. CANNING & PRESERVATION OF VEGETABLES
1838. CANNING OF MANGO PULP & MANGO SLICES
1839. CARBONATED BEVERAGS
1840. CASHEW FENI
1841. CASHEW NUT (DRIED & FRIED)
1842. CATTLE BREEDING
1843. CATTLE BREEDING & DAIRY FARM TO PRODUCE MILK
1844. CATTLE FEED FROM TAPIOCA
1845. CHEWING GINGER & AMLOKI
1846. CHEWING GUM
1847. CHILLI SAUCE
1848. CHILLI POWDER
1849. CHOCOLATE
1850. CIDER PLANT
1851. COCOA POWDER
1852. COCOA BUTTER & COCOA POWDER
1853. COCONUT SHELL POWDER
1854. COCONUT WATER
1855. COCONUT SWEET (WATERY)
1856. COCONUT MILK POWDER (DEHYDRATED)
1857. COCONUT PRODUCTS & BY PRODUCTS (INTEGRATED PLANT)
1858. COLD DRINK
1859. CURRY POWDER
1860. DAIRY FOR MILK PROCESSING (GHEE, BUTTER & PANEER)
1861. DAIRY PRODUCTS
1862. DAIRY PRODUCTS MILK PACKAGING IN POUCH (GHEE, BUTTER, ETC.
1863. DAIRY FARM TO PRDUCE MILK WITH PACKAGING (COW)
1864. DAIRY FARM TO PRDUCE MILK WITH PACKAGING (BUFALLOE)
1865. DAIRY FARM & MILK PRODUCTS
1866. DAL MOTH, CHANACHUR & BHUJIYA
1867. DEHYDRATION OF FRUITS & VEGETABLE
1868. DESICCATED COCONUT POWDER FROM COCONUTS
1869. DEHYDRATION & CANNING OF FRUITS & VEGETABLES
1870. DRY FRUIT ROASTING & PACKAGING
1871. DRYING OF RED CHILLIES, HALDI, DHANIYA, PEAS & GROUND NUT
1872. EGG POWDER
1873. FISH CANNING IN TIN & POUCHES
1874. FISH DEHYRATION (DRYING OF FISH)
1875. FISH MEAL
1876. FISH PROCESSING (BEAST FREEZING PROCESSES)
1877. FLAVOURS FOR FOOD INDUSTRIES
1878. FLOUR MILL (ROLLER)
1879. FROZEN MEAT
1880. FOOD DEHYDRATION (FRUITS & VEGETABLES)
1881. FRIED & ROASTED GROUND NUT, GRAMS, PEAR ETC.
1882. FRUIT JUICE MAKING & PACKAGING IN PLASTIC CONTAINER
1883. FRUIT JUICE IN TETRA PACK (DRINKS)
1884. FRUIT JUICE, SQUASHES, SAUCE & KETCHUP, JAM, JELLY, VINEGAR ETC.
1885. GARLIC FLAKES
1886. GARLIC POWDER
1887. GHEE & BUTTER
1888. GINGER (PULVERISED)
1889. GINGER GLAZING & PRESERVATION
1890. GINGER STORAGE
1891. GINGER PROCESSING
1892. GINGER OIL & GINGER DUST
1893. GINGER POWDER (DRY) & OLEORESIN
1894. GRAPE DEHYDRATION
1895. GRAPE CULTIVATION
1896. GRAPE JUICE
1897. HONEY PROCESSING & PACKAGING
1898. ICE CREAM & ICE CANDY
1899. ICE CUBE
1900. INVERT SUGAR
1901. IDLI MIX, DOSA MIX SAMBHAR MIX, VADA MIX, GULAB JAMUN MIX
1902. INSTANT COFFEE & INSTANT TEA

1903. INSTANT NOODLES
1904 INSTANT SOUPS
1905. IODIZED SALT FROM CRUDE SALT
1906. JAM CHUTNEY PICKLES & SQUASHES
1907. KATHA MANUFACTURING
1908. LECITHIN (SOYA BASED)
1909. LEMON & ITS PRODUCTS
1910. MACARONI MANUFACTURING
1911. MACARONI, SPAGHETTI, VERMICELLI & NOODLES
1912. MAIZE & ITS BY PRODUCTS MALTING PLANT
1913. MANGO PAPPAD (AAM PAPPAD)
1914. MANGO POWDER RIPE
1915. MANGO POWDER
1916. MANGO PROCESSING & CANNING (MANGO PULP)
1917. MEAT PROCESSING (CHICKEN MUTTON)
1918. MEAT PROCESSING (BUFFALO)
1919. MENTHOL BOLD FROM MENTHOL FLAKES
1020. MILK POWDER
1921. MILK POWDER & GHEE
1922. MILK POWDER, GHEE & SPICES
1923. MILK PRESERVATION & MARKETING TO WHOLE SELLERS
1924. MILK PRESERVATION & MARKETING TO WHOLE SELLERS (IN POUCHES)
1925. MILK TOFFEE MANUFACTURES
1926. MINERAL WATER
1927. MINERAL WATER IN POUCHES
1928. MINI FLOUR MILL ATTA MAIDA, SUJI & WHEAT BRAN
1929. MITHAI/HALWAI (SWEET & NAMKEEN)
1930. MUTTON PROCESSING
1931. PAN MASALA (MEETHA, SADA, ZARDA) MAKING & PACKING
1932. PAN MASALA AND POUCH MAKING
1933. PANEER (CHEESE)
1934. PAPAD & BARIYAN
1935. PAPAD PLANT
1936. PEPSICOLA IN POLYTUBES
1937. PETHA PACKAGING
1938. PICKLES
1939. PIGGERY/MEAT/CHICKEN PROCESSING
1940. PINE APPLE JUICE CANNING
1941. POTATO & ONION POWDER
1942. POTATO & ONION FLAKES
1943. POTATO CHIPS
1944. POTATO GRANULES
1945. POUCH FILLING FOR SAUNF SUPARI ILAICHI ETC.
1946. PRESERVATION OF RAWS MANGO JUICE
1947. PROCESSED CHEESE & MARINE PDTS.
1948. PULP FROM TARMARIND
1949. READYMATE PROCESSED FOOD
1950. RICE & CORN FLAKES
1951. RICE BASMATI (TRADING)
1952. RICE POLISHING & PACKAGING IN POUCH
1953. ROASTED/SALTED/MASALA/ CASHEW NUTS ALMONDS & PEA NUT
1954. ROLLER FLOUR MILL

INFOTECH/IT PROJECTS

1955. MEDICAL TRANSCRIPTION
1956. E-COMMERCE
1957. CYBERCAFE
1958. INTERNET SERVICE PROVIDER (ISP)
1959. COMPUTER EDUCATION CENTRE
1960. PORTAL (WEBSITE DESIGN)
1961. CALL CENTRE

TERMS AND CONDITIONS

FOR INDIA

1. Please ask for Quotations/ Proforma Invoice for Each *Market Survey Cum Detailed Techno Economic Feasibility Report.* Payable in advance through Draft/M.O./Cash in favour of 'ENGINEERS INDIA RESEARCH INSTITUTE', Delhi. Delivery by Regd.Post/Courier within 2 Days. (Postage Free)

2. Ask for a Hi Tech Projects, monthly magazine. Each issue covers approx. 75 project profiles.

FOR OVERSEAS

1. Please ask for Quotations/ Proforma Invoice in US $ for Each *Market Survey Cum Detailed Techno Economic Feasibility Report.* Payable in advance through Bank Draft in favour of 'ENGINEERS INDIA RESEARCH INSTITUTE', Delhi. (Payable in India). Delivery by Regd. Air Mail Post/Courier within 3 Days. (Postage Free)

2. Ask for a Hi Tech Projects, monthly magazine. Each issue covers approx. 75 project profiles.

ENGINEERS INDIA RESEARCH INSTITUTE

4449, Nai Sarak (D), Main Road, Delhi - 110 006 (India)
Phones: 91-11- 2391 8117, 2391 6431, 2384 0361
Fax: 91-11- 2391 6431 E-Mail : eirisidi@bol.net.in Website:www.eiriindia.org
Also at : 4/54, Roop Nagar, Delhi - 110 007 (India)
Ph:. 23840361 Mob: 098114 37895

PATRON: YOU CAN ALSO DEPOSIT THE AMOUNT IN "EIRI" ACCOUNT WITH UTI BANK LTD. CA-05401020000 6248 OR ICICI BANK LTD. CA-022705000598 OR UNION BANK OF INDIA CA-307201010015149 AND JUST SMS US ON PH. 09811437895

LIST OF PUBLICATIONS/BOOKS PUBLISHED BY

ENGINEERS INDIA RESEARCH INSTITUTE 4449, NAI SARAK, MAIN ROAD, DELHI - 6 (INDIA)

Name of Books	Rs.	US$
EXPORT ORIENTED INDUSTRIES/PROCEDURES		
* Hand Book of Export Oriented Industries	1300/-	150
* Start Your Own Export Business (How To Export)	350/-	50
SPICES & COLD STORAGE		
* Hand Book of Spices & Packaging with Formulaes	650/-	90
* Start Your Own Cold Storage Unit	375/-	50
TEXTILE AUXILIARIES & CHEMICALS		
* Textile Auxiliaries and Chemicals with Processes and Formulations	950/-	100
PHARMACEUTICALS & DRUGS		
* Pharmaceuticals and Drugs Technology with Formulations	950/-	100
LEATHER & LEATHER PRODUCTS		
* Hand Book of Leather & Leather Products Technology	850/-	100
BIOTECHNOLOGY/BIOFERTILIZERS		
* Hand Book of Biotechnology	900/	100
* Hand Book of Biofertilizers and Vermiculture	900/-	90
AYURVEDIC MEDICINES		
* Ayurvedic & Herbal Medicines with Formulaes	750/-	90
* Hand book of Ayurvedic Medicines with Formulation	900/-	100
RUBBER & RUBBER INDUSTRIES		
* Rubber Chemicals & Processing Industries	400/-	60
* Technology of Rubber & Rubber Goods Industries	900/-	100
FIBRE GLASS MOULDING		
* Hand Book of Fibre Glass Moulding	450/-	60
MINERAL & MINERALS		
* Hand book of Minerals and Minerals based Industries	975/-	100
FISH FARMING		
* Hand Book of Fish Farming and Fishery Products	650/-	65
ORGANIC FARMING/FOOD		
* Hand Book of Organic Farming & Organic Foods with Vermi-Composting and Neem Products	1100/-	110
INDUSTRIAL TRADE DIRECTORIES IN CD ROMS		
* **All India Directory of Food, Bakery, Food Processing, Beverages, Agro Products** Manufacturers, Exporters and Importers with Machineries Suppliers and Foreign Importers	975/-	

Name of Books	Rs.
* **All India Directory of Plastics and Polymers** Manufacturers, Exporters and Importers with Machineries Suppliers and Foreign Importers	975/-
* **World Importers Directory (International Buyers) and Indian Exporters**	1200/-
* **All India Directory of Textiles, Hosiery, Garments, Fabries, Thread, Yarn, Dyeing, Printing and Other Textile Products**	975/-
* **All India Directory of Manufacturers, Exporter & Traders**	1250/-
* Delhi & Around Mfrs. & Exporters Directory	750/-
* All India Directory of Chemicals Industry	1000/-
PROJECT REPORTS IN CD-ROM	
* Lucrative New 92 Project Reports in Cd	16,500/-
* 45 Infotech/IT, Hospitality, Hospital, College, School & Club	11,000/-
* 23 Profitable Construction Projects	11,000/-
* 56 Agro Based & Food Process Projects	11,000/-
* 52 Food, Dairy, Bakery, Confectionery & Snacks Foods	11,000/-
* Profitable Plastics, Polymers & Allied 100 Projects	16,500/-
* 45 New Chemicals & Allied Project Reports	11,000/-
* 44 Textile, Garments, Hosiery & Allied	11,000/-
* 21 Dairy Farm and Milk Products	11,000/-
* 29 Paper, Pulp & Paper Converting Prod.	11,000/-
* 31 Essential Oils, Perfumes, Flavours & Aromatic Compounds	11,000/-
* 63 Profitable Packaging & Allied Projects	11,000/-
* 36 Profitable Printing & Allied Projects	11,000/-
* 28 Surgical & Disposable Medical Projects	11,000/-
* 99 Profitable Printing & Packaging Projects	16,500/-
* 42 Electroplating, Anodizing & Allied Proj.	11,000/-
* 20 Profitable Plantation & Cultivation Proj.	11,000/-
* Profitable 55 Products (Agro/Ind. Wastes)	12,000/-
* 35 Gums, Adhesives, Sealants & Resins	12,000/-
* 43 Iron, Steel, Casting, Fabrication, Wire Drawing & Rolling Mills Projects	12,000/-
* 54 Paint, Varnish, Solvents, Lacquers, Resins, Enamels, Pigments, Thinner & Powder Coating Projects	12,000/-
* 26 New Educational Projects (School etc.)	11,000/-
* 12 Mosquitoes Preventive Projects (Coils, Mats, Liquids, Agarbatti, Nets, Spray etc.)	7500/-
* 52 Cosmetics (Herbal & Synthetics) Technology Projects (52 Proj. Reports)	12,000/-
* 67 Rubber & Rubber Goods Industries	12,000/-
* 21 Bakery & Allied Projects Reports	7,500/-
* 37 Aluminium & Aluminium Based Ind.	11,000/-
* 14 Potato & Potato Based Industries	8,500/-
* 50 Electrical, Electronic & Computer/IT Based Industries (50 Projects Reports)	12,000/-
* 5 Power Plant Projects (Thermal,Hydro, Solar, Wind Energy & Lignite Coal Based	11,000/-
* 35 New Profitable Industries (35 Reports)	11,000/-
* 10 Molasses Based Lucrative Projects	11,000/-
* 24 Fruits/Veg. & Allied Food Dehydration Projects (24 Projects Reports)	11,000/-
* 160 New Exports Oriented Units & Most Profitable Projects (160 Projects Reports)	21,000/-

Send Draft in favour of "Engineers India Research Institute, Delhi" (Postage Rs. 50/- Extra)

ENGINEERS INDIA RESEARCH INSTITUTE

Regd. Off : 4449, Nai Sarak (B), Main Road, Delhi - 110 006 (India)

* Ph: 9811437895, 91-11-23918117, 23916431, 23840361 * Fax: 91-11- 23916431 * E-Mail : eirisidi@bol.net.in

YOU CAN DEPOSIT THE AMOUNT IN EIRI ACCOUNT WITH UTI BANK LTD. CA - 054010200006248

ICICI BANK LTD. CA-022705000598 OR UNION BANK OF INDIA CA-307201010015149

BOOKS ON ELECTROPLATING, CANDLE, BUILDING MATERIALS & OILS/ FATS

TECHNOLOGY OF BUILDING MATERIALS AND CHEMICALS WITH PROCESSES

ISBN. 81-86732-54-3 + Rs. 950/-

Details of Construction Chemicals, Super Plasticizers in Concrete, Flyash Lime Bricks, Rigid PVC Foam Sheets, Precast Hollow Core Slabs, Calcium Silicate Bricks, Ready Mixed Concrete, Timber Subsitutes, Clay-Flyash Bricks, Reinforced Concrete Door & Window Frames, Ferrocement Door Shutters, Details of Machineries, Cement Plant, High Alumina Cement, Brick, Glazed Ceramic Tiles, Suppliers of Machinery & Raw Materials etc.

ELECTROPLATING, ANODIZING AND SURFACE FINISHING TECHNOLOGY

ISBN. 81-86732-33-0
Rs. 750/- or US $ 75/-

Principles of electroplating, technology of cleaning, pickling & dipping, electrolytic & chemical processes for the polishing of metals, nickel plating, chromium plating, hard chromium plating, copper plating, electro forming, brass plating, silver plating, gold plating, cadmium plating, zinc plating, anodic oxidation of aluminium, phosphating processes, manufacturers/suppliers of machinery & electroplating chemicals & materials etc.

HAND BOOK OF OILS, FATS & DERIVATIVES WITH REFINING & PACKAGING TECHNOLOGY

ISBN. 81-86732-56-X + Rs. 950/-

Oil Bearing Materials Derivated, Oilseeds carrying Soap making Oils, Oilseeds from Shrubs, Vegetable Oils, Oilseeds from Fruits, Oils/Fats Extraction, Fats and Oil Refining, Hydrogenation, Packaging, Fatty Acids, Glycerine, Fat Splitting, Protein Meals, Oleochemicals, Coconut Oils, Ghani Oils, Groundnut Oil, Plant Economics and Suppliers Addresses of Machinery etc.

CANDLE MAKING PROCESSES & FORMULATIONS HAND BOOK

ISBN. 81-86732-62-4 ★ Rs. 380/-

Introduction, Equipment & Materials, Raw Materials, How to Manufacture, Candle Making Process, Wax Melting, Moulded Candles, Surface Techniques, Novelty candles, Chemicals Colours Used, Candle Power, Waxes Used, Moulds, Selected Formulations, Coloured Candles Manufacture, Perfumed Candles, Magic Candles, Project Profiles, Imported Machinery Suppliers of Machinery, Suppliers of Raw Materials etc.

BOOKS ON PACKAGINGS

HAND BOOK OF PACKAGING TECHNOLOGY

 # ISBN. 81-86732-67-5 # Rs. 900/-

Packaging Materials, Eco-Friendly Packaging, Folding Board Cartons, Corrugated Board, Multiwall Paper Sacks, Plastics, PVC, Expanded Polystyrene, Flexible Packaging, Shrink & Glass Containers, Aluminium Foil, Wooden Containers, Aerosol Packaging, Packaging of Horticultural Crops, Packaging of Cosmetic, Soaps & Detergents, Packaging of Hazardous Chemicals, Fertilizers & Pesticides Industry, etc.

HAND BOOK OF FOOD PACKAGING TECHNOLOGY

ISBN 81-86732-90-X
Rs. 900/- or US $ 100/-

Packaging of Coffee, Tea & Spice, Preservation of fresh foods, Shelf life assessment of processed foods, Packaging of fish for retailing, Aseptic packaging, Long life milk, Metal containers, Carton board, folding cartons for food packaging, Thermoformed & blow moulded containers, Blow moulded containers, Jumbo bags, Packaging of fish products, milk products, cereals, Post harvest technologies etc.

औषधीय एवं सुगन्धित पौधों का व्यवसायिक कृषिकरण

A Complete Hand Book of Medicinal & Aromatic Plants Cultivation

ISBN No 81-86732-86-1
 # Rs. 800/- or US $ 100/-

START YOUR OWN EXPORT BUSINESS (HOW TO EXPORT)

ISBN. 81-86732-57-8 # Rs. 350/- or US $ 50/-

Latest methods including Rules for Successful Exporting, Brief Details for Starting Export Business, Registration of Exporters, Appointing Overseas, Agents, Obtaining an Export Licence, Obtaining Export Credit Insurance, Finance Arrangement for Exports, Procuring/Manufacturing Goods for Export & their Inspection by Government Authorities, Packing and Marking Goods for Export, Excise Procedure etc.

HAND BOOK OF LEATHER AND LEATHER PRODUCTS TECHNOLOGY

ISBN 81-86732-87-X # Rs. 850/- or US $ 100/-

Leather Processing, Leather Manufacture, Vegetable Tannins, Vegetable Dyes, Preparation of Chrome Liquor, Manufacture of Exotic Leather from Ray Fish, Formaldehyde Free Finishing Recipe For Glazed Kid Leather, Canvas Shoes, Shoe Upper Leather, PVC Footwear, Industrial Hand Gloves, Leather Chappals, Leather Garments, Football (Leather), Suppliers of Plant, Equipments & Machineries and Raw Materials etc.

स्मॉल एवं कॉटेज स्केल इण्डस्ट्रीज (लघु उद्योग)

ISBN. 81-86732-55-1 ★ Rs. 525/-

यह पुस्तक हिन्दी भाषा में नया व्यवसाय शुरू करने वालों के लिए छापी गयी है। पुस्तक में लघु उद्योग शुरू करने से सम्बन्धित सभी जरूरी जानकारियां दी गई है। संक्षिप्त विवरण: मार्गदर्शन, पंजीकरर्ण, सहायतार्थ संस्थाएं, कपड़े धोने और स्नान के साबुन, फिनायल, लिपस्टिक, शैम्पू तथा हेयर वाश, हेयर आयल्स व ब्रिलियण्टाइन, काली मेहंदी, फेस टैल्कम तथा बेबी पाउडर, टूथ पेस्ट तथा माउथ, स्याही उद्योग, फिनायल उद्योग, गंधरहित डमी अगरबत्तियां, धूपबत्तियां, कृत्रिम सुगन्धों, पोली बैग, कॉरोगेटेड बोर्ड और डिब्बे, पेन, बालपेन व रिफिल, पटेटो चिप्स तथा वेफर्स, कॉर्नफलेक्स, डेयरी प्रोडक्ट्स, आइस कैण्डी उद्योग, दियासलाई उद्योग, रेडीमेड गारमेण्ट उद्योग, निटिंग, सुगंधित सुपारी, मशीनों व कच्चा माल के बनाने व बेचने वालों के पते। आय व्यय योजना (प्रोजेक्ट प्रोफाइल)।

ENGINEERS INDIA RESEARCH INSTITUTE Mobile : 9811437895

4449, Nai Sarak, Main Road, Delhi - 110 006 (INDIA) Ph./Fax : 91-11- 23918117, 23916431, 23840361

BOOKS ON PRINTINGS, OFFSET, SCREEN, FLEXO & GRAVURE TECHNOLOGY

HAND BOOK OF
PRINTING TECHNOLOGY
OFFSET, SCREEN, FLEXO, GRAVURE, INKJET & DIGITAL
ISBN 81-86732-75-6 # Rs. 975/-

Typographic, Pre-Press Processes, Camera, Scanning, Offset Plate Making, Presses, Offset Press, Proof & Proofing Techniques, Newspaper Printing: Gravure & Packaging, Screen Printing, Plant Economics, Suppliers of Machineries & Raw Materials etc.

HAND BOOK OF
OFFSET PRINTING TECHNOLOGY
ISBN : 81-86732-82-9
 # Rs. 500/- or US $ 50/-

Desktop Publishing Proof-Reading, Pre-Press Processes, Camera, Scanning, Offset Plate Making, Presses, Offset Press, Proof & Proofing Techniques, Newspaper Printing, Plant Economics, Suppliers of Plant & Machineries, Suppliers of Raw Materials etc.

HAND BOOK OF
SCREENPRINTING WITH PROCESSES & TECHNOLOGY
ISBN. 81-86732-63-2 ★Rs. 350/-

Screen Printing Methods, Screen- Process Stencils, Screen Printing Stencils, Chemicals Adhesives, Screen Printing On Glass, Colour Combination, Silk Screen Photo Stencil Preparation, Plant Economics Suppliers of Plant & Machinery & Raw Materials.

HAND BOOK OF
PRINTING PROCESSES TECHNOLOGIES & INDUSTRIES
ISBN. 81-86732-07-1 # Rs. 375/-

The book covers latest technology of almost all the printing technology viz; screen, offset, velvet cloth, sheetfed offset. Project profiles on various printing industries are also provided. Suppliers of machinery are also given.

BOOKS ON PLASTIC COMPOUNDING, PROCESSING, MOULDS, POLYMER, FIBRE GLASS, PVC & PET PRODUCTS

PLASTIC COMPOUNDING MASTER BATCHES, PET & OTHER PLASTIC PROCESSING INDUSTRIES
ISBN. 81-86732-49-7 • Rs. 750/-

Extrusion, Injection, Blow & Rotational Moulding, Additives for Polymers, PVC Compounding, Colour Master Batch, PET, Suppliers of Machineries, Suppliers of Raw Materials etc.

PLASTIC PROCESSING AND PACKAGING INDUSTRIES
ISBN. 81-86732-11-X
Rs. 450/- or US$ 50/-

Introduction, Plastic Processing, Injection & Blow Moulding, Compounding & Processing of PVC, PU, Project profiles and directory section. The book is covering with the 54 fully detailed chapters etc.

TECHNOLOGY OF
PVC COMPOUNDING AND ITS APPLICATIONS
ISBN 81-86732-88-8
Rs. 900/- or US $ 100/-

PVC Resins Processing of PVC, Additives for PVC, Compounding, Compounding of PVC, Testing of Resins and Compounds, Speciality Plastic Compounds & Masterbatches, PVC compounds, Xlpe cable compound, jelly filled telecommunication cable compound & sheating compound, Plastic Granules Applications of PVC, Suppliers of Machineries/Raw Materials etc.

MOULDS DESIGN & PROCESSING HAND BOOK
ISBN. 81-86732-23-3
 # Rs. 495/- or US$ 50/-

Classification of Moulds, Production Schedule of Plastic Injection Mould, Steel for Injection Mould, Trouble, Injection Mould Design, Compression/Transfer Mould, Blow Mould Design, Standard Mould Parts, Conversion Table etc.

PET PREFORM & ITS PRODUCTS MANUFACTURING
Rs. 1300/-
US$ 100/-

Processing and manufacturing technology of PET Bottles, Preform and market study with Project Profiles of PET bottles, preform & others. Suppliers of Machinery & Raw Materials etc.

ENGINEERS INDIA RESEARCH INSTITUTE Mobile : 9811437895
4449, Nai Sarak, Main Road, Delhi - 110 006 (INDIA) Ph./Fax : 91-11- 23918117, 23916431, 23840361

VARIOUS PROJECT REPORTS IN CD-ROMS

37 ALUMINIUM AND ALUMINIUM BASED INDUSTRIES Rs. 11000/-

Aluminium powder, AAC & ACSR aluminium conductors, Aluminium silicate, Aluminium utensil, Aluminium wire drawing, Aluminium paint, Aluminium ingots from scrap, Aluminium alloy & ingots, anodizing of aluminium, Aluminium chloride, Aluminium channels, aluminium rolling mill, Aluminium bottles, Aluminium foil cutting & roll making, Aluminium end caps, Aluminium door,Window, Aluminium colapsible tube, Aluminium phosphide, Aluminium ingots from bauxite, Aluminium caps, Aluminium furniture & hardware, aluminium beverage cans, Aluminium cans for capacitors, Aluminium & Aluminium alloys from aluminium scraps to make utensils,(induction furnace melted),Aluminium hot & cold rolling mill (aluminium sheets & circles), Anodic aluminium labels, aluminium slugs & circles, Aluminium printing plate for offset printing machine, Aluminium foils, Aluminium wire and rods, Brass and aluminium hinges, Hard anodizing on aluminium, Pilfer proof caps, Piston assembly (Aluminium alloy), Pressure die casting Al., Paper coated al.wire, Pressure cooker.

14 POTATO AND POTATO BASED PROJECTS (14 PROJECT REPORTS) Rs. 8500/-

Alcohol from potatoes, Dextrose powder from potatoes, Frozen finger chips, I M F L (whisky) from potatoes, Liquid glucose, Potato chips/waffers, Potato powder (automatic plant), Potato starch, Potato chips, Potato and onion flakes, Potable beer (alcoholic) based on potato & barley/malt, Potato powder, Sago seeds (saboo dana), Vodka from potatoes

21 BAKERY & ALLIED PROJECTS Rs. 7500/-

Automatic bread and biscuit unit, Automatic biscuit plant, Baking powder, Biscuit unit (pineapple) automatic pineapple biscuit making plant, Bread plant, bakery unit (rusk, Pastries,Bread, Buns cake, toffee, etc. confectionery industry, Confectionery industry (toffee & candy), Chocolate, Custard powder, Candy hard boiled, icing sugar, Jelly powder, Lecithin (soya based), Mithai/halwai (sweet & namkeen), Milk powder & ghee, Mini flour mill (maize, sorghum, millet), Namkeen industry (bhujia, Chana chur etc.), Potato chips/waffers, Roller flour mill (mini flour mill), Yeast from molasses.

5 POWER PLANT PROJECTS Rs. 11000/- (THERMAL, HYDRO, SOLAR, WIND ENERGY AND LIGNITE COAL BASED)

Power plant (thermal), Power plant from lignite coal, Power plant (hydro based), Solar power plant, Wind energy power project (capacity: 10 mw).

12 MOSQUITOES PREVENTIVE PROJECTS (COILS, MATS,LIQUIDS, AGARBATTI, NETS, SPRAY ETC.) Rs. 7500/-

Mosquito coils using eucalyptus leaves, Mosquito coils and mats, allethrin mosquito repellent oil, Mosquito repellent mats, aerosol & mosquito repellent spray (baygon, hit, Mortein type), pest control, Allethrin mosquito mat recharger, Mosquito net, mosquito larva destroyer, Mosquito repellent oil, Mosquito coil agar batti (incense sticks), Mosquito & flies repellent agarbatti (incense sticks)

10 MOLASSES BASED LUCRATIVE PROJECTS Rs. 11000/-

Animal feed (cattle, Poultry, sheep or pig),(liquid feed) (molasses based), Acetic acid from molasses, Absolute/neutral alcohol (purified ethyl alcohol)from sugar cane juice or molasses, Citric acid from molasses, Country liquor from molasses, Ethanol (biofuel) from molasses, Industrial alcohol (rectified spirit), Oxalic acid from molasses, Octanol (octyl alcohol) from molasses, yeast from molasses.

24 FRUITS/VEG. & ALLIED FOOD DEHYDRATION PROJECTS Rs. 11000/-

Banana powder, Curcumin & turmeric oil from turmeric, Dehydration of jack fruit, Dehydration of figs by sun drying method, dehydration of onion and garlic, Desiccated coconut powder, Dry ginger powder and oleoresin, Dry ginger (ginger powder), Onions & onion powder, Egg powder, Fruit juice powder, Fruits and vegetable dehydration, Glucose-d powder, Garlic flakes and powder (dehydrated), Grape dehydration, Instant food, Mango powder, mustard powder, Milk powder & ghee, Potato powder, Turmeric powder (edible grade), Tamarind juice powder, Tomato powder, yeast dry powder from maize.

PROFITABLE NEW 35 INDUSTRIES Rs. 11000/-

Aluminium ingots from bauxite, Ayurvedic dant manjan (red colour - dabur type), Angora rabbit wool, Aluminium powder, Aluminium Foils, Besan plant, Bee keeping, Corn/maize oil, Cotton yarn, corn flakes, Detergent cake & powder, Dairy farming, Dehulled sesame seeds, Dairy products, Dry ginger (ginger powder), Egg powder, Fish farming, Fruit juices bottling plant, Fruits and vegetable dehydration, Goat farming, Honey processing and packaging, Mango processing & canning (mango pulp), Neem oil from seeds, Packed coconut water, Peanut butter, Pappad plant (automatic), Potato and onion flakes, Plastic buttons (by injection moulding methods), Potato powder, Pickles, Processed food, Rabbit farming, Sanitary napkins, Tamarind kernel powder, Tamarind juice powder.

ENGINEERS INDIA RESEARCH INSTITUTE Mobile : 9811437895

4449, Nai Sarak, Main Road, Delhi - 110 006 (INDIA) Ph./Fax : 91-11- 23918117, 23916431, 23840361

VARIOUS PROJECT REPORTS IN CD-ROMS

50 ELECTRICAL, ELECTRONIC AND COMPUTER BASED INDUSTRIES Rs. 12000/-

Air conditioners & parts, AAC & ACSR aluminium conductors, business process outsource (B.P.O.), cyber cafe, Call centre (international), Call centre (domestic), Ceiling fan, Chokes & patties, Chokes & starters, Choke of fluorescent tubes, Compact disk, Computer education institute, Computer assembly, Computer continuous stationery, Computer software, Cello tape, Compact fluorescent lamps, Distribution transformer, Domestic transformer, Electrical panel boards, Electrical domestic appliances, Electric energy meters, Electric fans, Electric motors, Electric switches and sockets, Electronic choke (ballast), Electronic toys (E.O.U), Electrical stamping for transformer, Electrical repairing, Epoxy transformers, F.H.P. motors, GLS lamps, GLS lamps & fluorescent tubes, H.T. & l.t. insulator, HT air brake switches d.o. fuse, Lightening arrestor, Integrated circuits, Light emitting diodes (L.E.D.), Miniature circuit breaker, Mixer/grinder (mixi), Medical transcription, printed circuit boards (PCB), PVC wires and cables, power inverters, Power transformer, Portal, Solar cells, Tubular poles for electrical transmission, Telephone (push button & cordless), un interrupted power supply, Servo controlled stabilizer, Voltage stabilizer.

54 PAINT, VARNISH, SOLVENTS, LACQUERS, RESINS, ENAMEL, PIGMENTS THINNER & POWDER COATING PROJECTS Rs. 12000/-

The content cover in cd rom- automobile paints, Aluminium paint , Acrylic copolymer emulsion, Acrylic emulsion paints, Bituminous based corrosion resistant, Cement paint, Clear transparent lacquer for coating on brass bangles to make it weather-resistant, Copper phthalocyanine blue & green , Dry distemper and cement paint, (water based) in liquid form for electrophoretic coating application on metal plates, Enamel removers, Enamelling of copper wire, Epoxy resins, Glass putty, glass coating solution, Hammertone paints, Insulating varnish, insulating varnish, (Poly Vinyl butyral based, ffc grade), Lime colour/cement colour (synthetic- red iron oxide) used for Šflooring , Lacquer emulsion (high shine and medium shine) for leather finishing & N.C.lacquer for leather finishing (formulation & manufacturing processes), Naphtha based thinner, N.C.putty , N.C. thinners used in automobiles , Oil-bound distemper paints, Paint industry paint removers, Paint driers, powder coating paints, Paint and reducer, Primer paints, Enamel paints & distemper, Powder coating primer paints & enamel paints, Poly vinyl acetate emulsion, Pigments binders for textile printing putty and water proofing paint, Phenol formaldehyde resin, Poly amide resin, Refractory paint (graphite based), Red oxide pigments from iron pickling plant waste, Stoving paint, Silicone emulsion for textile, Stainer for paints, Solvents & thinners, Texture paints, thinners,thinners (ethyl alcohol based), Thinners (white spirit based), Urea formaldehyde resin, Unsaturated polyester resins, varnish (clear) for wood (flame-retarding type), Wood primer for paints, Wall putty, Wire enamel.

67 RUBBER AND RUBBER GOODS INDUSTRIES Rs. 12000/-

Auto tyre tubes & flaps, Autorubber moulding parts & steel jacks, Auto tubes, Coir foam (rubberized coir), Crumb rubber, Crumb rubber modified bitumen (crmb), Cycles tyres and tubes, Field rubber converted to the 60% latex rubber, Gaskets, Hawai chappals, hard rubber battery container, Hose pipe Rubber (Radiator),(Rubber Hoses for Automobiles), Latex foam rubber (spong rubber), Latex rubber thread, Latex rubber based adhesive, latex rubber condoms, Latex foam rubber stabilizer, Microcellular sheets(rubber sheets for shoe soles, Oil seals,'o' ringss, Rubber powder, Rubber hose pipe, Rubber auto gaskets, Rubber eraser, rubberised cork sheet, Rubberised foam for manufacture of mattresses, Cushion etc., Rubber auto parts, Rubber goods from waste rubber, Rubber band, Rubber plantation, Rubber process oil, rubber hoses for automobiles, Rubber reclaiming, Rubber ball, rubber beading for automobiles, Rubber epdm auto parts, Rubber transmission belt & v-belt, Rubber stereo, Rubber & plastic sheets, Mats & flaps, Rubber sheet for automobiles, Rubber balloon, Rubber cots and aprons, Rubber roller for textile mills & paper industrie, Rubber flooring, Rubber solutions, rubber adhesive for plywood, Rubber rollers & ebonite rollers, rubberized cloth, Rubber hose pipe & rubber glazing, Rubber moulding & lining of rubber sheeting, Rubber adhesive (all purpose) neoprene & isoprene basedrubber moulding & lining of rubber sheeting, Rubber chappel and rubber sheet, Rubber sheet and allied hospital rubber goods, Rubber caps (closures) for pharmaceutical uses, Rubber plastic stamp & pad (automatic), rubber compound for toys (using plaster of paris), Rubber sheets for shoe soles (eva) (ethylene vinyl acetate sheet for sole), Surgical examination gloves (disposable), Synthetic rubber adhesive, Silicon rubber nipple/teats, Tyres, tubes & flap (moped to truck), Tyre retreading materials (tread rubber, Cushion, gum (compound) rubber solution pre-cured rubber),Tyre & tubes, Tyre retreading by cold process, Vulcanising adhesive formulation vulcanizing rubber solution/cement for automobile tyres, V-belts water based latex adhesives.

52 COSMETICS (HERBAL & SYNTHETICS) TECHNOLOGY PROJECTS (52 PROJECTS REPORTS) Rs. 12000/-

After shave lotion, Antiseptic cream (boro plus type), Ayurvedic dant manjan (red colour - dabur type), Anti-dandruff cream, Aloe vera gel stabilized, Ayurvedic medicines, Body creams and lotions, Baby oil (body oil), Cosmetics industry (modern), Cold creams, Car shampoo, Coconut oil from copra, Detergent cake & powder, Enamel removers, Extraction of essential oil (cardamon, jeera, ajowan, ginger oil etc.) & packing of ground spice,Face mask (liquid form) strawberry flavour (milk mask, Cleansing mask, butter milk mask,paw paw mask & others), Face cream and body cream , Herbal cosmetic , Henna paste making, Hair oils, Hair dye in form of hair oil, Herbal face paste, Herbal shampoo & creams, hair removing cream, Hair fixer (hair gel for afro hair), Hair removing wax, Hair colour mate (formulations and process), Herbal tooth paste & tooth powder, Hair dye liquid, herbal extracts, hair dye powder, Hair colour mate (formulations and process), keshkala tel (vasmol or godrej keshkala tel type), Kali mehandi powder (hair dye powder), Lipsticks , Liquid soap, liquid bindi & sindur, Liquid toilet cleaner (Harpic type), Mustard oil, Nail enamel (nail polish), Rose water, Shampoo, Shaving Cream, scents and perfumes, Spray (perfume), Toilet soap industry (soap from soap stock), Toilet & herbal soap, Tooth powders, Tooth paste gel type (like colgate, close-up etc.),Tooth paste (calcium carbonate base), Toilet soap with glycerine transparent soap, Talcum powder (face & toilet powder).

ENGINEERS INDIA RESEARCH INSTITUTE Mobile : 9811437895

4449, Nai Sarak, Main Road, Delhi - 110 006 (INDIA) Ph./Fax : 91-11- 23918117, 23916431, 23840361